Embr

Embryo

A Pink Floyd Chronology
1966–1971

NICK HODGES & IAN PRISTON

CHERRY RED BOOKS

THE RED OAK PRESS LIMITED

First published in Great Britain in 1999 by

CHERRY RED BOOKS
a division of Cherry Red Records Ltd
Unit 17, Elysium Gate West,
126–8 New King's Road
London sw6 3jh
E-mail: iain@cred.demon.co.uk

in association with The Red Oak Press Ltd

Photographs taken at Mike Leonard's house are reproduced by
kind permission of *Terrapin* magazine © Irene Winsby

A catalogue record for this book is available from the British Library.

ISBN 1 901447 07 3

Typeset in Adobe Garamond by
Strathmore Publishing Services, London n7

Printed and bound in Great Britain by
Whitstable Litho, Whitstable, Kent

Contents

List Of Plates

The plates are placed between pages 246 and 247

Rehearsals at Mike Leonard's house on or about 20 January 1967

IT 11 promoting the '14 Hour Technicolour Dream'

Syd Barrett's Pink Floyd in flower-power garb for *Record Mirror* on 12 August 1967

Poster advertising the premiere of *The Committee* at the Cameo Poly, Oxford Circus, London

Indecipherable and strange: the poster for 2–4 August 1968

San Diego Community Concourse, 17 October 1971

Acknowledgements

Ian would like to convey special thanks to Michael Christensen, Thomas Muller, and Dave Taylor for their valuable assistance in compiling information for this book which he dedicates to Jane as thanks for her patience and encouragement when it kept going wrong!

Nick would like to thank his many correspondents over the years, as well as the numerous organisations whose staff have assisted in the job of researching the sometimes convoluted career of the band. Thanks also to my parents for valuable advice and technical assistance, and Kay, who still managed to enjoy the week in France despite the fruitless search for *Le Livre* ...

The authors would welcome correspondence on any aspect of the accuracy of this book.

Preface
Whither The Sixties Underground

The music of Pink Floyd between 1966 and 1971 serves as a brilliant illustration of life and human experience. It is saturated with the pain and exaltations of living, obsessions with death and the terror of loneliness. The romanticism of their early work allowed fluid boundaries between past and present, reality and unreality, the conscious and unconscious. *The Dark Side Of The Moon* brought these concerns to the surface in 1972 and 1973 in a somewhat unnatural and highly unified form. It ushered out the otherworldly, replacing previously loose connections and inter-connections with minutely controlled transitions: seamless webs.

It was only after Christmas 1971 that the group turned their attention to *The Dark Side*: a development which was to irrevocably alter the band's direction and send them on a path which would give them the commerical success which they always craved. It could be argued that we stop before the real drama begins. Many observers, however, seem to share our view that the Floyd's output before 1972 is more aesthetically and intellectually satisfying.

It is this journey that is so often neglected by biographers and has so fascinated us for the last five years.

Our observations of what was to make this era special have perhaps been overly nostalgic at times and for that we can make no excuse. We hope, however, that you will find our efforts to be both insightful and entertaining!

IAN PRISTON AND NICK HODGES
April 1999

Introduction
The Man And The Journey

To understand the early Floyd is to understand 'The Man And The Journey'. This piece was arguably the most significant opus in the history and development of The Pink Floyd, yet to most casual fans, and many not-so-casual, it remains unknown. Even to those who have heard it the piece remains an enigma to which the band themselves have seldom made reference.

Yet it marks both the culmination and the genesis of the band's 'themed pieces', which were to become more and more explicit, resulting in 1983 in the polemical and lambasting *Final Cut*.

We hope to shed some light upon the themes prevalent in the band's concept work, and perhaps go some way towards explaining 'The Man And The Journey'.

PART 1: GAMES FOR MAY

The history of Floydian theme pieces may be traced back as far as 1967, when the band staged an event entitled 'Games For May: Space Age Relaxation For The Climax Of Spring' at the Queen Elizabeth Hall, London. While it may be somewhat conjectural to cite this as the true beginning of the band's interest in the song cycle, it is clear that they made substantial efforts to tie their performance into some kind of coherent whole, creating recorded pieces to greet the audience and bid them farewell, while members of the band's entourage also entered the auditorium – as a gorilla, or to distribute daffodils to a bemused public – involving the audience in an experience which allowed them to participate rather than observe, as was, and is, the norm on such occasions.

The music was also tied into performance to a greater extent than the simple act of the band being on stage playing – during 'Tape Bubbles', a pre-recorded piece by Wright, the auditorium was filled with soap bubbles through which light refracted into curious oil shapes; the light show was not only visual but tactile, the result being synethesthetic disorientation in which the audience was the main participant.

The show began with a Waters-composed tape effect called 'Tape Dawn' which, he recalled in *Q* Magazine, August 1992, was 'to be played in the Theatre's foyer as the audience was coming in'. Significantly, the themology of this recording – essentially birdsong at half speed – was to reflect the very human concerns which were to dominate Waters' approach to concept pieces – life, death, day, night ...

While the majority of the show comprised the band's 'greatest hits' one can see some reason for the particular order in which they chose to perform them. With the audience seated, the show properly began with 'Matilda Mother' – a song concerned with the morning of life: childhood. 'Flaming' came next, a classic song, which is both laden with images gleaned from childhood, seen through the distorted lens of psychedelics, space-age, and a lyrical eulogy to nature and the joys of spring. This was ideally complemented by 'Scarecrow': a song about a straw man in more senses than the obvious.

While many nominate 'Jugband Blues' as, in the words of Pete Jenner, 'the ultimate self-diagnosis of schizophrenia', 'Scarecrow' is more poignant for me at least – our first indication of the chinks in Syd's armour.

While it remains undocumented, it is here that I feel the band took the interval, since the mood of the performance becomes far more up-beat with the arrival of 'Games For May'.

'Games For May' was of course written specially for the performance, suggesting perhaps more than anything, that the band wished the event to say something more than an average gig. Since it was rewritten for release as 'See Emily Play' it is difficult to say quite what its intent was, other than to celebrate the season of rebirth.

'Bike', on the other hand, is far more straightforward – hopeful of love with a desperate undercurrent. Significantly Barrett displays his fascination with childhood, and one suspects that it sums up his yearning for a meaningful relationship, despite its whimsical, almost nonsense, phrasing. That he refers back to a friendly mouse, an image that also appears earlier in 'Scarecrow' bears mention. While it may be over-stressing it, mice – passive and gentle creatures – seem the only thing able to move him; that the mouse is 'getting old' further indicates the sad predictability of life – those closest to us will ultimately be rendered nothing more than dust. The mechanical completion of the piece could be said to reflect that ultimate hippie fear, technology at the hand of The Others ('most of them have got one') in which mankind will find its inevitable damnation.

'Arnold Layne' and 'Candy And Currant Bun' were to follow – this was more due to the fact that they were the band's latest release, and their appearance in the suite is to our mind a consequence of this fact, rather than to any thematic purpose, since the next song was 'Pow R Toc H' – a space piece to all intents and purposes. Toc H is, to those who did not realise already, a benevolent fund for old soldiers (a point which would not have been lost on Waters, one can be sure). As such it represents two things, old age and death. The cycle has almost come full circle, with one thing left – salvation?

'Interstellar Overdrive' is a metaphor for a number of things: the inner journey – enlightenment; 'space-age relaxation' – a musical 'trip' in its many senses; and nirvana – a state many believe is found in death. This is further confirmed by the placing of 'Tape Bubbles' at this point – something I have earlier touched upon. The bubbles themselves may indicate peace – contentment, and heavenly euphoria – similar as they are to the clouds upon which the Kingdom of Heaven may be found, if so desired.

The show ended, prosaically, with a Barrett-composed piece entitled 'Tape Ending' – an enigmatic track about which I can claim no knowledge, and about which I make no comment.

If this reading of the show is to be accepted, the encore is the band's musical joke – 'Lucifer Sam'; there is no heaven, only hell, and a plaintive desire for death amidst the 'shifting sands'. Life is a hard taskmaster.

Part 2: A Saucerful Of Secrets

The next attempt by the band to create a structured piece was in the following year, with the piece 'A Saucerful Of Secrets' from their second 'difficult' album. Given the last twelve minutes of the album as a gift by the record company to do with what they wanted, the band chose to explore in further detail the themes discussed above.

Unlike 'Games For May' or others of the band's later concept pieces, 'Saucerful' is, of course, wholly without lyrics – vocals only appearing as instruments to convey feeling. This realised, anyone wishing to understand the song must rely upon the music, and song titles (as found upon the *Ummagumma* version a year later) to make sense of the piece.

The piece opens with the sound of quiet wind chimes, bringing to mind memories of a child's crib. If one speeds the track up many times, the timpani rumble takes on the sound of chiming bells. This may be regarded as an awakening, or birth – while the song becomes increasingly frantic, symbolising in our mind the fear a baby experiences as it enters the real world, with all its strange noises and disjointed experiences. As the song reaches full consciousness there is a gentle realisation of safety, before the band launch into 'Syncopated Pandemonium', focused around Nick's cyclic drumming, reminiscent of a heartbeat.

The ensuing minutes are a maelstrom of white noise and dissonant keyboard – life is flashing before your eyes, disappearing into a haven of peace and tranquillity – the 'Storm Signal' arrives too late – perhaps it is a last look back.

Rick's keyboard makes its entrance, bearing all the hallmarks of Anglican church music – the inference is too strong to ignore: 'Celestial Voices' is the entrance to heaven at the end of life. In one way 'Saucerful' is a concentrated acid vision – birth, fear, nirvana and death. In another it strongly symbolises the crystallisation of the band's preoccupation with that very earthly theme of life itself.

Part 3: The Man And The Journey

1969 began in earnest on Saturday 18 January with 'Turn On The Tap Zap: An Event By The Pink Floyd', a Middle Earth night at the band's old haunt, The Roundhouse. The event was an all-nighter – 10.30 pm 'til dawn – plenty of time to perform any manner of 'events'. Quite what they performed is an enduring enigma. Perhaps it was here that 'The Man And The Journey' began to take shape ...

It was, in its embryonic, and to our mind most fulfilling, form complete by April of that year, when it made its debut on Monday 14th at The Royal Festival Hall, just up the road from the Queen Elizabeth Hall on London's South Bank. The show had been preceded by a number of low key dates in the UK and on the continent, and ran virtually concurrent with eight days of sessions at which they recorded the sound-track to Barbet Schroeder's seminal film *More*.

Many of the tracks recorded for *More* were to make their first appearance as part of 'The Man And The Journey' suite, properly called 'The Massed Gadgets Of Auximenes ... More Furious Madness From Pink Floyd'. Of the suite, three tracks were already part of their repertoire – 'Beset By Creatures Of The Deep' (Careful With That Axe, Eugene), 'The Pink Jungle' (Pow R Toc H) and 'The End Of The Beginning' (Celestial Voices, from the 'Saucerful Of Secrets' suite).

The development of 'The Man And The Journey' and that of *More* was highly integrated, indeed, the copy of the programme held by the Royal Festival Hall archive features hand-written notes which detail *More*'s working titles next to those given by the band for the 'Massed Gadgets' cycle, indicating that by the 14th, the band had already started work on the film sound-track (and that they were having fun doing it!).

'Sleeping' features the note 'Quicksilver', while 'The Beginning' ('Green Is The Colour') has the legend 'Stephan's Tit'(!) alongside, and 'Doing It' is also labelled 'Up The Khyber'. There is little doubt that while the songs featured in two contexts, that of the film and that of the suite, they were intended to develop the intent of both in their own ways.

Quite by virtue of the piece's title it is clear that the 'concept' is straight-forward, and the individual elements feature titles which label the steps our pilgrim makes through their life and on their journey. The facts are well docu-mented elsewhere, so we will refrain from describing the set list, apart from where it benefits the following argument.

Seven tapes of the suite are in common circulation amongst collectors, the first and rarest being of the Royal Festival Hall debut, the second being of a perfor-mance at the Manchester Free Trade Hall on 22 June. The third tape – of 'The Final Lunacy', at the Royal Albert Hall, is relatively easy to find, while another, most common recording, taken from a VPRO radio broadcast of a performance at Amsterdam's Concertgebouw on 17 September complements an incomplete audience recording which does feature music cut from the radio show. A part performance at the Plumpton Blues and Jazz Festival has survived in rather fine quality, while the last tape is almost a footnote; an often forgotten performance at the Théâtre Des Champs Elysées in January 1970. Thanks to our illicit friends it is relatively easy to trace the development of the show as the year passed.

The development of the show was not as dramatic as that of *Eclipse* – essentially, the greatest differences to be found are in terms of the band's confidence as they become more familiar with the piece. Roger has admitted that the Royal Festival Hall debut was more like a rehearsal than a proper performance, and Dave's guitar in particular is allowed to wander and find its own way, which I find particularly refreshing. 'Doing It' and 'Sleeping' bear closest relationship with their partners on *More* at this gig; by the time the band played at the Concertgebouw the links were far more tenuous as the suite became something altogether its own.

'Grantchester Meadows' (here titled 'Daybreak') opened the show, following extended birdsong around the auditorium. For Roger and David the song is very much one associated with childhood; it is a matter of record that they regularly visited Grantchester on bikes as young teenagers, and the area is a virtual idyll, located as it is on the banks of the Cam, about four miles from the city of Cambridge. The association between childhood and morning is a common one, both for the band and literature in general. 'Daybreak' could just as easily have been a piece written for 'The Journey' as 'The Man', indeed there are strong

indications that 'The Man And The Journey' is more a retreading of the old
birth, life, death theme than one describing an average day and a fantastic
journey. This argument will be taken further in the course of our discussion.

'Daybreak' is rudely shattered by 'Work' which again works on two levels. The
obvious, that given by the title, is of a rail journey and factory labour. The track,
not present on all tapes (but particularly evidenced on the Royal Festival Hall,
Manchester and Concertgebouw audience recordings), is highly percussive, indus-
trial, and conceived with the sound of a steam train whistle. It is this locomotive
image which leads to our second, Freudian reading of the track – that it is also a
reference to the fact that the 'average man' thinks of sex about once every six
minutes (particularly so when work is repetitive and boring).

'Work' leads into 'Afternoon', available elsewhere as 'Biding My Time' on the
Relics compilation. 'Afternoon' is not simply about 'any afternoon', but the afternoon of our lives – 'I'll never pine for the sad days and the bad days, when we
was working from nine to five'. Retirement beckons – it is sad that our hero only
finds love, 'the warm light of the firelight in her eyes', so late in the day. The song
gets gradually more bawdy, turning almost into a French burlesque towards the
end; love and sex cannot be divided, and so we begin 'Doing It'.

The track is a unique drum solo in most cases, but appears as an improvisation by Wright and Mason (recalling 'Up The Khyber') at the Festival Hall. Cliff
Jones has described the Cockney origins of the phrase 'Up The Khyber' and it is
clear that in this context it is a (short!) paean to the reproductive act. Which all
too soon leads to 'Sleeping'.

'Sleeping' is a wonderful instrumental which the band played in many forms
during 1969, alternatively as 'Quicksilver' during the 'trip' sequences in *More* and
'One One', an outtake from *Zabriskie Point* which one suspects was a variation
on the 'Love Scene'. As an instrumental the track is extremely versatile, on the
one hand hedonistic (associated with drugs and sex) and on the other, gentle.
In its form as part of 'The Massed Gadgets' it is possibly the most interesting
moment of any within the annals of Floydian history, since it features the first
appearance of the 'schoolteacher' rant which was to appear again ten years later
on *The Wall*. Clearly the image was one which particularly haunted Roger, and
one which he felt deserved greater exposure.

Naturally then, it is 'Nightmare' ('Cymbaline') which follows this sequence.
The song is particularly personal to Roger, being an early expression of his dis-
illusionment with the music business, and his fear of failure. 'Nightmare' also
sets the stage for the ensuing journey in much the same way as 'Daybreak' which
opened the piece. One could make much of Waters' association between dreaming and travel (reaching its zenith with *The Pros And Cons Of Hitchhiking*, of
course). Here, however, it serves to illustrate a fear of the unknown. One gets the
feeling that the sleep of 'Nightmare' is the sleep of death – our 'Man' asks to be
woken as if it is something outside of his control, that if he is allowed to continue
he will never wake again. The inference of death (and ravens, the parasitic carrion
crow) is countered by the image of 'a butterfly with broken wings', at once fragile
and needing care – care which one is powerless to provide, given that there are so
many other distractions and pressures to deal with.

Introduction

'Nightmare' gives way to 'Daybreak' (reprise), essentially just a denouement and sound effect of an alarm clock. The circle is made and the day begins again.

It was at this point that the band took their interval, and it is unclear whether or not 'The Journey' was intended to take up where 'The Man' ended, or whether it is a piece in its own right. 'The Man' seems unhappy in his role as worker and uncomfortable in that of the lover, while he dreams of travel. It is not inconceivable that he should take a journey, especially one where he shall find fulfilment, as seems the case on one level in the second part of the suite. 'The Journey' is fantastic and there are numerous elements which point to it not being an externalised, but an internalised one.

It begins, somewhat obviously, with 'The Beginning' ('Green Is The Colour'). The subject of the song is, essentially, hope. The final line gives the clearest indication of its meaning: 'heavenly is the bond between the hopeful and the day' – the line twixt dream and reality. This song, like many around this time, features a strong religious, almost evangelical subtext – 'the canopy of blue', before which stands a woman (an angel or guardian) through whose dress shines light so bright you must cover your eyes. The second verse seems to have been written with its appearance in *More* in mind, since it would appear to be describing Estelle's drug use. With hope, or a vision, our 'Man' embarks upon his journey.

It is apparent, however, that the mission is not to be without danger, since our hero takes his first steps only to be 'Beset By Creatures Of The Deep' (Careful With That Axe, Eugene). Perhaps, as in Bunyan's *Pilgrim's Progress*, he must face out the danger in order to attain enlightenment. The theme is common to many concept pieces of the progressive movement, recalling Yes' 'Close To The Edge' (but better!). The danger, however, is not immediately obvious – the ominous bass theme is almost imperceptible at first, and it is extremely difficult to tell quite where 'The Beginning' ends and 'Beset' begins. It is only after having come close to death, one assumes, that 'The Man' reaches land (with a momentary degree of familiarity, and greater security) and enters 'The Pink Jungle'.

'The Pink Jungle' is the earliest piece included in the suite, being a heavier version of 'Pow R Toc H', a track the band had been playing three years earlier at the Free School. Here it is a sound-picture indicating a surreal environment, and harking back to the psychedelic pursuits of expanding horizons and taking on new experiences. Given this link, it is unsurprising that it ends with a scream and a descent into a place which would appear to be within oneself: 'The Labyrinths Of Auximenes'.

'Labyrinths' brings to mind 'Heart Chakra', a track by Tim Leary on the sound-track to the film *Turn On, Tune In, Drop Out*. Waters' strong bass line recalls the heartbeat, while the image of the 'labyrinth' suggests the human mind. Our hero is actually coming face to face with himself as a result of his experiences, and finds the experience a fearful one, at least at its inception. Auximenes, it has been suggested, was the Greek king Oxymenes – perhaps Waters may have wished to draw a parallel with Theseus' encounter with the Minotaur. In many ways 'The Journey' is Waters' *Iliad*, Homer's odyssey of enlightenment.

'The Labyrinths Of Auximenes', like 'Sleeping' was also to be used extensively for a number of years in different forms. Even while it featured in 'The Massed

Gadgets' the band performed it as part of 'A Celebration For Moon-night', an *Omnibus* special for the BBC's evening of programmes celebrating the Apollo 11 moon-landing on 20 July. Later it was to re-appear as an instrumental on their 1971 tour which has subsequently been christened by bootleggers as 'Corrosion'. Others have noted that elements were to be incorporated into the bass-line of 'Money' on *Dark Side Of The Moon*. It would seem the case that when necessary, the band were quite happy to mine a seam until it was exhausted, despite any intervening years.

It is Gilmour's strong and tranquil guitar wash which heralds 'The Man's' ultimate salvation. 'Behold The Temple Of Light' is clearly a vision of utopia: which may be seen, but not yet experienced. 'The Temple Of Light' may be read objectively as final enlightenment and ultimate contentment. It quickly gives way to 'The End Of The Beginning'. This oxymoron would suggest that while the journey has come to an end, it is never over. While 'The Journey' is complete, the obstacles encountered will not disappear and there is always the risk that one will have to surmount them again to maintain one's new-found contentment.

The thoughts above may seem conjectural to some. Our main aim here is to encourage a re-evaluation of early themes and concept pieces in the band's history – things which often tend to be ignored in the light of their later, more narrative works.

Perhaps, by a thorough knowledge of the chronological facts, this will become an easier and more accessible task for those inclined to set a mind to it. Hopefully the following examination of the band's activities will aid in this process.

AUTHORS' NOTE

Throughout this book, where concert dialogue is transcribed the following legend is used to identify cuts or truncations to tracks, and inaudible dialogue on any available recordings:

><	Recording cut between tracks.
>	Beginning of track cut.
<	End of track cut.
[...]	Dialogue inaudible.

1965
The Beginning – part one

There are seven known occasions on which The Pink Floyd Blues Band / The Tea Set / The Pink Floyd played in 1965. For further details the reader should consult Povey and Russell.[1] The entries that follow reflect the relevant known recorded output around this time.

- **Jokers Wild 5-track single sided LP recorded at Regent's Sound Studios, London, UK.**

  The band released fifty (or forty – no one, not even Clive Welham, their drummer, is sure) copies of this, probably the most scarce Floydian release (RSLP 007). Dave has kept the master tape, though it's unlikely he'll ever give it a proper release.

  Private LP, 11.36, Why Do Fools Fall In Love, 1.53, Walk Like A Man, 2.11, Don't Ask Me, 2.58, Big Girls Don't Cry, 2.16, Beautiful Delilah, 1.54

  Two tracks from the album were also pressed up on a single sided EP (RSRO 031), also in a limited edition of fifty copies.

  Private EP, 4.53, Why Do Fools Fall In Love, 1.53, Don't Ask Me, 2.58

SUMMER

- **'Syd's First Trip' filmed by Nigel Lesmoire-Gordon in a disused quarry outside Cambridge.**

  This received a limited official release by Vex Films in 1993. Cliff Jones in *Mojo* magazine told a convoluted tale about the experiences inspiring 'Astronomy Domine'.[2]

OCTOBER

- **'Lucy Leave' and 'King Bee' recorded.**

  7.00, Lucy Leave, 3.57, King Bee, 2.53

  This 'test recording' has been widely bootlegged. It could have been recorded in November rather than October. EMI engineer Phil Smee has no doubt about their authenticity: 'These are the demos that Peter Jenner said were not good enough to submit to anyone.'[3]

'Lucy Leave' might be the same recording as 'Lucy Lee In Blue Tights' which we have entered under 31 October 1966.

1966
The Beginning – part two

SUNDAY 30

- **Giant Mystery Happening, Marquee Club, Soho, London, UK.**

FEBRUARY

SUNDAY 27

- **Spontaneous Underground, Marquee Club, Soho, London, UK.**

John Hopkins recalled in his oft-quoted 'Psychedelphia' article that:

> The Pink Floyd had been gigging around for a year or two on the London Art
> College Scene when Steven Stollman got them to play at one of his Marquee
> Club happenings. That was almost exactly a year ago. Somehow word got
> around that what they were doing was different. It was. They played mainly
> instrumentals and numbers would sometimes last for half an hour each.
> Guitars played with cigarette lighters, etc.[4]

MARCH

FRIDAY 11

- **Rag Ball, Essex University, Colchester, Essex, UK.**

Roger Waters: 'In 1966 we did a gig at Essex University. We'd already become
interested in mix media, as it were, and some bright spark down there had
done a film with a paraplegic in London, given this paraplegic a film camera
and wheeled him round London filming his view. Now they showed it up on
screen as we played.'[5]

SUNDAY 13

- **Spontaneous Underground, Marquee Club, Soho, London, UK.**

The Floyd would play such things as 'extraordinarily loud and muffled versions of "Louie Louie", "Roadrunner" and the Chuck Berry songbook with instrumental numbers which built up layer upon layer of electronic feedback.'

The flyer for the gig read 'TRIP bring furniture toy prop paper rug paint balloon jumble costume mask robot candle incense ladder wheel light self all others March 13th 5 pm'.

Interviewed in July 1995, Nick Mason commented, in reaction to being shown an ad for this gig, that:

> There were elements of the underground that we did tune into. The main one was mixed media. We may not have been into acid but we certainly understood the idea of a Happening. We supplied the music while people did creative dance, painted their faces, or bathed in the giant jelly. If it had been thirty years earlier Rick would have come out of the floor in front of the cinema screen playing the organ.[6]

SUNDAY 27

- **Spontaneous Underground, Marquee Club, Soho, London, UK.**

APRIL

THURSDAY 7

- **Spontaneous Underground, Marquee Club, Soho, London, UK.**

Rick's comments about 'a private affair' at the Marquee in June may explain why the Marquee's advertisements omit mention of any performances at the venue by any band on the dates the Floyd are known to have played until late December, when the band's profile became more established, and events entered the public domain.

MAY

- **Syd goes to watch experimental avant-garde band AMM record their debut LP with Joe Boyd.**

Keith Rowe, AMM's guitarist, is said to have had an influence on Syd. Their LP *AMMUSIC* now fetches very high prices, though this doesn't stop it from being bloody awful to most ears. It was issued on CD a few years back with additional session outtakes.

EARLY SUMMER

- **Goings On Club, Archer Street, London, UK.**

Underground: The London Alternative Press 1966–1974 describes Miles:

> having made contact with a group of students at the nearby Architectural
> Association ... went to see them play at the Goings On Club in Archer Street,
> a tiny place largely frequented by poets. They were called the Abdabs,
> specialised in serious experimentation in sound and light, wore white coats,
> and would discuss their work, post-performance, with the equally serious
> audience.[7]

This recollection, while interesting, is also somewhat confusing ... the
truism 'if you can remember the 60s you probably weren't there' springs
to mind! Most likely Miles is mistaken about the band's name – the group
had certainly been using the name 'The Pink Floyd' prior to the summer of
66, and the event seems similar to the Sound / Light Workshops which were
presented at the London Free School in November. Nigel Fountain, the
author of *Underground*, mentions how the week after Miles reviewed the gig
for *East Village Other*, the US underground paper, the band changed their
name to The Pink Floyd.

Sue Miles in *Days In The Life* describes how 'anybody could get up and
do anything they wanted. It was actually very good in a funny sort of way.
There were all sorts of poets, bits of magic – Spike Hawkins dropping bits of
broken egg down Johnny Byrne's back.'[8]

JUNE

- **Marquee Club, Soho, London, UK.**

Richard Wright has told how 'It was when we were playing a private affair at
the Marquee that we met managers Peter Jenner and Andrew King.'[9]
Interviewed in *zigzag 25*, Jenner recalled that:

> It was in June, I remember, because I was in the middle of the crucifyingly
> boring chore of marking examination papers ... Anyway, I decided to pack
> it in for the evening and go along to this mad gig at the Marquee, which was
> being run by people like Steve Stollman and Hoppy ... I arrived around 10.30
> and there on the stage was a strange band, who were playing a mixture of
> R&B and electronic noises ... and I was really intrigued because in between
> the routine stuff like 'Louie Louie' and 'Roadrunner', they were playing these
> very weird breaks; so weird that I couldn't even work out which instrument
> the sound was coming from. It was all very bizarre and just what I was looking
> for – a far out, electronic, freaky, pop group ... and there, across the bass amp
> was their name: 'The Pink Floyd Sound'.[10]

Peter Jenner told the story again for *The Story Of Pop*, a BBC radio documentary broadcast in 1994.[11] He confirms there that at the time the band were known as 'The Pink Floyd Sound'.

LATE SUMMER

- **Peter Jenner takes a demo tape of the band to Joe Boyd.**

Joe Boyd recalled in the 1994 *Omnibus* documentary that he received a tape of the band at around this time. We suspect that there may be some confusion between this tape and the account of the Syd Barrett demo tapes, which appears under '1967'. The two might be one and the same.

Joe Boyd referred to the same (or a subsequent!) tape again in 1997. In part two of a documentary series called *Joe Boyd: A World Of Music*,[12] he commented that shortly after October 1966 he 'took the Pink Floyd to Jack Altman and he wasn't interested. But then when I left Elektra [in October of 1966], I carried on taking Floyd tapes to people and got Polygram interested and ended up recording the Pink Floyd ...'[13]

The version of 'Interstellar Overdrive' featured in the CBC Radio documentary described under 'Early 1967' might be sourced from either of the above recordings.

SEPTEMBER

FRIDAY 30

- **All Saints Hall, London Free School, Powis Gardens, Notting Hill Gate, London, UK.**

The correct postal address for All Saints Hall is Powis Square rather than Gardens – we have followed convention. Some people refer to it as being at 26 Powis Terrace, this address being where many of the educational courses and information-giving of the school took place. All Saints Hall was knocked down in the early 80s. Anybody particularly interested in the 'scene' might like to search for the recently reprinted *Days In The Life*.

The gig was advertised as a 'Celebration Dance' featuring the 'Pink Floyd Sound and others'.

A flyer for the gig is reproduced in Miles. His reproduction of *IT* 8 behind the flyer has nothing to do with the gig.

OCTOBER

TUESDAY 11

- *International Times* **newspaper launched.**

International Times, or *IT* as it was more commonly known, was to become the voice of the London underground, in the same way as the *Village Voice* was to articulate the interests of the Eastern US counter-culture.

As a fund-raiser the newspaper organised an event to be held at the Roundhouse in Chalk Farm, London – its announcement was a customarily bold statement of intent, as was the fashion at the time:

> Eleven pm October 15 Round House Chalk Farm. Lovers of the world unite. Costumes. Popstars. All night rave to Launch International Times. The Soft Machine, The Pink Floyd, Steel bands, Strips, Trips, Happenings, Movies. Bring your own poison & flowers & gas-filled balloons & submarine & rocket ship & candy & striped boxes & ladders & paint & flutes & feet & ladders & locomotives & madness & autumn & blowlamps. Pop / Op / Costume / Masque / Fantasy / Loon / Blowout / Drag Ball / SURPRISE FOR THE SHORTEST BAREST COSTUMS [*sic*] AT – The Round House, Chalk Farm Underground. 11 pm onwards.

The Roundhouse was a vast railway shed, owned by British trade unionist Arnold Wesker, who intended setting it up as a centre for bringing 'art' to the working class. He called the venue Centre 42, but did little with it – it was in a bad state of repair and he couldn't raise funds for refurbishment. The Underground, however, borrowed the keys and moved in, much to Wesker's embarrassment – rehearsal space for London's orchestras, not free-form happenings, were what he'd had in mind for the building. In *Underground: The London Alternative Press 1966–74*, Miles later told Nigel Fountain how 'Centre 42 had the place for years and had done fuck-all with it. Through Michael Henshaw we got permission to have a party there. Later on Arnold Wesker severely regretted this.'[14]

FRIDAY 14

- **All Saints Hall, London Free School, Powis Gardens, Notting Hill Gate, London, UK.**

Syd's set list, reproduced in Miles, would indicate that the band performed 'Pink', 'Let's Roll Another', 'Gimme A Break', 'Piggy Back', 'Stoned Alone', 'I Can Tell', 'The Gnome', 'Interstellar Overdrive', 'Lucy Leave', 'Stethascope', 'Flapdoodle Dealing', 'Snowing', 'Mathilda Mother', 'Pow R Toc H', and 'Astronomy Domine'.

The repertoire was to remain more or less the same through the early days of UFO and the Free School.

SATURDAY 15

• *International Times'* **First All-Night Rave, Roundhouse, Chalk Farm, London, UK.**

A flyer produced for the event promised a 'pop op costume masque drag ball et al, strip trip, happenings, movies, Soft Machine, Pink Floyd Steel Band'.

It was the Floyd's first major gig – they played before 2,500 people. Admission was 10d – 5d for anyone in costume. The ancient power supply gave up during 'Interstellar Overdrive' bringing their set to a dramatic end. According to Pip Carter, a friend of the band, 'The Floyd were playing mad interpretations of well-known songs – psychedelic blues such as 'Cops And Robbers' with Syd improvising like hell. He was using his Zippo [a metal cigarette lighter] on his guitar as well as running ball bearings down the neck to produce controlled feedback.' [15]

Melody Maker reviewed the above two gigs, giving the band their first ever national press, passing comment that 'the Floyd need to write their own material – "psychedelic" versions of "Louie Louie" won't come off ...', comments which have been widely quoted elsewhere. At the All Saints Hall:

> the slides were excellent – colourful, frightening, grotesque, beautiful – and the group's trip into outer space sounds promised very interesting things to come. Unfortunately all fell a bit flat in the cold reality of All Saints Hall, Powis Gardens, Notting Hill, but on Saturday night at Chalk Farm's Roundhouse things went better when thousands of people turned up to watch the show.

Mick Farren, a popular figure in the underground at the time, was to describe his experience at the gig in his 1972 book *Watch Out Kids*:

> A band called the Soft Machine played from the floor as a weird biker rode round and round them. Another band, called Pink Floyd, took possession of the stage. They played music that sounded like a guitar solo by The Who, only it was a solo without any song to go round it – like a sandwich without bread. They honked and howled and tweeted, clanked with great concentration. They were very loud with no musical form save that every forty minutes they stopped, paused a while and started again. Across the room an Italian film crew filmed a couple of nubile starlets stomping in a mess of pink emulsion paint. As we lurched into shot we were told by the producer: 'Fuck off, you're spoiling the spontaneity.' [16]

A sizeable proportion of latter day general descriptions of the gig – who was there, etc. – seem to have been initially sourced from the review published in *IT* 2 very shortly after the event. The Pink Floyd get a brief mention:

> The Pink Floyd, psychedelic pop group, did weird things to the feel of the event with their scary feedback sounds, slide projections playing on their skin (drops of paint run riot on the slides to produce outer space / prehistoric textures on the skin), spotlights flashing on them in time with a drum beat.

Perhaps the best report on the event which we have come across was Richard Boston's article printed in *New Society*[17] (later to become *New Statesman*). Boston not only comments on the gig, with the amusing detachment of many who must have passed the throngs of partygoers as they converged on The Roundhouse, but spoke to John Hopkins about the Free School ('a non-organisation existing in name only, with no elected officers and no responsibilities') and *IT*'s politics.

Of the event he wrote that:

> The music was by two groups – the Soft Machine and the Pink Floyd, which is a 'psychedelic pop group': that is to say, if I understand rightly, they produce sounds and lights which resemble hallucinations in psychedelic experiences.
>
> Men outnumbered women substantially, and all the girls seemed firmly attached. Certainly it was not a good place for a pick-up. A mini-skirted girl, who had presumably just repulsed a prowling male, was heard to say to her even more mini-skirted friend, 'What a corny approach.' ... In an area off at one side, out of sound of the music, films were being shown. There was a Feiffer film (called *The Feiffer Film*), and another called *Towers Open Fire* in which William Burroughs talked junk. There were probably others as well, but it was not easy to see over the heads of the crowd at the back, especially as some heads kept getting between the projector and the screen.

SUNDAY 16

- **First nationally published interview with the group in the *Sunday Times* newspaper, UK.**

This interview, made following the *IT* launch party, and widely quoted, was published on 30 October.

FRIDAY 21

- **All Saints Hall, London Free School, Powis Gardens, Notting Hill Gate, London, UK.**

The London Free School's reputation grew very quickly. Roger Waters: 'There were about twenty people there when we first played, the second week one hundred and then three to four hundred and after that many couldn't get in.'

FRIDAY 28

- **All Saints Hall, London Free School, Powis Gardens, Notting Hill Gate, London, UK.**

Some Americans turned up with a collection of non-moving psychedelic slides at one of the All Saints gigs around this time. So as to improve their effect, the band managers went out and bought some sealed beam spotlights and a white sheet for the slides.

MONDAY 31

- **Blackhill Enterprises is established.**

Peter Jenner and Andrew King sign a six-way partnership with the band. Some have suggested that the then lighting man, Joe Gannon, was also party to this original agreement – early articles on the band often referred to him as the fifth band member – however, this seems unlikely. To our knowledge this has not been substantiated, least of all by Jenner who commented in 1994 that, '… we originally had a six-way partnership, which they have never queried. They're incredibly honourable. The Floyd's yearly royalty cheques have kept the wolf from the door on many occasions.'[18]

The name 'Blackhill' was taken by King from a Welsh border cottage that he owned. Other, thorough details may be found in *Days In The Life*.[19]

- **Thompson Private Recording Studios, Hemel Hempstead, UK.**

The studios were very basic – actually a basement in someone's house!

Let's Roll Another One and improvisations, 3.15

'Let's Roll Another One' would, of course, later be renamed 'Candy And A Currant Bun'. The quality of the recordings was by some accounts dreadful, and by King's account in *Crazy Diamond*, quite good – 'similar to things people do on home portastudios today'. The recording of 'Let's Roll Another One' in circulation bears the former suggestion out.

However, 'Interstellar Overdrive' as later appeared on *San Francisco* in April 1968, is of reasonable quality.

San Francisco, Interstellar Overdrive, 15.22

We have five different recordings of the soundtrack, timings of which range from 14 min. 34 sec. to 16 min. 14 sec. All are identical but for the 16mm film source or tape copy running at different speeds. The most reliable length, we would suggest, is that given above (timed by the authors at a private viewing of an original print). Further details regarding the film are given under April 1968.

It is likely that the band also recorded 'Lucy Lee In Blue Tights' and 'I Get Stoned'. Joe Boyd, whom the band knew from his involvement in the UFO, suggested that Blackhill record some high quality masters which could be sold to a record company for immediate release. Years later, according to *Crazy Diamond* 'King and the studio owners waged a bitter legal battle for the rights to the tapes.'[20]

FRIDAY 4

- **All Saints Hall, London Free School, Powis Gardens, Notting Hill Gate, London, UK.**

A poster for the gig – possibly the most valuable that exists – may be seen behind Peter Jenner in his interview for the BBC's 1994 *Omnibus* documentary.[21]

Turn On, Tune In, Drop Out
FRIDAY, 4 and TUESDAY, 8
Free School
Powis Gardens, W.11
Sound/Light Workshop
SATURDAY, 5
Wilton Hall, Bletchley
Blackhill Enterprises 289.0179
41 Edbrooke Road, W.9

Advertisement in *Melody Maker*, 5 November 1966

SATURDAY 5

- **Wilton Hall, Bletchley, Buckinghamshire, UK.**

- **Fiveacre Psychedelic Nudist Colony, Watford, Hertfordshire, UK.**

Guy Fawkes night special!

TUESDAY 8

- **All Saints Hall, London Free School, Powis Gardens, Notting Hill Gate, London, UK.**

FRIDAY 11

- **All Saints Hall, London Free School, Powis Gardens, Notting Hill Gate, London, UK.**

TUESDAY 15

- **All Saints Hall, London Free School, Powis Gardens, Notting Hill Gate, London, UK.**

The ad for this gig and for the one on the 22nd describes the occasions as being a 'Sound / Light Workshop – experimentalists welcome'.

FRIDAY 18

- **Philadelic Music For Simian Hominids, College of Art, Hornsey, London, UK.**

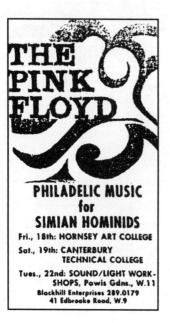

THE PINK FLOYD

**PHILADELIC MUSIC
for
SIMIAN HOMINIDS**

Fri., 18th: HORNSEY ART COLLEGE
Sat., 19th: CANTERBURY
TECHNICAL COLLEGE
Tues., 22nd: SOUND/LIGHT WORK-
SHOPS, Powis Gdns., W.11
Blackhill Enterprises 289.0179
41 Edbrooke Road, W.9

The next three gigs were advertised in an attractive advert placed in *Melody Maker* on the 19th.

It was Mike Leonard – their former landlord and a lecturer at Hornsey College of Art whose experiments with combined sound and lightshows first inspired the band to use the idea in their own shows.

Nick Mason was to comment in a *Melody Maker* interview in early 1967 that 'We were very disorganised then until our managers materialised and we started looking for a guy to do the lights full time. The lighting man literally has to be one of the group. When we were in our early stages we didn't play a lot of our electronic "interstellar" music and the slides were still rather amateurish.'[22]

SATURDAY 19

- **Technical College Dance, Canterbury Technical College, Canterbury, Kent, UK.**

The Floyd played in front of a fifteen-foot high tinfoil Buddha, and were supported by a band called the Koalas.[23] The *Kent Herald* printed an extensive review, and interviewed the band for a feature on the 23rd.

At last the psychedelic sound has come to Canterbury – and how! To my mind, the most powerful instrument of the group is the organ, played by Rik Wright [*sic*]. The strong, loud vibrating sounds drone continuously and build up the main sense of weirdness'.

The journalist goes on to say how 'it is becoming increasingly difficult to describe the music produced by groups today, and in this case the only real solution is for everyone to experience for themselves the effect of psychedelic music.'[24]

TUESDAY 22

• **All Saints Hall, London Free School, Powis Gardens, Notting Hill Gate, London, UK.**

TUESDAY 29

• **All Saints Hall, London Free School, Powis Gardens, Notting Hill Gate, London, UK.**

With their increasing renown and the growth in underground venues around the capital this would be the last time the band would appear at the Free School, probably to the relief of the vicar, who was in the habit of throwing them out at 11 pm.

Norman Evans reviewed the gig in *IT* 5:

Since I last saw the Pink Floyd they've got hold of bigger amplifiers, new light gear and a rave from Paul McCartney. This time I saw them at Powis Gardens, W11 on Tuesday 29th. The last of their regular shows there.

Their work is largely improvisation, and lead guitarist Sid Barrett [*sic*] shoulders most of the burden of providing continuity and attack in the improvised parts. He was providing a huge range of sounds with the new equipment from throttled shrieks to mellow feedback roars.

Visually the show was less adventurous. Three projectors bathed the group, the walls and sometimes the audience in vivid colour. But the colour was fairly static and there was no searching for the brain alpha rhythms by chopping the focus of the images.

The equipment that the group is using now is infant electronics: let's see what they will do with the grownup electronics that a colour television industry will make available.[25]

DECEMBER

• **The Architectural Association, Bedford Square, London, UK.**

• **Royal College of Art, Kensington, London, UK.**

SATURDAY 3

• **Psychodelphia versus Ian Smith, Roundhouse, Chalk Farm, London, UK.**

PSYCHODELPHIA
versus IAN SMITH
GIANT FREAK OUT!
AT THE ROUNDHOUSE
CHALK FARM ROAD. N.W.1
DECEMBER 3rd. 10 p.m. on.
Screaming THOUSANDS, Under-
ground Films, Poets, HAPPEN-
INGS, with the PINK FLOYD and
the RAM HOLDER MESSENGERS.
Bring your own happenings and
ecstatogenic substances.
Drag optional
Tickets at Indica Books
Housemans, Better Books, and Collets

Organised by the Majority Rule for Rhodesia Committee, an anti-apartheid coalition.

The flyer meanwhile looked forward to 'the biggest party ever, fancy dress optional. Pink Floyd – Films. Madness etc.'

Advertisement in *Melody Maker*, 3 December 1966

MONDAY 12

- **You're Joking? A Show For Oxfam, Royal Albert Hall, Kensington, London, UK.**

This was the Floyd's first appearance at a large and prestigious venue.

According to Rick Sanders,[26] they shared the bill with John Bird, Eleanor Bron, Peter Cook and Dudley Moore and members of the Royal Shakespeare Company.

THURSDAY 22

- **Marquee Club, Soho, London, UK.**

Their first appearance at the club since Spontaneous Underground – the event ran from 7.30 until 11.00 pm, with The Iveys also performing. John Hopkins was to offer the band a contract to supply mixed-media for his new club, UFO.

Advertisement in *Melody Maker*, 24 December 1966

- **UFO Presents Night Tripper, The Blarney Club, Tottenham Court Road, London, UK.**

The club's opening night; John Hopkins and Joe Boyd set up UFO as a response to the increasing popularity of the Free School, and the success of events at the Roundhouse. The idea was originally intended to run over Christmas, with two nights at the Blarney booked. It quickly became evident that the club was what the underground needed, and UFO almost immediately became the heart of the London underground. A detailed account of the early days of the club may be found in *Days In The Life*.[27]

Miles reported in *IT* 29 that 'December 23rd saw "Night Tripper" at Tottenham Court Road, advertised by a poster and display ad in *IT* 5 and by pamphlets handed out on the Portobello Road in Notting Hill. There was no indication as to who would be there performing, the audience attended because they 'knew' who would be there and 'knew' what was happening.'

The true meaning of the acronym UFO has never been convincingly told … suggestions have included Unlimited Freak Out, Underground Freak Out or, more obviously, Unidentified Flying Object.

Chris Welch wrote at length on the Club in the *Melody Maker*,[28] including interviews with Joe Boyd and Dave Howson. A nice but blurred photo of a band that *looks* like the Floyd (!) accompanies the piece.

The ad for the gig, and that on the 30th, appeared in *Melody Maker* on 24 December and promised 'films, slides, heat, food'. 'Night Tripper' started at 10.30 pm and finished at 4.30 am. Membership was free on the opening night. Support was provided by Soft Machine.

THURSDAY 29

- **Marquee Club, Soho, London, UK.**

An advertisement in *Melody Maker*[29] advises that it was scheduled to run from 7.30 – 11.00 pm. Early enough for ravers to catch the last tube home. The band were supported by Syn.

FRIDAY 30

- **UFO Presents Night Tripper, The Blarney Club, Tottenham Court Road, London, UK.**

Following this gig the Blarney Club was renamed UFO and became a regular event.

Miles in *IT* 29, 'the name change to the UFO occurred the next week and the first UFO advertised the Pink Floyd, Fanta and Ood, the Giant Sun Trolly and Dave Tomlin improvising to government propaganda.'

U F O presents

NIGHT TRIPPER

with

PINK ● films slides heat food

FLOYD

10/- admission
with free membership opening night
Friday, Dec. 23 & 30. 10.30-4.30
31 Tottenham Court Road

Advertisement in *Melody Maker*,
24 December 1966

Until this point, the Blarney Club, which was more used to hosting Irish dances on Thursdays and Saturdays, attracted little or no attention from the nearby Tottenham Court Road Police Station. As the weeks went by, the police would increasingly succumb to the temptation to search the strange-looking people who queued patiently outside the Berkley and Continental cinemas above the club, but would stop at going inside.

SATURDAY 31

- **New Year's Party, Cambridge Technical College, Cambridge, Cambridgeshire, UK.**

- **Psychedelicamania, New Year's Eve All Night Rave, Roundhouse, Chalk Farm Road, London, UK.**

The Pink Floyd supported The Who and The Move. A large and interesting advert was placed in *Melody Maker* on the 24th and the 31st to promote the event, which was scheduled from '10.00 pm till dawn'.

The *Daily Mail* newspaper attended both gigs, and published an article warning of 'pop above the danger level'.

> Teenagers celebrating the New Year at two psychedelic pop music sessions in London were risking permanent damage to the ears. The music and light were arranged to create the psychedelic sensations similar to those experienced by taking the drug LSD.
>
> The lowest sound level in both clubs was 90 decibels on the edge of the dance floor. The highest was a steady 110 near the loudspeaker, where 20 to 30 young people were clustered in dazed immobility. The Pink Floyd group occasionally reached 120 at the 'Freak-out'.[30]

Nick Jones reviewed the gig in detail for *Melody Maker* on 7 January of the following year. Of the Floyd he wrote how 'on stage the Pink Floyd, The Who, and The Move each attempted to excite the audience into some positive action. The Pink Floyd have a promising sound, and some very groovy picture slides which attract far more attention than the group, as they merge, blossom, burst, grow, divide and die.'

LATE

- **Pearce Marchbank (later to design *Friends* and *Time Out*) plans an underground magazine to rival *IT*: the *Wall Street Journal.***

The magazine, which to the best of our knowledge didn't get off the ground, was to include posters by various artists including Nick Mason.

1967
Doing It!

- **The Swinging London Set, a feature at Madame Tussaud's Waxworks Gallery, London, UK.**

  'The Swinging London Set' by James Butler, an installation of 'blown-up photos of various pop figures' was unveiled at Madame Tussaud's in September 1966. Miles asserts that the band were on the mural in 1967. This is mistaken – the archive department at Madame Tussaud's has no record of Pink Floyd being involved – the Beatles certainly were however.

- **RTBF radio broadcast, Belgium.**

  The show was simply a Belgian broadcast of excerpts from the BBC's *Look Of The Week* programme. A number of other European broadcasts contemporary or otherwise, are often passed off as being 'different'. The commentary confirms that the copy in general circulation is from a rebroadcast. Whether or not there is or was an 'original' we don't know.

  RTBF broadcast, Astronomy Domine with introduction, 4.23

- ***Pop Colour Mix*, ZDF TV, Wiesbaden, West Germany.**

  A colour television ZDF test transmission, the band are seen performing 'Interstellar Overdrive' 'live' in the studio. Never rebroadcast, this remains a dusty gem which few have ever seen.

- **Syd Barrett solo demos recorded for Joe Boyd.**

  The only track known to be on this tape was 'Boom Tune', written for The Purple Gang. Sadly, the recordings appear to have been lost. It has been suggested that it was recorded in the summer of 1967, although an earlier date may be more likely. 'Boom Tune' is doubtless an alternative title for 'Here I Go', in view of the latter's line, 'What a boom this tune'.[31] Incidentally, while The Purple Gang achieved some success in the underground with their anthem 'Granny Takes A Trip' their sound was pure jugband, and unlikely to be of interest to even the most ardent student of the counter-culture.

  Joe Boyd recounted in *Days In The Life*: 'Just before UFO began I had set up Witchseason Productions when I thought I had signed the Pink Floyd to Polydor. That's why I had set up the company. The deal fell apart.'[32]

  Perhaps Syd made the recording in late 1966 'just before UFO began'. It could be that the tape was also a demo for Polydor.

EARLY

• **CBC Radio, Canada.**

Probably the earliest radio interview with the band and Pete Jenner, this was rebroadcast as part of Capital Radio's *The Pink Floyd Story*, in December 1976.[33] The interview features a unique recording of 'Interstellar Overdrive'.

9.16, featuring Interstellar Overdrive

There is also another version of this recording, possibly taken from the original master, which has recently surfaced, featuring a longer version of 'Interstellar Overdrive', but omitting much of the interview with Peter Jenner. In *The Pink Floyd Story* version, 'Interstellar Overdrive', the reader will have probably noted, fades very shortly after Peter Jenner says 'we think we can do both'. While this first copy continues for a moment or so, the second continues for a further 1 min. 1 sec. and ends with a particularly unaggressive crescendo, as opposed to the version of 'Interstellar' that appears on *Tonite Let's All Make Love In London*.

The recording is plainly early but is not the same as that which appears on the *San Francisco* soundtrack. Trying to attribute a date to it is problematic – perhaps it too, was recorded at their first 31 October 1966 recording session or the reader might like to refer to our entry regarding Peter Jenner's demo tape(s) under Summer 1966.

7.06, with longer version of Interstellar Overdrive

JANUARY

SUNDAY 1

• **'Spotlight On The Pink Floyd And The Move', written by Chris Welch and Nick Jones, published in *Melody Maker* magazine, UK.**

An article that concentrates more on The Move than Pink Floyd. Nick Mason and Roger Waters comment on the psychedelic scene.

The piece concludes that, 'The Move and Pink Floyd are two of today's groups. You may find their attitudes frightening or refreshing – fun or phoney. But by thunder – it's rhythmical!' The authors agree with gusto!

THURSDAY 5

• **Marquee Club, Soho, London, UK.**

An advert in *Melody Maker* on 24 December 1966 indicates that Eyes Of Blue provided support.

Like all week-day events at The Marquee the club was open from 7.30 to 11.00 pm.

Friday 6

- **Freak Out Ethel, Seymour Hall, London, UK (7.30 pm).**

An attractive 'photoposter' advertising this gig is available. Sadly, it is a composite, combining a period picture with a blow-up of the flyer.

Sunday 8

- **Uppercut Club, Forest Gate, London, UK.**

Monday 9

- **Rehearsals, London, UK.**

We have attached the date to what follows by deduction. Joe Boyd speaking on Independent London Radio in 1982:

> We were rehearsing at Polydor's studios in Stratford Place, getting what was, I think, two days from the session. Andrew and Peter, who were managing the Pink Floyd, called me up and said that they had just signed with an agency – the Bryan Morrison Agency – and the agents wanted to come down and meet me and meet the group, etc. These three guys walked in from the Bryan Morrison Agency and there was an immediate, intense dislike between myself and those three, and they were saying, 'Well, we don't think this Polydor deal is very good and we can get you a better deal etc., etc., and who are you? Listen to us and everything's going to be a lot better ...'
>
> And the next thing I knew was that Andrew and Peter were calling me up saying that the band were not going to sign the Polydor deal and that Bryan Morrison was putting up the money for an independent recording, which we would then go and deal as a master and sell to a record company. And the record was produced and they then sold it to EMI. The same agents then came down and immediately said, 'You can't have them at UFO anymore.'

Wednesday 11

- **Sound Techniques Studios, Chelsea, London, UK.**

Joe Boyd speaking in 1997, explained that after the *IT* launch party, he 'continued taking Pink Floyd tapes to people and got Polygram interested and ended up recording the Pink Floyd. Originally it was supposed to be for Polygram (Polydor at the time) but by the time we actually made the record there had been interest from EMI who kind of gazumped Polydor.' [34]

The Floyd recorded 'Interstellar Overdrive', 'Let's Roll Another One', and 'Arnold Layne'. 'Let's Roll Another One' would later be rewritten as 'Candy And A Currant Bun', after the BBC refused to play the single because they felt the B side was advocating illegal drug use.

THURSDAY 12

- **Sound Techniques Studios, Chelsea, London, UK.**

Accounts of the date of recording 'Interstellar Overdrive', 'Let's Roll Another One' and 'Arnold Layne' are historically quite clear – the 11th is the correct date. The lengthy version of 'Interstellar Overdrive' and 'Nick's Boogie' were not known to have been in existence until about 1994, as was the existence of this second date. Peter Whitehead only filmed and recorded the latter two for his film – indeed he helped finance the session for the purposes of including the band in *Tonite Let's All Make Love In London*. We would suggest that it is reasonable to surmise that three songs were recorded on one day and two on the other, but in which order we do not know.

FRIDAY 13

- **UFO Club, Tottenham Court Road, London, UK.**

The flyer read, 'Gape at the film MARILYN MUNROE, thrill to the GIANT SUN TROLLEY, gasp at the horrible crawling SLIDES.'
    The Giant Sun Trolley, an avant-garde 'medieval' group would later change their name to The Third Ear Band, and sign to Harvest records, home of the Floyd.
    The footage of the band that may be seen in the 'See For Miles' video *The Pink Floyd – London 66–67* was filmed at this gig.

SATURDAY 14

- **Reading University, Reading, Berkshire, UK.**

MONDAY 16

- **Institute of Contemporary Arts (ICA) Clubroom, St James, London, UK.**

In the tradition of serious art which the ICA promoted the band were to answer questions about their performance and their music after they'd done the show.

TUESDAY 17

- **Music In Colour, Commonwealth Institute, Kensington, London, UK.**

> **TICKETS 10/-**
> at door or from
> DOBELLS
> BETTER BOOKS
> COLLETS
> INDICA, or
> CHRISTOPHER
> HUNT LTD.
> Tel. GUL 1748
>
> Christopher Hunt presents
> Music in Colour *by*
> **THE PINK FLOYD**
> **COMMONWEALTH INSTITUTE**
> Kensington High Street
> **TUESDAY, JAN. 17th — 8 p.m.**

While in the course of our research the Commonwealth Institute's archive department was contacted. It would appear that no records of this concert were kept as it was a private booking. This gig was the band's first association with Classical promotor Christopher Hunt, who was later to help with the 'Games For May' extravaganza.

THURSDAY 19

- **Marquee Club, Soho, London, UK.**

90 Wardour Street   London W.1

Thursday, January 19th (7 30-11 0)
★ **THE PINK FLOYD**
★ MARMALADE
Friday, January 20th (7 30-11 0)
★ **SONNY CHILDE**
and the TNT
★ FELDER'S ORIOLES
Saturday, January 21st (8 0-11 30)
★ **THE NEAT CHANGE**
★ **THE BUNCH**
Sunday, January 22nd (8 0-10 30)
★ SUNDAY SPECTACULAR
★ An Evening with
★**BEN WEBSTER** AND
★**BLOSSOM DEARIE**
with the
★**RONNIE SCOTT**
QUARTET

Monday, January 23rd (7 30-11 0)
★**THE HERD**
★THE ULTIMATE
Tuesday, January 24th (7 30-11 0)
FIRST APPEARANCE AT THE MARQUEE
★ **JIMI HENDRIX**
★SYN
Wednesday, January 25th (7 30-11 0)
★ MARTIN WINSOR
★ RED SULLIVAN
plus SPECIAL GUESTS

marquee artists Agency and Management
18 Carlisle Street, W.1

FRIDAY 20

- **UFO Club, Tottenham Court Road, London, UK.**

Director Joe Durden-Smith filmed the show for the Granada TV documentary *Underground: Scene Special*, broadcast on 7 February. The documentary, an overview of the extended underground, featured footage from the 'Cosmic Poetry Visitation' at the Royal Albert Hall in June 1965, experimental theatre and a 'legalise pot' rally!

The Floyd are heard performing an early live version of 'Matilda Mother', which appears as background music and is unfortunately of risible quality. Various underground luminaries interrupt the music in order to give their view of the 'scene'. A happening at Piccadilly Circus can also be heard; it is over footage of this that the track is played. The version is often mistakenly referred to as being 'Percy The Ratcatcher', which is, of course, an early title for 'Lucifer Sam'.[35] The excerpt shows all the signs of being a live rendition but the sound quality and ambience is quite different to the recording of 'Interstellar Overdrive' later in the programme. This said, it is most likely that both are from the same gig.

The sequence featuring 'Interstellar Overdrive' comprises some excellent footage of the band performing four minutes of the track before a small but animated audience. 'Interstellar' is used as an anchor for the documentary's climactic argument. The narrator tells us that 'One of the aims ...' presumably of the Floyd, '... is to make music a felt experience', and he goes on to describe the music as that of 'experience rather than melody'. The thirty second reprise may be heard over the credits at the end of the programme. Some bootleg versions of the piece have a section of each excerpt segued together. The segue sounds reasonable but denies the listener the entirety of the music.

An alternative explanation to the long-term assertion that the footage is from the above date may be found under our entry for the 27 January.

Underground: Scene Special, 29.58, Matilda Mother, 2.41, Interstellar Overdrive, 4.13, Interstellar Overdrive reprise, 0.34

On 24 June 1988 the UK's Channel 4 TV station featured a minute of 'Interstellar Overdrive' in the programme *Wired*.

Wired, Interstellar Overdrive, 1.00

The band were supported on this occasion by Marmalade.

- **Irene Winsby photographs the band rehearsing.**

The photographs, by Irene Winsby, from the early pages of Miles were photographed on or about this date. An additional three photographs from a large private collection from the period found their way onto the London market in early 1995. The photographs would probably not have passed the photographer's quality control – Rick's eyes, for example, are closed in one – and are, as a consequence, perhaps all the more interesting. Syd changes his shirt during the session and is obviously very stoned by its end. Some other examples may be found between pages 246 and 247.

January 1967

SATURDAY 21

- **Birdcage Club, Portsmouth, Hampshire, UK.**

SUNDAY 22

- **Rehearsals, London, UK.**

MONDAY 23 – WEDNESDAY 25

- **Sound Techniques Studios, Chelsea, London, UK.**

THURSDAY 26

- **Rehearsals, London, UK.**

FRIDAY 27

- **UFO Club, Tottenham Court Road, London, UK.**

Miles clearly asserts that the band were filmed for *Underground: Scene Special* on the 20th. However, *Melody Maker* in the news section of its 28 January issue commented:

> Granada Television is to make a documentary programme about London's UFO Club, the mixed media centre in London's Tottenham Court Road. The film will be made at the club tomorrow (Friday).
> Material filmed at the club will be used in the TV documentary which will be broadcast on February 7.

'Tomorrow (Friday)' suggests the 27th. Actual publication date for *Melody Maker* has always been a week previous to the date on its cover, as is the case with many publications. It would be unreasonable to conclusively back either date. The credits on the programme itself don't help.

SATURDAY 28

- **University of Essex, Wivenhoe Park, Colchester, Essex, UK.**

SUNDAY 29

- **Sound Techniques Studios, Chelsea, London, UK.**

MONDAY 30

- **Photo session and rehearsal, London, UK.**

TUESDAY 31

- Sound Techniques Studios, Chelsea, London, UK.

FEBRUARY

WEDNESDAY 1

- The Pink Floyd turn professional.

  Roger left college. He had completed five years out of seven on his architecture course. A number of commentators assert that Syd had written nearly all of the songs which he recorded with the Pink Floyd over the preceding six months.

- Sound Techniques Studios, Chelsea, London, UK.

THURSDAY 2

- Cadenna's, Guildford, Surrey, UK.

FRIDAY 3

- Queen's Hall, Leeds, Yorkshire, UK.

MONDAY 6

- *Jackie* photo sessions, London, UK.

TUESDAY 7

- Broadcast of Granada TV's *Underground: Scene Special*.

- *Fabulous* photo sessions, London, UK.

WEDNESDAY 8

- Rehearsals, London, UK.

THURSDAY 9

- New Addington Hotel, Croydon, London, UK.

February 1967

FRIDAY 10

- Leicester College of Technology, Leicester, Leicestershire, UK.

SATURDAY 11

- Sussex University, Falmer, Brighton, East Sussex, UK.

MONDAY 13

- Photo sessions, London, UK.

THURSDAY 16

- Southampton Guildhall, Southampton, Hampshire, UK (cancelled).

FRIDAY 17

- St Catherine's College Valentine Ball, Dorothy Ballroom, Cambridge, Cambridgeshire, UK.

THE VALENTINE BALL IS EVERYBODY'S BALL
at
THE DOROTHY
THIS FRIDAY, 10 p.m. to 3 a.m.
THE PINK FLOYD
BOB KIDMAN
ALEXIS KORNER BLUES INC.
PEARL HAWAIIANS, etc.
DISCOTHEQUE BAR CABARET BUFFET
Double Tickets 3½ guineas from Martin Wakeling, St. Catherine's College, Miller's, or the Dorothy

Advertisement in *Cambridge Evening News*, 15 February 1967

A battered copy of the poster for the concert was sold at a London memorabilia shop for £1500 in 1995.

SATURDAY 18

- California Ballroom, Dunstable, Bedfordshire, UK.

Roger recalled in an interview with *zigzag* magazine in 1973: 'The California Ballroom, Dunstable was the one where they were pouring pints of beer on to us from the balcony, that was most unpleasant, and very, very dangerous too … we actually had broken beer mugs smashing into the drum kit.'

Nick Mason in *Mojo* magazine:

Audiences often turned quite hostile, about 20 to 30 minutes into the set.
Sometimes it was expressed by the throwing of objects, sometimes by their
leaving the facility. Therefore, the conclusion must be that either they didn't
fit or the audience didn't understand. It was very curious.[36]

Monday 20

• **Adelphi Ballroom, West Bromwich, West Midlands, UK.**

Tuesday 21 – Wednesday 22

• **EMI, Studio 3, Abbey Road, London, UK.**

Recording 'Matildas Mother'. It should be noted that where necessary we
use the original and exact titles listed by Malcolm Jones, as taken from the
original session sheets; in this way we hope to track the development of the
songs as their titles evolve over time.

Thursday 23

• **EMI, Studio 3, Abbey Road, London, UK.**

'Matildas Mother' mono and stereo mixing sessions.

Friday 24

• **Ricky-Tick Club, Thames Hotel, Windsor, Berkshire, UK.**

June Bolan, Blackhill's secretary and the band's occasional van driver recalled
in *Days In The Life* how 'you'd do three gigs a night: a club called Rikki-Tik
[*sic*] in Windsor and another Rikki-Tik [*sic*] (I think in Hounslow) and then
your third gig for the night, at two o'clock in the morning, would be UFO
in Tottenham Court Road.'[37]
   While the band's schedule was certainly hectic at the time, Bolan's recollection is not altogether convincing – reliable evidence suggests that the band
played Hounslow on the 25th – to our mind it is unlikely that they played
there on consecutive nights.

• **UFO Club, Tottenham Court Road, London, UK.**

The advert for the gig in *IT* 14 describes the event as 'the return of the invisible Pink Floyd'. They were supported by the Brothers Grimm while there
were also to be 'films, etc'. The poster emblazons the Floyd's name (amongst
others) on a cross-section of a cauliflower!

February 1967

- **Ricky-Tick Club, Hounslow, Middlesex, UK.**

Despite June Bolan's comments, perhaps it is wise to trust this as the true date of the band's performance at the Hounslow Ricky-Tick, since it is after Malcolm Jones' record taken from the Floyd's own date sheets.

MONDAY 27

- **Sound Techniques Studios, Chelsea, London, UK.**

Two takes of 'Arnold Layne' (one of which would form the A side of the single released on 11 March) were recorded, as was 'Candy And A Current Bun' (that released as the single B side) and a take of 'Chapter 24'. The sessions were engineered by John Woods, who co-owned Sound Techniques. The band also recorded an alternative version of 'Interstellar Overdrive', later released by EMI-France in July 1967. Both Miles and Watkinson and Anderson mistakenly describe this version of 'Interstellar Overdrive' as never having been released.[38]

Recently a shorter, edited version of 'Arnold Layne' has been discovered, allegedly taken from an acetate, the edit is somewhat crude, and it is possible that it is bogus.

Arnold Layne, rejected edit from acetate, 2.24, 2.29

Along with the above, an 'original' version of 'Candy And A Currant Bun' which is both shorter and with substantially different (more overtly drug inspired) lyrics has surfaced. We assume that it was recorded on this date since the backing track is identical to the official release, excepting the omission of the central keyboard break, though we can find no documentary evidence as such to support this.

Candy And A Currant Bun, uncensored, 1.50, 1.54

TUESDAY 28

- **Blaises Club, Queensway, London, UK.**

LATE

- **The Floyd sign for EMI.**

None of the biographies or major journalistic accounts name the actual date on which the Floyd signed on the dotted line, though it was presumably on the 28th giving time for recording on the 27th and their being in an EMI studio on 1 March. Caroline Boucher in an article entitled 'Waters In The

Pink', published in *Disc & Music Echo* on 8 August 1970, confirms that the band were only 'semi-professional' on the 27 February.

In his article about the band in *IT* 10, John Hopkins suggests that the *News Of The World* 'social deviants' article – 'Pop Stars And Drugs' – that was published around this time delayed the band's signing with EMI.

The band, most commentators agree, were signed by EMI for an advance of £5,000 and that the contract required the band to produce albums rather than just singles – an exceptional sum and exceptional terms for the time. Waters later described the deal as 'bloody stupid'.[39]

Numerous fans argue that EMI filmed the signing and that they retain a copy of the same in their archive. Footage that is said to be from this date may be seen in the 1994 Vex film. Overdubbed material that looks equally contemporaneous appeared in the 1990 Knebworth film. About a minute long in all, and probably sourced from three different shoots, the band (and a couple of female friends) are seen in the back garden of a very Hampstead-ian looking house, and then later walking about a park which would appear to be Regent's Park in North London. The footage concentrates on Syd, who plays up for the camera.

MARCH

- **SRP3 radio, Stockholm, Sweden, interview Nick Mason.**

  Interview, 1.23

WEDNESDAY 1

- **EMI, Studio 3, Abbey Road, London, UK.**

  The band worked on the final stereo and mono mixes of 'Chapter 24' and 'Interstellar Overdrive'.

  Chapter 24 magazine no. 4 printed an excellent interview with Phil Smee by David Parker. David asked Phil how he'd become involved in the *Opel* album – it had begun with a meeting at EMI:

  > 'This is the sort of thing we've found,' they said, and played me a tape of a 1967 Pink Floyd instrumental! I was told it was an unfinished backing track from their first EMI recording session, though it sounded like a finished recording to me. The whole thing lasted about four minutes and sounded a bit like the middle section of 'See Emily Play'.

  The interviewer understood that this track was part of a cassette that had been circulating within EMI containing unissued Syd Barrett and/or Pink Floyd recordings.

- **The Dance Hall, Eel Pie Island, Twickenham, Middlesex, UK.**

THURSDAY 2

- Assembly Rooms, Worthing, East Sussex, UK.

FRIDAY 3

- Market Hall, St Albans, Hertfordshire, UK.

SATURDAY 4

- Poly Rag Ball 1967, Regent Street Polytechnic, London, UK.

SUNDAY 5

- Saville Theatre, Shaftsbury Avenue, London, UK.

MONDAY 6

- *The Rave*, Granada TV Studios, Manchester, Greater Manchester, UK.

  As was often the case in the mid-sixties, pop bands would occasionally be given their own pop shows, onto which they would invite guests to perform. *The Rave* was The Move's show, and they were to give the Floyd some early exposure. It is thought that 'Arnold Layne' was shown, though only briefly.

TUESDAY 7

- Malvern Big Beat Sessions, Winter Gardens, Malvern, Worcestershire, UK.

THURSDAY 9

- Marquee Club, Soho, London, UK.

FRIDAY 10

- UFO Club, Tottenham Court Road, London, UK.

  The ad for the gig in *Melody Maker* promised, 'Films – Lights – raids – subversives'.

SATURDAY 11

- 'Arnold Layne' / 'Candy And A Currant Bun' single released in the UK.

  Melody Maker ran a review and interview with Syd shortly after.

- **Technical College Dance, Canterbury, Kent, UK.**

The band were supported by Spectre Quinn.

The *Kent Herald* reviewed the concert and spoke to the band afterwards – their reporter seems to have been impressed!

> When the Pink Floyd played at Canterbury in November they were good, but when they returned on Saturday to the Canterbury Technical College dance they were even better … The music, a mixture of high droning sounds and exciting build ups, teamed with flashing and unusual colours projected on to the back of the stage, go to make up an exciting improvised act.
>
> As the music starts people listen uninterestedly, but after about three minutes the sound is so strong that it is impossible not to go with it.

The band were to comment after the gig how they too felt that they had developed since their previous visit. All of this went under the rather amusing headline, 'The pagan effect of the Pink Floyd'.[40]

The *Kentish Gazette*'s preview on 10 March quoted the band as saying,

> I suppose that if we had to have some kind of definition, you could say The Pink Floyd were lights and sounds. The two mediums complement each other and we definitely don't use them together as a gimmick. Our aim is simply to make our audiences dig the effect.[41]

SUNDAY 12

- **Agincourt Ballroom, Camberley, Surrey, UK.**

MONDAY 13

- **The often quoted and much reproduced 'The Pink Floyd Versus Psychedelphia' article by John Hopkins appears in *IT* no. 10.**

TUESDAY 14 – WEDNESDAY 15

- **EMI, Studio 3, Abbey Road, London, UK.**

Working once again on 'Chapter 24' and 'Interstellar Overdrive' (short version). It is possible that this session, and not that from the 27th, is the origin of 'The French EP' version of 'Interstellar Overdrive'.

THURSDAY 16

- **EMI, Studio 3, Abbey Road, London, UK.**

'Interstellar Overdrive' was recorded, along with a track logged by EMI as 'Flame', both were produced by Norman Smith.

Peter Jenner in 1994: 'They played it twice, one version recorded straight on top of the other. They doubletracked the whole track. Why? Well it sounds pretty fucking weird doesn't it? That big sound and all those hammering drums.' [42]

- **Middle Earth, Covent Garden, London, UK.**

The poster for this gig is illustrated in Michael English's book *3D Eye*. [43]

FRIDAY 17

- **Kingston Technical College, Kingston-upon-Thames, Surrey, UK.**

SATURDAY 18

- **Enfield College of Technology, Queensway, Enfield, Middlesex, UK.**

SUNDAY 19 – MONDAY 20

- **EMI, Studio 3, Abbey Road, London, UK.**

The band were pretty busy during these sessions, managing to get work done on 'Take Up Thy Stethoscope' (two versions) and 'The Gnome', along with first takes of 'The Scarecrow' and 'Power Toc H'.

MONDAY 20

- **'Arnold Layne' promotional film is completed.**

This film – which is thought of as the standard 'Arnold Layne' promo (with the band and a mannequin dressed as undertakers in a short reminiscent of a silent-movie), was filmed by the BBC for *Top Of The Pops*. It was scheduled to be shown on 6 April. Unfortunately, by the time of the broadcast the single was dropping down the charts and the film was pulled at the last minute. It was eventually shown on French TV's *Bouton Rouge* on 21 May.

The filming date is confirmed in *Melody Maker* on 25 March: 'On Monday the Pink Floyd finished filming a short promotional clip for the single'. 'Finished' suggests that filming it might have taken more than a day.

Arnold Layne, 1.33, video

Many collectors have incomplete (1 min. 10 sec.) copies of the video, sourced from the 1990 Knebworth film.

TUESDAY 21

* **EMI, Studio 3, Abbey Road, London, UK.**

  Further work on 'Power Toc H'.
  Mark Lewishohn in *The Complete Beatles Recording Sessions* writes how on this day

  > Norman Smith was working elsewhere in Abbey Road during this evening, producing ... 'The Piper At The Gates Of Dawn'. At around 11 pm he brought in his young group to sheepishly meet the Beatles and exchange what Hunter Davies noted as 'half-hearted hellos'.[44]

  Melody Maker suggests in its 25 March issue that the Floyd had been dropped in upon by Paul McCartney on several occasions. We've read about six differing accounts of the 'drop-in' and find Mark Lewishohn's to be the most convincing. Nick Mason: 'It was a bit like meeting the Royal family.'[45]

WEDNESDAY 22

* **EMI, Studio 3, Abbey Road, London, UK.**

  'Interstellar Overdrive' – mono and stereo mixdowns.

THURSDAY 23

* **Rotherham College of Technology, Rotherham, Yorkshire, UK.**

FRIDAY 24

* **Ricky-Tick Club, Hounslow, Middlesex, UK.**

SATURDAY 25

* **Ricky-Tick Club, Thames Hotel, Windsor, Berkshire, UK.**

* ***Melody Maker* updates the public on progress on *Piper*.**

  > The Pink Floyd, whose first single 'Arnold Layne' hit the Pop 50 at number 33 this week, have now completed five tracks of their first album. Beatle Paul McCartney has already dropped into several of the sessions and reports say the album is a 'knock-out'.

  Following our description of the progress thus far, those five tracks were probably 'Matildas Mother', 'Chapter 24', 'Interstellar Overdrive', 'Flame' and either 'Take Up Thy Stethoscope' or 'The Gnome' from the sessions on 19 and 20 March. The band, within a month of starting, were almost half way towards completing the substance of the album.

SUNDAY 26

- EMI, Studio 3, Abbey Road, London, UK.

- Rex Ballroom, Bognor Regis, Sussex, UK.

MONDAY 27

- EMI, Studio 3, Abbey Road, London, UK.

TUESDAY 28

- Easter Rave, Chinese R & B Jazz Club, Corn Exchange, Bristol, Avon, UK.

News Flash — Easter Rave
CHINESE R & B JAZZ CLUB
BRISTOL CORN EXCHANGE
Tonight (March 28) ★ ★ ★
It's New — It's Great
THE PINK FLOYD
The New Rage

The advertisement promised 'It's New – It's Great, The Pink Floyd, The New Rage'.[46]

WEDNESDAY 29

- EMI, Studio 3, Abbey Road, London, UK.

  Mono and stereo mixing sessions for 'The Gnome', 'Power Toc H', 'The Scarecrow' and 'Take Up Thy Stethoscope And Walk'.

- The Dance Hall, Eel Pie Island Hotel, Twickenham, Middlesex, UK.

THURSDAY 30

- An article about the band appears in *Hit Week*, a Dutch music magazine.

- EMI, Studio 3, Abbey Road, London, UK.

FRIDAY 31

- Top Spot Ballroom, Ross-on-Wye, Herefordshire, UK.

APRIL

SATURDAY 1

- **EMI launches the group to the press.**

- *Melody Maker* **publishes an article about the band entitled 'Freaking Out With The Pink Floyd'.**

- **The Birdcage, Portsmouth, Hampshire, UK.**

MONDAY 3

- **BBC TV Studios, London, UK.**

- *Monday Monday,* **live broadcast from the Playhouse Theatre, Northumberland Avenue, London.**

The broadcast was presented by Dave Cash and produced by Don George. It was aired between 1.00 – 2.00 pm. 'Arnold Layne' and 'Candy And A Currant Bun' were played. The broadcast was not recorded by the BBC and seems not to have survived elsewhere.

TUESDAY 4

- **BBC TV Studios, London, UK.**

WEDNESDAY 5

- **BBC TV Studios, London, UK.**

THURSDAY 6

- **First appearance on** *Top Of The Pops,* **BBC 1 TV, London, UK (cancelled).**

The Floyd were advertised in *Melody Maker* on 8 April as making their debut on *Top Of The Pops* on the 6th.
  Melody Maker confirmed the cancellation on 15 April with the following report:

> Producer Stanley Dorfman told MM on Monday: 'We filmed the Floyd and the Move before last week's show because they were both playing out of town on Thursday night. Naturally we wanted to get the film in the can in case their records entered the chart. In fact on our combined chart the Floyd dropped three places so it ruled them out of the show.'

April 1967

- **Salisbury City Hall, Salisbury, Wiltshire, UK.**

- **Floral Hall, Belle Vue, Belfast, County Antrim, Northern Ireland.**

Waters told *Melody Maker* how 'we played in Belfast recently and the reception there was great. The same thing happened when we played in Abergavenny. We had screamers and everything.' The article also confirms that the band hired a plane to take them to the gig.[47]

- **An article about the band appears in *Go* magazine, USA.**

- **Plans for *The Life Story Of Percy The Ratcatcher*, a feature film produced by the band, are revealed in the press.**

Melody Maker reports that 'Plans have moved ahead quickly for the group to start shooting sequences for their first feature film on April 24. The provisional title of the half-hour film is *The Life Story Of Percy The Ratcatcher*.'

- **Rhodes Centre, Bishop's Stortford, Hertfordshire, UK.**

- **Roundhouse, Chalk Farm, London, UK.**

Support and mixed media was provided by The Flies, Earl Fuggle and the Electric Poets, The Block, Sandy and Narda dancers, and Sam Gopal tabla. Films and lights were by Patrick Trevor.[48]

- **Britannia Rowing Club, Nottingham, Nottinghamshire, UK.**

- **Bath Pavilion, Bath, Avon, UK.**

- **EMI, Studio 3, Abbey Road, London, UK.**

'Astronomy Domine' recording sessions – two takes made on this date, along with one of 'Percy The Ratcatcher' – an early version of 'Lucifer Sam'.

WEDNESDAY 12

- **EMI, Studio 3, Abbey Road, London, UK.**

Vex Films' 'Syd's First Trip' video includes footage of the band outside Abbey Road Studios which is said to have been shot by Nick Mason sometime during the sessions around this date.

THURSDAY 13

- **Tilbury Railway Club, Railway Hotel, Tilbury, Essex, UK.**

The ticket for the gig described the Floyd as 'The Next projected sound of '67', and added that 'This ticket entitles the bearer to free Fan Club Membership'. It is quite probable, we suppose, that the fan club is the same one that gets a mention in *Melody Maker* on 22 February 1969.

FRIDAY 14

- **Club-A-Go-Go, Newcastle-under-Lyme, Staffordshire, UK (cancelled).**

This show was rescheduled on 19 May.

SATURDAY 15

- **Kinetic Arena – K4 Discoteque, West Pier, Brighton, Sussex, UK.**

Melody Maker listed this gig as the last of eight in an article on 8 April. It is likely that this show was hastily scheduled following the cancellation of the Brighton Arts Festival. The Brighton Arts Festival's grant was refused after tabloid stories about the 'dangers' of psychedelia.

MONDAY 17

- **EMI, Studio 3, Abbey Road, London, UK.**

Mixes for 'Astronomy Domine'.

TUESDAY 18

- **EMI, Studio 3, Abbey Road, London, UK.**

The band continued work on the mono and stereo mixes of 'Astronomy Domine' in the morning. In the afternoon they worked on 'Lucifer Sam' (two versions / takes were produced as a result of this session). They also recorded the unreleased song 'She Was A Millionaire', later mooted as their next single.

Syd was later to attempt to re-record the latter for his *Barrett* LP.[49]

Interestingly, also in this session the band worked upon crossfades from 'Interstellar Overdrive' into the 'Bike Song'. It would appear the band saw the two tracks as being together on the album, but seem to have abandoned this idea pretty early on.

WEDNESDAY 19

- **Bromel Club, Court Hotel, Downham, Bromley, Kent, UK.**

THURSDAY 20

- **Queens Hall, Barnstaple, Devon, UK.**

FRIDAY 21

- *IT* 11 **runs a cover story promoting the forthcoming '14 Hour Technicolor Dream'.**

- **The Starlite, Greenford, Middlesex, UK.**

- **UFO Club, Tottenham Court Road, London, UK.**

The poster for this gig is illustrated in *3D Eye.*[50]

SATURDAY 22

- **An interview with Roger Waters appears in the Dutch magazine *Kink*.**

- **Benn Memorial Hall, Rugby, Warwickshire, UK.**

Brain Damage no. 39 printed a 'reader flashback' on the night. The writer, who had reviewed the gig and interviewed the band for the *Rugby Advertiser* reproduced his article:

> The boys appeared only once – but the 45-minute stint was about all the average onlooker could take. Flipping throughout their repertoire, which included 'Interstellar Overdrive', 'Candy And A Currant Bun' and their latest 'Arnold Layne'.

SUNDAY 23

- **Starlight Ballroom, Crawley, West Sussex, UK.**

The advertisement details that the band were to provide 'their own psychodelic lighting'. It further informed the uninitiated that attendees could expect,

'Music to fit the mood, mood to fit the music' and 'great hallucinatory effects'. There was also to be a 'full supporting cast'.[51] Nothing about good clean fun!

MONDAY 24

- **The band spend the day working on**
  ***The Life Story Of Percy The Ratcatcher.*[52]**

- **Blue Opera Club, The Feather's Pub, Ealing Broadway, London, UK.**

  zigzag 32, in an interview with Roger:

  > The worst thing that ever happened to me was at The Feathers Club in Ealing, which was a penny, which made a bloody great cut in the middle of my forehead. I bled quite a lot. And I stood right at the front of the stage to see if I could see him throw one. I was glowering in a real rage, and I was gonna leap out into the audience and get him. Happily there was one freak who turned up who liked us, so the audience spent the whole evening beating the shit out of him, and left us alone.[53]

  The ad for the gig, meanwhile, described the band as 'the new chart sensation'. There was no support.

TUESDAY 25

- **The Stage Club, Oxford, Oxfordshire, UK.**

FRIDAY 28

- **Tabernacle Club, Hillgate, Stockport, Cheshire, UK.**

SATURDAY 29

- **Recording for *Fan Club*, Nederland 1 TV, Holland.**

  The band performed 'Arnold Layne' live in the studio for a later broadcast. Nick was to recall in *Mojo* magazine, July 1995: 'We had played a gig in Holland that same night and we didn't get to Alexandra Palace until three in the morning.' Peter Jenner tells much the same story in the May 1994 issue of the same magazine.

SUNDAY 30

- **14 Hour Technicolor Dream Free Speech Festival, Alexandra Palace, Muswell Hill, London, UK.**

  A benefit for 'London's own hip newspaper' the *International Times.*

14 Hour TECHNICOLOR DREAM
8pm Saturday APRIL 29 onwards
ALEXANDRA PALACE N22

Alexis Korner* Alex Harvey* Creation* Charlie Browns
Clowns* Champion Jack Dupree* Denny Laine* Gary
Farr* Graham Bond* Ginger Johnson* Jacobs Ladder
Construction Co* Move* One One Seven* Pink Floyd*
Poetry Band* Purple Gang* Pretty Things* Pete Townshend
Poison Bellows* Soft Machine* Sun Trolley* Social Deviant
Stalkers* Utterly Incredible Too Long Ago Sometimes

INTERNATIONAL TIMES

£1 advance tickets only
FROM HIP SOURCES & BOOK SHOPS

Shouting at People* Young Tradition* Lincoln Folk Group*
Noel Murphy* Dave Russell* Christopher Logue* Barry
Fantoni* Ron Geesin* Mike Horovitz* Alex Trocchi* Mike
Kemshall* Yoko Ono* Binder Edwards & Vaughn* 26 Kingly
St* Robert Randall* love from Allen Ginsberg* Simon
Vinkenoog* Jean Jacques Lebel* Andy Warhol* The Mothers
of Invention* The Velvet Underground* and famous popstar
who cant be mentioned for contractual reasons* guess who

Advertisements proclaimed the event 'A Giant Benefit Against Fuzz Action' and a 'Festival Of Light Machines', while Richard Neville was to describe how:

> Seven thousand ravers at a guinea a head turned up to record their new found spontaneity for handy randy BBC cameras, yet only £1,000 found its way into the *IT* coffers. With classic subterranean cool, no one ever asked what happened to the rest, but the following weeks saw a surprising number of new business ventures sprouting from the undergrowth.[54]

zigzag 25 goes into quite some detail describing the event:

> The whole thing just burned into my memory for ever ... it hit you as soon as you walked into the place – lights and films all over the walls and blitzing volume from 2 stages with bands playing simultaneously! ... as dawn

started to shine a shimmering eerie light at the windows, the Pink Floyd came on: 'It was a perfect setting,' says Jenner. 'Everyone had been waiting for them and everybody was on acid; that event was the peak of acid use in England ... everybody was on it – the bands, the organisers, the audience – and I certainly was.' Of course, the Floyd blew everybody's mind.[55]

Others gave the experience an alternative spin ... June Bolan in *Mojo* magazine, May 1994 tells a rather different story:

> First of all we couldn't find Syd, then I found him in the dressing room and he was so gone. I kept saying, Syd, it's June. Look at me. Roger Waters and I got him on his feet, got him out to the stage. We put the white Stratocaster round

his neck and he walked on stage and of course the audience went spare because they loved him. The band started to play and Syd stood there, he just stood there, tripping out of his mind. They did three, maybe four numbers and we got him off. He couldn't stand up for a set, let alone do anything else.

Further detail and more extensive quotes may be found in *Days In The Life.*[56]

Ronald Maxwell of the *Sunday Mirror* suggested that 'in fact the whole thing was rather like the last struggle of a doomed tribe trying to save itself from extinction'. *Melody Maker* meanwhile, vehemently disagreed; Nick Jones reviewed the event for *Melody Maker* – he gives scant mention to the Pink Floyd but did comment that the 'Alexandra Palace isn't the best place for acoustics, most of the sound echoing up into the huge dome and away.'[57]

Robert Wyatt in *Days In The Life*:

I got a short-back-and-sides haircut and a suit and tie to do that gig. That was my avant-garde gesture. The Floyd had those pyramids as far as I recall. They were doing very slow tunes.[58]

It has been said that the whole show was filmed by BBC 2 for its *Man Alive: What's A Happening?* show. Footage from the event was featured in the *Pink Floyd 1966–1967* video.

IT 13 reflected on the event the following month. Although there is no direct reference to the Floyd in the piece the following quote might intrigue:

Receipts from the *IT* film of the occasion, already in demand from US television companies and worldwide film distributors, are expected to gross another £5,000 within 3 months and may well amount to £20,000 in the long run.

To whom, we wonder, was the film sold – if at all? It is not known whether *IT* and the BBC made their own separate efforts or whether *IT* sold their film to the BBC. It would be necessary to see the *Man Alive* video to confirm either way. Unfortunately the BBC are 'no longer in possession' of the film, as is the case with much of their pre-1970s archive.[59] Colin Miles – who was of course very much involved in *IT* – produced the *London 66–67* video, which featured non-Floydian footage from the event. For the time being, we would suggest that the only way that Pink Floyd footage from the 'Dream' will reach the light of day, would be if Peter Whitehead (who filmed *London 66–67*) discovers that he has a bit more of it stashed away, in the same way that he did with the Sound Techniques footage.

It is not known *what* the Floyd played that night – all the reviewers decline to name any tracks. Phil Smee, in his *Chapter 24* interview, did however mention that they played 'Set The Controls For The Heart Of The Sun'.[60] Perhaps it was performed as the sun rose over London ...

• **Plaza Teen Club, Thornton Lodge, Huddersfield, Yorkshire, UK.**

MAY

- **'Arnold Layne Was Just Us Say The Pink Floyd'**, *Beat Instrumental* newspaper, UK.

  An extended review of 'Arnold Layne', and an interview with Waters, Wright and Barrett.

  'Incidentally,' continued Roger, 'the next record will probably be completely different. We don't want to get stuck in a rut with just one sound. What sound it will be, we just don't know. All we'll do, is go into the studio with an arrangement, and see what sounds appear. If we think it's right for that particular time, we'll use it. If not, we'll try something else.'

- **'At The Very Centre Of The Scene: The Pink Floyd', article written by Dandy Richards, publication unknown.**

  Dandy Richards was a contemporary of the band from art college, where he had worked with Mike Leonard on early light shows. The article, written after 'Games For May', featured an extensive interview with Nick, giving particular attention to this performance.

WEDNESDAY 3

- **Moulin Rouge, Ainsdale, Southport, Lancashire, UK.**

THURSDAY 4

- **The Locarno, Coventry, Warwickshire, UK.**

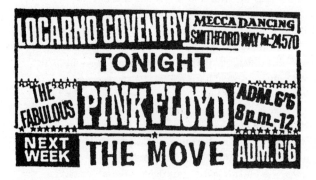

The exact venue for this gig is proven by a copy of an ad which was first reproduced in *Chapter 24* no. 4.

SATURDAY 6

- **Advert in *Melody Maker* newspaper for 'Games For May'.**

  The advertisement promised 'electronic compositions, colour and image projections, girls and The Pink Floyd'.

- **Kitson College, Leeds, Yorkshire, UK.**

SUNDAY 7

- **King And Queen Mojo A-Go-Go, Tollbar, Sheffield, Yorkshire, UK.**

FRIDAY 12

- **'Games For May', Queen Elizabeth Hall, South Bank, London, UK.**

'Games For May – Space Age Relaxation For The Climax Of Spring'. The first quadraphonic sound system in Britain was used at this show, but stolen almost immediately afterwards!

According to records kept by the venue, the programme started at 7.53 p.m. and ended at 10.06 p.m., with an interval from 8.35 – 8.57 p.m. The show lasted then an hour and fifty-three minutes; quite a length for a pop event at the time. Records kept by the Performing Rights Society, completed by the band for royalty purposes, detail the set list performed, which makes for extraordinary reading. Titles are here recounted exactly as they appear on this sheet.

The show began with a tape effect track entitled 'Tape Dawn', written by Roger Waters. He was to remember his preparations for the concert twenty years later in *Q* magazine:

> I was working in this dank, dingy basement off the Harrow Road, with an old Ferrograph. I remember sitting there recording edge tones off cymbals for the performance – later that became the beginning of 'Saucerful Of Secrets'. In those days you could get away with stuff like chasing clockwork toy cars around the stage with a microphone. For 'Games For May' I also made 'bird' noises recorded on the old Ferrograph at half-speed, to be played in the theatre's foyer as the audience was coming in. I was always interested in the possibilities of rock 'n' roll, how to fill the space between the audience and the idea with more than just guitars and vocals.[61]

The rest of the concert comprised, in this order, 'Matilda Mother', 'Flaming', 'Scarecrow', 'Games For May', 'Bicycle', 'Arnold Lane', 'Candy And A Currant Bun', 'Pow R Toc H' and 'Interstellar Overdrive'. The show ended with 'Tape Bubbles' – a pre-recorded piece by Wright and 'Tape Ending' by Barrett. The band were to encore with 'Lucifer Sam'.

Anthony Thorncroft of the *Financial Times* – not an organ normally given to coverage of underground pop music – gave a complimentary review the following day:

> The proceedings began with one of the two acolytes who travel with the four man group to superintend the electrical equipment and assist in the effects, throwing flowers at the audience. Then came a long period of blackness and hysterical laughter, which suddenly terminated in the musical sound of the Floyd.

They remained largely invisible in the first half, their figures dimly deciphered behind the brilliant colours which flickered over them. On a backcloth shapes like amoeba under a microscope ebbed and flowed with the glimpse of an occasional human form. The colours were primary and brilliant.

In between some pounding instrumental excursions ... the group wandered around the stage playing with friction cars, and water, and blowing bubbles against a recorded cacophony. The bubble, in fact, with the flower, was a symbol of the evening ... The performance was billed as a salute to spring, but this was all far removed from nature. It was instead a triumph of the mechanical and the belligerently avant-garde. The audience, which filled the hall – was beautiful, if strangely subdued, and to enjoy them was alone worth the price of a ticket.

The *IT* 13 review very much reflected the times:

The choice of the Queen Elizabeth Hall for the GAMES FOR MAY event was really good thinking, for it was a genuine twentieth-century chamber music concert. Acoustically, the hall is probably better for amplified sound than natural sound and the cleanness of presentation of the hall itself was perfect for the very loose mixed media.

The performance consisted, basically of the Pink Floyd, a tape machine, projections, flowers, and the Queen Elizabeth Hall, all combined rather leisurely. The first half was a fairly straight presentation of their sound and light show, but the second half moved right into the hall and into the realm of involvement. Musically the second half was really bordering on pure electronic music and very good at that.

On the whole it was good to see the strength of a hip show holding its own in such a museum like and square environment. More of this.[62]

Nick Mason has observed how 'it was the beginning of the concept that we ended up spending the next 20-odd years doing.'[63]

Peter Jenner recalled in a conversation with *zigzag* some years later how 'the owners of the hall ... went absolutely bananas because the bubbles which had filled the place had left marks all over their posh leather chairs, and some of the flowers which had been handed out to the audience had been trodden into the carpets.'[64]

SATURDAY 13

- **St George's Ballroom, Hinkley, Leicestershire, UK.**

SUNDAY 14

- *Look Of The Week*, **BBC 1 TV, London, UK. Shown at 11.10 pm.**

The band also recorded the show on this date. All of the many rebroadcasts have, to our knowledge, been incomplete. Floydian content was as follows:

10.27, Pow R Toc H and introduction by Robert Robinson, 1.20, Introduction by Dr. Hans Keller, 1.06, Astronomy Domine, 4.02, Interview with Syd and Roger and closure of Floyd piece, 3.51

Seven or eight minutes are typically rebroadcast and are easily available on video. Perhaps the best footage was that included on the *Sounds Of The Sixties* BBC 2 documentary, 1993:[65]

8.03, Continuity announcer, 0.17, Pow R Toc H and introduction by Robert Robinson, 0.44, Introduction by Dr. Hans Keller, 1.01, Astronomy Domine, 4.02, Interview with Syd and Roger, 1.40, video

WEDNESDAY 17

- **Broadcast of *Man Alive: What's A Happening?*, on BBC 2 TV, UK.**

  Film from the '14 Hour Technicolor Dream Free Speech Benefit' was broadcast. Footage from the show was also aired in France on the *Bouton Rouge* show on 12 December 1967.

THURSDAY 18

- **Sound Techniques Studios, Chelsea, London, UK.**

  Sessions for 'See Emily Play'.

FRIDAY 19

- **Club-A-Go-Go, Newcastle-upon-Tyne, Northumberland, UK.**

SATURDAY 20

- **Floral Hall, Southport, Lancashire, UK.**

- ***Melody Maker* reports that 'See Emily Play' and *Piper At The Gates Of Dawn* are to be completed within the week.**

  The Pink Floyd complete the recording of their new single and their first LP this week. Peter Jenner told the MM on Monday: 'We will complete about fourteen tracks altogether and then take a new single and the album from that.'
  The single, following up the Floyd's 'Arnold Layne' hit, will be rush released on either May 26 or June 2, and the album will be issued in mid-June.

  'See Emily Play' was released on 16 June and *Piper* was released on 5 August.

SUNDAY 21

- **Sound Techniques Studios, Chelsea, London, UK.**

'See Emily Play' completed. Although EMI log this track as the 23rd, Rick mentioned in an interview in *Beat Instrumental* at the time that 'See Emily Play' was recorded at Sound Techniques after several days of working on it. The tape was handed over to EMI on the 23rd (hence EMI recording it as the latter). The band also worked on 'The Bike Song', though once again it is possible that it was actually only handed over to EMI on this date, and could have been recorded a few days earlier.[66]

When Dave was back in England picking up supplies for his band in France he popped in on the recordings, and was distressed to find that Syd didn't recognise him.

- ***Bouton Rouge*, ORTF TV, France.**

The Floyd's French television debut, a broadcast of the 'Arnold Layne' promo made for, but not shown on, *Top Of The Pops*.[67]

- **The Regent, Brighton, East Sussex, UK (cancelled).**

MONDAY 22

- **Sound Techniques Studios, Chelsea, London, UK.**

TUESDAY 23

- **Sound Techniques Studios, Chelsea, London, UK.**

'See Emily Play' handed over to EMI.

One of the authors possesses an acetate of 'See Emily Play' which was pressed on the 23rd. The acetate adds a sublime openness to the sound and has an additional five seconds at the song's end; a different and cleaner ending that features additional guitar ringing through an echo unit.

Ian's EMIdisc acetate, See Emily Play, 2.51

Another alternative acetate exists, which is shorter, and to many sounds like a 'different mix'. We are somewhat dubious about its legitimacy.

Acetate, See Emily Play, 2.35

- A Psychedelic Experience In Technicolor, Town Hall, High Wycombe, Buckinghamshire, UK.

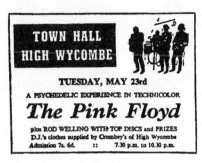

Advertisement in the *Bucks Free Press*, May 1967

WEDNESDAY 24

- Bromel Club, Court Hotel, Downham, Bromley, Kent, UK.

THURSDAY 25

- Gwent Constabulary Dance, Cross Ash, Abergavenny, Monmouthshire, Wales, UK.

FRIDAY 26

- Empress Ballroom, Winter Gardens, Blackpool, Lancashire, UK.

SATURDAY 27

- Bank Holiday Beano, Civic Hall, Nantwich, Cheshire, UK.

SUNDAY 28

- Sound Techniques Studios, Chelsea, London, UK.

MONDAY 29

- Barbecue '67, Tulip Bulb Auction Hall, Spalding, Lincolnshire, UK.

Pink Floyd were last on the bill, supporting the Jimi Hendrix Experience. Also appearing were the Move, Geno Washington And The Ramjam Band and Cream along with Zoot Money And The Big Roll Band (later to release the much sought after 'Madman Running Through The Fields' single as Dantalions Chariot).

JUNE

- **Pathé Pictorial broadcast a colour promo for 'The Scarecrow'.**

Pathé Pictorial, 2.15, Introduction, 0.13, The Scarecrow, 2.02, video

The film was shot in the county of Suffolk, UK and was introduced, in classic fashion, as follows:

> And as another mallard flies off on its predestined course, we take you to something else that could be strictly for the birds: pop group The Pink Floyd performing 'The Scarecrow' from their latest LP have taken their improbable psychedelic colours into the open air.

A bit inaccurate with regard to the 'latest LP'!

A number of collectors lay claim to having a brief Barrett comment from this film. A bit of a joke; the comments bear the distinct voice of Storm Thorgeson and have been lifted from a rebroadcast we would date as from the 1980s. The Knebworth film featured a 1 min. 17 sec. excerpt.

- **Chiswick House, Chiswick, London, UK (cancelled).**

A report in *Melody Maker* suggested that the Floyd were planning 'another "Games For May" type happening at Chiswick House, in June … retitled "Games For June" including light shows, etc.' [68]

If the event happened, which we strongly doubt since it doesn't get another mention in the press, the Floyd didn't play at it.

THURSDAY 1

- **EMI, Studio 3, Abbey Road, London, UK.**

The band worked on mixes for 'Lucifer Sam' and 'The Bike Song'.

FRIDAY 2

- **UFO Club, Tottenham Court Road, London, UK.**

The poster for this gig appears in *3D Eye*.[69] A half-page display ad for the gig may be found in *IT* 15. 'UFO is the place to go but get there early to avoid sensory disorientation all night blab blab blab'.

Peter Jenner often recalls this show as being the first at which he realised that Syd's health was failing. Syd was renowned for having twinkling eyes, but on this occasion it seemed to Jenner as if the blinds had been pulled, while Syd didn't seem to notice him.

A review of the gig appeared in *IT* 15:

> The Pink Floyd played last week (June 2) to the largest crowd that U.F.O. has ever held. At times queues stretched for yards up Tottenham Court Road, and twice the box office had to close because the floor was completely packed.
>
> The audience included Jimi Hendrix, Chas Chandler, Eric Burdon, Pete Townshend, and members of the Yardbirds.
>
> Appeals by Susy Creamcheese and Joe Boyd were made to the rather emotional crowd to prevent them taking any action against John Hopkins' imprisonment,[70] until after his appeal had been heard.
>
> It is a pity that with all this happening the Pink Floyd had to play like bums. The Soft Machine also appeared briefly to perform a poem for John Hopkins, The Tales of Ollin dance group played for about 40 minutes and completely captured the audience's imagination, also on the bill was the Hydrogen Jukebox.

The same issue of *IT* also reported (somewhat obscurely):

> A Soho strip club is featuring an 'L.S.D.' act consisting mainly of a chick writhing about around a giant spike while strobes and coloured lights play on the stage. The record used is 'Arnold Laine' [*sic*].[71]

MONDAY 5

- **EMI, Studio 3, Abbey Road, London, UK.**

Mixes for 'Chapter 24'.

WEDNESDAY 7

- **EMI, Studio 3, Abbey Road, London, UK.**

Further sessions – the band continued work on 'Matilda's Mother', 'Chapter 24' and 'Flaming'.

FRIDAY 9

- **College Dance, College of Technology / College of Commerce, Hull, Yorkshire, UK.**

SATURDAY 10

- **The Nautilus, South Pier, Lowestoft, Suffolk, UK.**

June 1967

- **UFO Club, Tottenham Court Road, London, UK.**[72]

SUNDAY 11

- **The Immage, Terneuzen, Holland.**

  A report in *Melody Maker* suggests that the band were scheduled to also be in Holland on the 10th so as to play two concerts – we assume that their plans were revised and they played both on the same night, as other sources confirm.[73]

- **Concertgebouw, Vlissingen, Holland.**

TUESDAY 13

- **Blue Opera Club, The Feather's Pub, Ealing Broadway, London, UK.**

THURSDAY 15

- **Free Concert, Abbey Wood Park, Abbey Wood, London, UK.**

FRIDAY 16

- **'See Emily Play' / 'Scarecrow' released in the UK.**

- **Tiles Club, Oxford Street, London, UK.**

  It is rumoured that a film of the band performing at this gig was made by Rediffusion for their *Come Here Often?* show, broadcast later in July – however, the recording of 'Astronomy Domine' circulating is really an alternative broadcast of the *Look Of The Week* performance.
  The club was open between 7.30 pm and 2.30 am that night and the Floyd were supported by Sugar Simone And The Programme. The ad for the gig, which is reproduced in the 1973 *Shelter* programme, made no reference to the 'See Emily Play' release party which is rumoured to have taken place on the night.

SATURDAY 17

- **Dreamland Ballroom, Margate, Kent, UK.**

SUNDAY 18

- **Radio London Motor Racing and Pop Festival, Brands Hatch, Kent, UK.**

TUESDAY 20

• **Magdalen College Commemoration Ball, Oxford, Oxfordshire, UK.**

WEDNESDAY 21

• **Bolton College of Art Midsummer Ball, Horwich, Bolton, Lancashire, UK.**

THURSDAY 22

• **Bradford University, Bradford, Yorkshire, UK.**

FRIDAY 23

• **Rolls-Royce Ball, The Locarno, Derby, Derbyshire, UK.**

SATURDAY 24

• **César's Club, Bedford, Bedfordshire, UK.**

Steve Peacock commented in *Sounds* in August 1974,

> I remember seeing them at the bowling alley in Bedford … play an aggressive set to a cowed audience. They seemed to take a gloomy kind of pleasure in it: in the dressing-cupboard afterwards, Roger Waters made the grim comment: 'At least we frightened a few people tonight.'[74]

SUNDAY 25

• **Mister Smiths, Manchester, Lancashire, UK.**

MONDAY 26

• **Warwick University, Coventry, Warwickshire, UK.**

TUESDAY 27

• **EMI, Studio 3, Abbey Road, London, UK.**

'Flaming' sessions.

WEDNESDAY 28

• **The Dance Hall, Eel Pie Island Hotel, Twickenham, Middlesex, UK.**

THURSDAY 29

- **EMI, Studio 3, Abbey Road, London, UK.**

  Mixing sessions. The band got through quite a few tracks: 'The Bike Song', 'Flaming', 'Matilda Mother' (correct title listed for the first time), 'Wondering And Dreaming' (an alternative 'Matilda Mother'?), 'Sunshine' and 'Lucifer Sam'. It is believed that 'Sunshine' was later reworked as 'Remember A Day' during the 'Saucerful of Secrets' sessions later in the year.

JULY

- **Unique 3-track 'Arnold Layne' EP released by EMI-France.**

  This highly sought after item features a unique edit of 'Interstellar Overdrive' unavailable on any other releases, European or otherwise.

  Arnold Layne, 2.49, Candy And A Currant Bun, 3.39, Interstellar Overdrive, 5.20

  'Interstellar Overdrive' was recorded on 27 February 1967 and is essentially the same as the album version though shorter and featuring a slightly different mix during the fade.

- **An interview with Richard Wright appears in *Beat Instrumental* magazine, UK.**

- **An interview with Roger Waters appears in *New Musical Express* newspaper, UK.**

- **An article about Syd Barrett appears in *Les Rockers*, a French music publication.**

  An English translation of the article appeared in *Chapter 24* no. 3. The content of the interview suggests that it was done around about this time, but it is not known when it was published.

- **DJ Pete Murray denounces Pink Floyd as a con on the influential *Juke Box Jury* television programme (UK).**

SATURDAY 1

- **The Swan, Yardley, Birmingham, West Midlands, UK.**

SUNDAY 2

- **Civic Hall, Birmingham, West Midlands, UK.**[75]

MONDAY 3

- **EMI, Studio 3, Abbey Road, London, UK.**

  Mono and stereo mixdowns for 'The Bike Song' and 'Interstellar Overdrive'.

- **Bath Pavillion, Bath, Avon, UK.**

WEDNESDAY 5

- **EMI, Studio 3, Abbey Road, London, UK.**

  Work on further mono and stereo mixes, on this occasion for 'Astronomy Domine' and 'Lucifer Sam'.

- **The Dance Hall, Eel Pie Island Hotel, Twickenham, Middlesex, UK.**

THURSDAY 6

- ***Top Of The Pops*, BBC 1 TV Studios, London, UK. Live broadcast.**

  The band's first appearance on *Top Of The Pops*, performing 'See Emily Play'. An original poor recording from the programme exists, and is owned by many on audio tape.

  See Emily Play with brief introduction, 2.33

FRIDAY 7

- **Portsmouth, Hampshire, UK.**[76]

SATURDAY 8

- **An interview with Roger Waters appears in *Record Mirror* magazine, UK.**

- ***Hit Parade* TV Show, UK.**

  The Floyd played 'See Emily Play'.

- **Memorial Hall, Nantwich, Cheshire, UK.**

SUNDAY 9

- **The Roundhouse, Chalk Farm Road, London, UK.**

  The gig was recorded by BBC 2, though it is not known if, or when, it was broadcast.

THURSDAY 13

- **The band hand EMI the first version of their
  Piper At The Gates Of Dawn album.**

  EMI's library notes for the album feature a different running order, and it is clear that this original master was replaced with what we know as the 'true LP master' some days later. The originally assembled album opened with 'Astronomy Domine' and featured five songs on side one, with 'Take Up Thy Stethoscope And Walk' the first track on side two, along with another five titles. Unfortunately EMI's library card does not spell out the complete tracklisting, but it does seem clear that the released album added an extra track, though which one is a mystery!

- ***Top Of The Pops*, BBC TV Studios, London, UK. Live broadcast.**

  Their second appearance of three, performing 'See Emily Play' – Syd by this time looking somewhat the worse for wear … and it was only downhill from here on.

- **An article about the band appears in Danish newspaper *Borge*.**

  Issue no. 14 of *Borge* touches on the band's appearances at the UFO and builds their readers' expectations of their first LP.

SATURDAY 15

- **Stowmarket Carnival, Stowmarket, Suffolk, UK.**

- *Disc* magazine reports that the Floyd intend creating a touring circus – doing shows around the country under a big top.

A subsequent article in *Disc* reported:

> Pink Floyd's 'circus show' featuring their light and sound act under a giant marquee – has its 'premiere' at Paignton, Devon on September 1–2.
> The first show will also feature Tomorrow and Crazy World Of Arthur Brown, while the Floyd will be supported on September 2 by the Move.

The gigs were cancelled because the tent manufacturers pulled out.

- *Melody Maker* reports that the band are to play at the 1968 Youth Culture Festival of Music at the Olympic Games in Mexico City.

Danish newspaper *Borge*[77] told the same story on 17 August. Sadly, any plans which were made ended up being cancelled, and the band were never to play.

SUNDAY 16

- Redcar Jazz Club, Coatham Hotel, Redcar, Yorkshire, UK.

MONDAY 17

- *Come Here Often?*, Rediffusion TV broadcast, UK.

The show was a 30-minute documentary about the DJ at the Tiles Club, Mike Quinnin. It was filmed on 16 June, though it is unclear if any Floyd footage was included.

TUESDAY 18

- The final master of *Piper At The Gates Of Dawn* is passed to EMI.

The final album was handed over to EMI in two parts – each tape holding one side of the final album. These tapes replaced the previous album master entered into the EMI library on the 13th. Once again however, the track-listing of these tapes differs from the actual album! The first tape contained 'Interstellar Overdrive', 'The Gnome', 'Chapter 24', 'The Scarecrow' and 'Bike'. Side one, on the second tape (!), featured 'Astronomy Domine', 'Lucifer Sam', 'Matilda's Mother', 'Power Toc H', 'Take Up Thy Stethoscope' and 'Flaming'.

As you can see 'Flaming' was moved from the end of side one to after 'Matilda's Mother', pushing 'Power Toc H' and 'Take Up Thy Stethoscope' down the list. It is also of interest to note how some of the song titles were still in flux up until the last minute, when decisions had to be finalised in the designing of the album sleeve.

The album had taken five months to complete – an indulgently long time in comparison to many of their contemporaries. In 1994 Nick Mason suggested that 'because the Beatles were taking their time recording Sgt Pepper in the studio next door, EMI thought this was the way people now made records.'[78]

● **The Palace, Douglas, Isle of Man, UK.**

WEDNESDAY 19

● **The Floral Hall, Gorleston, Great Yarmouth, Norfolk, UK.**

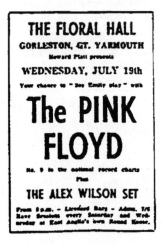

THE FLORAL HALL
GORLESTON, GT. YARMOUTH
Howard Platt presents
WEDNESDAY, JULY 19th
Your chance to " See Emily play " with
The PINK FLOYD
No. 9 in the national record charts
Plus
THE ALEX WILSON SET
From 8 p.m. - Licensed Bars - Adms. 7/6
Have Brackets every Saturday and Wednesday at East Anglia's own Round House.

The Floyd were supported by the Alex Wilson Set, and had to borrow their amplifiers as their own had broken down. An article in the *Eastern Evening News* on the 24th mentioned that 'a BBC 2 camera team were there preparing to record the freak-out' – nothing has been shown to substantiate this however. The paper's review describes what must have been a great gig:

> Suddenly it happened. As the curtains on the stage drew back the Pink Floyd launched themselves into a shuddering opening number, sending the decibels flying round the hall. Flashing green lights, the flashes linked to the rumbles of the guitars, burst around the group from all angles so that at times the different shadows thrown gave the impression that there was a whole crowd of people on the stand.

Roger complained to the reporter after the gig that 'the snag is on one-nighters you can't be sure the places where you play will be suitable for our projectors and other gear to have the full effect.'

Roger talked further after the gig about the group's plan for a travelling show [mentioned previously] to tour the country circus-style using a vast marquee. He said: 'although we have not yet approached them, we have thought of asking the Cream to join us and we have been in touch with Andy Warhol's group.'[79]

THURSDAY 20

● *Top Of The Pops*, **BBC TV Studios, London, UK. Live broadcast.**

The band's third, and final appearance on *Top Of The Pops* performing 'See Emily Play'. According to Waters, interviewed by *Melody Maker* and published in 1971, Syd 'didn't want to know. He got down there in a terrible state and said he wasn't gonna do it. We finally discovered the reason was that John

Lennon didn't have to do *Top Of The Pops* so he didn't'.[80] It is unknown whether he was eventually persuaded to appear on the show, or whether the rest of the band attempted to cover his parts without him.

'Tragically, the BBC apparently managed to wipe the footage in 1972/3, when they moved their archives to Brentford and apparently dumped two out of every three *Top Of The Pops* shows.'[81] It is rumoured that one of the shows may have survived in the US.

- **Two Red Shoes, Elgin, Grampian, Scotland, UK.**

First date of a short Scottish tour, 20–23 July.

Disc & Music Echo carried a review, published on the 29th: 'The teenagers aren't too sure about the Pink Floyd. "They're not bad – the Cream were better," says Jackie Errol, who comes across to the dance from Forres.'

The report continued that:

> The Pink Floyd aren't too sure about Elgin either. 'Terrible stage – we're going to give up ballroom gigs. Conditions are so bad. We'd really like to set up in a big tent, circus style, and take our show around the country … I suppose it's odd – us being up here when we've got a big hit going. Still, we're staying up here a couple of nights. Be a break really. No, the hotel people don't mind our clothes and hair. Think they'd be a bit disappointed if we didn't turn up in fancy dress.'[82]

FRIDAY 21

- **Ballerina Ballroom, Nairn, Highlands, Scotland, UK.**

SATURDAY 22

- **Syd Barrett appears in *Melody Maker*'s 'Blind Spot' feature.**

His comments have been reproduced in most of the biographies and probably all of the fanzines. Elsewhere in the newspaper, there's an ad for 'Pink Floyd – colour picture and exclusive feature' in *Disc & Music Echo*.[83]

- **The Beach Ballroom, Aberdeen, Grampian, Scotland, UK.**

SUNDAY 23

- **Cosmopolitan Ballroom, Carlisle, Cumbria, UK.**

MONDAY 24

- **The Maryland, Glasgow, Lanarkshire, Scotland, UK.**

TUESDAY 25

- **Press reports state that 'Old Woman in a Casket' or 'Millionaire'[84] are likely contenders for the next Floyd single.**

'Old Woman in a Casket' is also known to collectors as the song 'Scream Thy Last Scream' and 'Millionaire' is probably the same song as 'One In A Million', performed at The Starclub. Both songs failed to achieve any official release.

- **Greenock Palladium, Greenock, Lanarkshire, Scotland, UK.**

FRIDAY 28

- **Recording session for *Saturday Club*, presented by Keith Skues, BBC Radio, Playhouse Theatre, Northumberland Avenue, London, UK (cancelled).**

The session was commissioned by Phil Bebb and cancelled because Syd 'freaked out'.

Richard Wright in *Mojo*, 1994: 'We were supposed to do a session for the BBC one Friday, and Syd didn't turn up. Nobody could find him. He went missing for the whole weekend and when he reappeared again on the Monday, he was a totally different person.'

Syd might have gone missing for a day or so, but must have been present at Alexandra Palace on the 29th.

- **CIA vs UFO, UFO Club, Tottenham Court Road, London, UK.**

Melody Maker printed a letter about the gig from a disgruntled attendee. An in-concert photo of Waters and Mason is captioned 'PINK FLOYD: Their performance bore no connection with music'. After three 'ear-blasting numbers' the Coventry resident 'left in disgust' preferring 'rock and roll anytime'.

Elsewhere in the same issue, a more positive view was proffered by reviewer Roger Simpson:

> In a cacophony of sound played to a background of multi-coloured projected lights the Pink Floyd proved they are Britain's top psychedelic group before the hip audience at UFO Club, Tottenham Court Road, on Friday night.
> In two powerful sets they drew nearly every conceivable note from their instruments but ignored their two hit singles. They include 'Power Toc-H' and a number which received its first hearing called 'Reaction in G' which they say was a reaction against their Scottish tour where they had to do 'See Emily Play'. Bass player Roger Waters gave the group a powerful depth and the lights played on to them set an impressive scene.
> Many of the audience found the Floyd's music too much to sit down to

and in more subdued parts of the act the sound of jingling bells from their dancing masters joined in. It is clear that the Floyd prefer playing to UFO-type audiences rather than provincial ones and are at their best in an atmosphere more acceptable to them.[85]

Supporting the Pink Floyd were the Fairport Convention.

The poster for the gig is arguably *the* Pink Floyd poster to own. Often selling for vastly inflated prices, it is a silk screen classic by Haphash And The Coloured Coat and is the only poster from UFO that promotes the Floyd alone. A strange flying craft is animated above a beautiful angel in the foreground. In the background, there is another such craft that is circling a mythical castle with attendant UFOs. Pink Floyd is written in the trails of a biplane which flies through a scape of graduated red, orange and yellow. The border is semi-reflective silver. Watch out for fakes!

SATURDAY 29

• **Wellington Club, The Dereham Exchange, East Dereham, Norfolk, UK.**

Nick told how beer mugs were thrown at the drum kit in an interview with *zigzag* magazine some years later.

• **International Love-In, Alexandra Palace, Muswell Hill, London, UK.**

This was a twelve-hour music festival. Parts of the show were shown on French TV in December 1967.[86]

Roger, talking in *zigzag* 32 six years later:

> I'll never forget that night. We did a double header that night. First of all we played to a roomful of about 500 gypsies, hurling abuse and fighting, and then we did Ally Pally.
>
> Nick: We certainly weren't legendary there, Arthur Brown was the one. That was his great launching.
>
> Roger: There was so much dope and acid around in those days that I don't think anyone can remember anything about anything.

The poster was a psychedelic classic and was reproduced as a display ad in *IT* 17 [87] (illustrated on the next page). Tickets cost £1 – a lot to pay for a concert ticket at the time.

MONDAY 31

• **Town Hall, Torquay, Devon, UK.**

Following this performance the band cancelled all appearances through August, due to Syd's increasing unreliability.

AUGUST

TUESDAY 1 – WEDNESDAY 2

- **Scheduled promotional trip to Germany, most notably to appear on the prestigious *Beat Club News*, Bremen.**

  The trip was cancelled due to what was described at the time as Syd's nervous exhaustion.

FRIDAY 4

• **An interview with Syd appears in *Go* magazine, USA.**

Pretty forgettable stuff, discussing the nature of psychedelia amongst other things.[88]

SATURDAY 5

• ***Piper At The Gates Of Dawn* is released in the UK.**

As evidenced to many hitherto uncertain listeners by the release of the mono edition on CD in August 1997, the mixes on the mono and stereo versions are substantially different. An outtake which bootleggers have variously titled 'Instrumental '67', 'Class Act', 'Experiment', 'Madcaps Embrace' (particularly misleadingly), 'Sunshine' and 'In The Beechwoods' is reputed to be a rejected outtake from the LP.

Instrumental, 1.30

We certainly have the beginning and perhaps the whole track – it fades cleanly at the end and is very exact in its timing. The fade is abrupt but not unnatural, considering the production vogue of the time. It is best described after a first listen as sounding like work in progress, although the strong organ and backwards guitar that introduce it are more developed than this would suggest. It sounds a lot like one of those mad psychedelic shorts that appeared on Beatles albums from the period (*Strawberry Fields* for example) – perhaps this was its intended purpose: as a filler. Syd's guitar is archetypally him about 1967.

The copy in circulation would appear to have originated from Malcolm Jones. It was Jones who put together a cassette of unreleased Syd Barrett material, which probably formed the basis of all the bootlegs that appeared later, particularly in the mid 1980s. The same source would seem to have now been exhausted following the release of a pair of bootlegs in 1996.[89] Phil Smee commented on the song:

> Listening to the 4-track master the backwards noises that appear half way through don't seem to fit. I think this may have been a 3-track recording made over someone else's tape with the backwards noises coming from an unwiped previous recording. 4-track masters were often erased and reused once a final twin-track mix had been completed. I'm convinced the backwards sounds were not intended to be on there, someone just forgot to set the faders properly when the track was stuck on cassette.[90]

• **An article about the band appears in *Melody Maker* under the banner 'The Great Pink Floyd Mystery'.**

Floyd entries number several in the 5 August issue of *Melody Maker*.

August 1967

MONDAY 7

- **EMI, Studio 3, Abbey Road, London, UK.**

  'Scream Thy Last Scream' recording sessions. Malcolm Jones, in his excellent diary, *The Making Of The Madcap Laughs*, comments that 'the version I heard of this, to my ears, seems not to feature Syd on lead vocal, although he does seem to sing a line some way into the song.' The only recorded take of 'Set The Controls For The Heart Of The Sun' was also made on this date.

  For a detailed entry about 'Scream Thy Last Scream' and 'Vegetable Man' versions see 5–6 October.

TUESDAY 8

- **EMI, Studio 3, Abbey Road, London, UK.**

SATURDAY 12

- **The band appear in full flower-power garb on the cover of *Record Mirror* newspaper.**

  The photo-within-a-photo has often been poorly reproduced. The cover, oddly, is not supplemented by any sort of article about the band; a habit of the paper at the time.

- **Seventh National Jazz and Blues Festival, Balloon Meadow, Royal Windsor Racecourse, Windsor, Berkshire, UK.**

  Pink Floyd were to have been the ninth of ten bands, on this the Saturday night of the festival, but pulled out at the last minute. The programme shows that they were scheduled to play between 10.25 and 10.55 pm. It is perhaps a measure of how ill Syd was, that it was not possible for him to play for this relatively short amount of time.

TUESDAY 15 – WEDNESDAY 16

- **Sound Techniques Studios, Chelsea, London, UK.**

  The band would work on 'Jugband Blues', 'Apples And Oranges', 'Paintbox' and 'Remember A Day' – these songs would have undergone continued work during August and September.

SATURDAY 19

• **'Pink Floyd Flake Out' interview in *Melody Maker* newspaper, UK.**

Syd is described by a group spokesman as suffering from 'nervous exhaustion'.

SEPTEMBER

FRIDAY 1

• **UFO at the Roundhouse, Chalk Farm Road, London, UK.**

It was generally thought that this concert heralded the occasion on which the Floyd used sound effect tapes at a live show for the first time.[91] Our research for the 'Games For May' concert reveals conclusive proof to the contrary. It could be the case that at the time the band reserved such trickeries for larger concerts or venues such as the Roundhouse. Tomorrow were also on the bill.[92]

SATURDAY 2

• **UFO at the Roundhouse, Chalk Farm Road, London, UK.**

TUESDAY 5 – WEDNESDAY 6

• **Sound Techniques Studios, Chelsea, London, UK.**

THURSDAY 7 – FRIDAY 8

• **EMI, Studio 3, Abbey Road, London, UK.**

There are no reliable biographical accounts with regard to what went on at the above sessions. However …

TUESDAY 5 – FRIDAY 8

• **'Vegetable Man' recorded?**

Melody Maker reported that 'the group spent the first half of this week in the recording studios and their new single is expected to be chosen from the tracks they've cut.'[93]

We know that 'Scream Thy Last Scream' was recorded on 7 August. It could be, however, that 'Vegetable Man' was recorded between 5 and 8 October. Our alternative entry for 'Vegetable Man' under 5–6 October notes that it was recorded at Sound Techniques: perhaps at some point the recording month was confused and a date of 5–6 September is more accurate.

If both sides of the prospective single had indeed been recorded by this point, their new single could logically be 'expected to be chosen' from the tracks that they had cut.

Different cuts of 'Scream Thy Last Scream' exist, so it would not be amiss to suggest that more than one version of the songs were recorded on each occasion – given Syd's precarious state of mind the sessions over these months may have been harder than might be normally expected, especially given the perceived pressures to come up with 'product'. It is also likely that not all sessions at this time resulted in recordings which would have verified and documented the tracks attempted.

For a detailed breakdown of content and timings of both sides to the aborted single see 5–6 October.

Friday 8

• **The Floyd fly to Denmark.**

The Saturday 9 September issue of *Melody Maker* commented that 'The Pink Floyd fly off to Denmark on Friday for four days of concerts and TV appearances. Then the group go to Sweden for one day and return to Britain.'

If the Floyd were indeed to be away for five days, they probably returned to the UK on the 14th. Their schedule was evidently more flexible than *Melody Maker* suggests.

Saturday 9

• **Press Conference, Copenhagen, Denmark.**

• **Boom Cententer, Århus, Denmark.**

Sunday 10

• **Interview with Roger Waters on Tonarksvall P3, Stockholm, Sweden.**

3.10, Interview with excerpts from Arnold Layne

The interview, which is rather bland to be honest, contained this insight from Roger Waters:

> DJ: Could you please try in words to explain the kind of music you are performing?
> RW: No.

Perhaps we've been a bit unfair! – the interview is of very good sound quality and the copies in circulation are probably representative of a rebroadcast.

• **Gyllene Cirkeln, Stockholm, Stockholm, Sweden.**

MONDAY 11

- **Dutch TV, Copenhagen, Denmark.**

Promotional appearances to promote the European release of *Piper At The Gates Of Dawn*.

- **Restaurant, The Starclub, Copenhagen, Denmark.**

We have grave doubts as to the legitimacy of this entry. We can find no evidence to either prove or disprove this date, and include it in acknowledgement of the fact that a number of other chronologies list it as correct.

An article in Danish publication *Borge*,[94] confirms that it was the band's intention at the time of going to press, 17 August, to play on the 12th, 13th and 14th at the Starclub.

The same paper published on 28 September,[95] reported that the band were thrown out of Tivoli in Copenhagen for misbehaving at some point during their stay in Copenhagen. Apparently, at first they couldn't work out the admission fee, so somebody paid it for them. They then disobeyed a sign and walked on a lawn that they weren't supposed to. *Borge* further suggests that the band were attacked by some locals. The article was followed up in the 21 September issue, with the headline that the band didn't 'give a damn'. Gossip indeed!

TUESDAY 12

- **Restaurant, The Starclub, Copenhagen, Denmark.**

Malcolm Jones suggests that they played the Århus, Copenhagen on this date.

WEDNESDAY 13

- **Restaurant, The Starclub, Copenhagen, Denmark.**

This tape could be from one of four dates: 12, 13 or 14 (or, less likely, from the 11th).

37.45, Reaction In G Minor, 6.23, Arnold Layne, 3.07, One In A Million, 5.59, Matilda Mother, 6.01, Scream Your Last Scream, 5.18, Astronomy Domine, 7.29

Reaction In G Minor

Thank you. One.

Arnold Layne

This song is called 'One In A Million'. One, two, three, four!

One In A Million

Now this is called 'Matilda Mother' … I believe.

Matilda Mother

[Very quietly] One, two, three, four.

Scream Your Last Scream

Thank you.

Astronomy Domine

The first forty seconds of 'Reaction In G Minor' were later broadcast on the TV show *Beat Club News* [96] (whether this was a broadcast of an official recording or not remains in doubt). The programme was rebroadcast in Germany on 2 July 1993, and again on 4 June 1995.

Beat Club News 2 July 1993 rebroadcast, with voice over, Reaction In G Minor, 0.40

Beat Club News 4 June 1995 rebroadcast, without voice over, Reaction In G Minor, 0.39

It is possible that the band played instead at the Gyllenne Cirkeln, Stockholm on this date. Our entry under 8 September is persuasive in this respect.

THURSDAY 14

- **Restaurant, Starclub, Copenhagen, Denmark.**

A new date to many, which is given legitimacy by our entry under the 11th. The *Borge* article of 17 August invites attendees to enjoy the band's 'fantastic light show', suggesting that the Starclub gigs would have taken place in the evenings.

- **The band return to the UK.**

See our entry for 8 September; it is possible, of course, that they returned to England after their gig on the 13th and didn't play on the 14th, in readiness to make the journey to Ireland on the 14th. Whatever the truth of the matter, there can be no doubt that the band's schedule was particularly hectic at this time.

- **The band start a four-day tour of Ireland.**

Melody Maker, 9 September – 'On September 14 they go to Ireland for four days of promotion and dates.'

FRIDAY 15

• **Starlite Ballroom, Belfast, County Antrim, Northern Ireland.**

SATURDAY 16

• **Flamingo, Ballymena, County Antrim, Northern Ireland.**

SUNDAY 17

• **Arcadia Ballroom, Cork, County Cork, Eire.**

MONDAY 18

• **Belgian TV spectacular, Brussels, Belgium.**

Melody Maker, reported that the band 'are being flown especially from Ireland to Brussels on 18 September for a Belgian TV spectacular'.[97]
   If the band did indeed make the journey there doesn't seem to be any record in existence as to the content of the 'spectacular'. A similar entry appears under 8–12 November. Perhaps the two bookings are related in some way.

TUESDAY 19

• **Speakeasy, London, UK.**

This date may have been rescheduled from 21 August.

THURSDAY 21

• **Assembly Hall, Worthing, West Sussex, UK.**

FRIDAY 22

• **Tiles Club, Oxford Street, London, UK.**

SATURDAY 23

• **Saturday Scene, Corn Exchange, Chelmsford, Essex, UK.**

MONDAY 25

• **Playhouse Theatre, Northumberland Avenue, London, UK.**

Recordings were made which would be broadcast by the BBC on 1 October and 5 November 1967. See respective dates for details.

September 1967

TUESDAY 26

• **New York City Film Festival, New York City, New York, USA.**

Tonite Let's All Make Love In London receives its first screening, although it would be almost a year before it was eventually released.

WEDNESDAY 27

• **Fifth Dimension, Leicester, Leicestershire, UK.**

The poster for this gig is illustrated on page 28 of *3D Eye*.

THURSDAY 28

• **Skyline Club, Hull, Yorkshire, UK.**

SATURDAY 30

• **Imperial Club, Nelson, Lancashire, UK.**

OCTOBER

SUNDAY 1

• **Sundays at the Saville, Saville Theatre, London, UK.**

At least one of the band's two gigs at the Saville on this date was filmed by Yoko Ono!

• *Top Gear* **broadcast, presented by Pete Drummond and John Peel, BBC Radio 1, London, UK.**

Radio 1 had only gone on air the day before.
Broadcast of six out of the seven tracks recorded on 25 September 1967 at the Playhouse Theatre. The recordings were produced by Bernie Andrews and engineered by Dave Tate and broadcast between 2.00 and 5.00 pm. 'Apples And Oranges', the seventh track, was broadcast on 5 November 1967 on its own.[98]
The fact that *Top Gear* was co-hosted at this time goes some way towards explaining why the 'Reaction In G' and 'Set The Controls' recordings do not feature the familiar tones of John Peel. The show was repeated on *David Symonds* 13–17 November 1967 (Mon-Fri, 5.33–7.30 pm).
Some may be concerned that 'Reaction In G' might represent an edit, but the DJ in his introduction confirms that it is to be 35 seconds long.

3.52, Reaction In G, 0.35, Set The Controls, 3.17

In just thirty-five seconds time with Pat Doody [?] but here's 'Reaction in F Sharp Minor' by the Pink Floyd. Actually its 'Reaction in G' which is about four miles outside Carlisle. I didn't know that, you'll have to tell the AA, my boy.

Reaction in G

... called 'Set The Controls'. Are the controls set? Somebody's nodding in the other room. That means they are. So I guess they're alright.

Set The Controls

We have based the above entry on instinctual and educated guesswork: it may be that the two tracks are from a rebroadcast. The original broadcast is probably no longer in existence on tape bar the above two tracks, any other tracks purporting to be from this date being from the November rebroadcast. Comments made later, under our entry for 5 November, may prove to clarify the situation.

We are unaware of any tapes in existence that feature the David Symonds rebroadcast.

Monday 2

• **Photo session, London, UK.**

Thursday 5 – Friday 6

• **Sound Techniques Studios, Chelsea, London, UK.**

It is generally thought that 'Vegetable Man' was recorded during the October Sound Techniques sessions (though readers may wish to refer to our comments on 5–8 September). It was of course, never officially released.

Phil Smee has sewn up most queries about different versions of 'Vegetable Man'. The interviewer paraphrased, 'they found not one, but three versions ...The one we all know and love, a faster complete alternate take and an incomplete backing track. The latter was listed as an instrumental and "Sounds really chaotic with lots of sound effects whizzing around."' [99]

Sadly, Smee didn't comment about 'Scream Thy Last Scream'.

An interesting, though probably inaccurate, variation on the usual story about 'Vegetable Man' being intended as the B side of the Floyd's projected third single, was offered by Peter Jenner in *Mojo*, 1994:

The last Floyd song Syd wrote, Vegetable Man, was done for those sessions, though it never came out. He wrote it round at my house; it's just a description of what he's wearing. It's very disturbing, Roger took it off the album [*A Saucerful Of Secrets*] because it was too dark, and it is. It's like psychological flashing.

'Vegetable Man' was not the last thing that Syd *recorded* for the Floyd – it may have been suggested that it should be put on *A Saucerful Of Secrets*, and perhaps early on in the sessions, it was accepted that it wouldn't be suitable.

Both 'Vegetable Man' and 'Scream Thy Last Scream' were broadcast on the pirate radio station, Radio London, in 1975. The source of these recordings may be Peter Jenner, who, some suggest, felt the songs were too good to remain in the vaults.

There are two versions of each song which are available, featuring slightly different mixes or overdubs. The uninitiated may like to note that the studio versions of 'Scream Thy Last Scream' are the only ones to feature the 'laughing gnome' in the background. The BBC session recording omits this vital effect!

Scream Thy Last Scream, mono mix, 4.37, Scream Thy Last Scream, stereo mix, 4.42

Vegetable Man, 3.18, Vegetable Man with different vocal double track, 2.27

Tape collectors and bootleggers often get quite academic, passionate and persuasive about the proper titles for various versions of 'Scream They Last Scream'. We have listed all the ones that we are aware of. They could all originate from the same sources, but copied differently, or they might represent different recordings which were recorded on different dates (this latter explanation being somewhat doubtful). The most apparent differences between the versions is that some have perceptibly different uses of the stereo effect, and others have a more up-front vocal. We'd suggest that a sensible place to stop is with one 'stereo' and one 'mono' for 'Scream Thy Last Scream' and two radically differently timed versions of 'Vegetable Man'. When listed it all seems a little preposterous, but if the reader insists he or she could choose from the following 'Scream's' …

Scream Thy Last Scream, proposed final mix, 4.28

Scream Thy Last Scream, stereo outtake, 4.35

Scream Thy Last Scream, finished mix mono master tape version, 4.37

Scream Thy Last Scream, upgraded studio master recording, 4.38

Scream Thy Last Scream, our longest version yet, 4.43

FRIDAY 6

- **Top Rank, Brighton, East Sussex, UK.**

The band were paid £600 for this gig – at a time when Hendrix would play London for £35!

Nick would later complain how 'the Top Rank suites wouldn't let us drink in the bar, which made us bloody angry. We always swore we'd never go back, but we didn't keep to it.'[100]

- **The UFO Club closes.**

Mick Farren in *Watch Out Kids*:

> Even though a local black power group volunteered a squad of security men, gangs of skinheads attempting to break into the building every weekend made an already difficult situation impossible, and in October 1967 UFO finally closed.[101]

Richard Neville would later write in his seminal book *Playpower* that:

> The early days of UFO were an externalised acid trip – traumatic, familial, euphoric – but journalists were soon to headline it as London's answer to Haight-Ashbury, and the sensitive clientele vanished in the wake of German film crews, the Iron Cross boys, and drunken shore leave sailors, who mistook the girls' freedom and flamboyance for an invitation to forcibly abduct them from their friends.'[102]

SATURDAY 7

- **Victoria Rooms, Bristol, Avon, UK.**

New Style **VICTORIA ROOMS** Bristol presents Sat., Oct. 7th **PINK FLOYD** plus support group
Admission 8/6
7.45 to 11 p.m.

MONDAY 9 – WEDNESDAY 11

- **EMI, Studio 3, Abbey Road, London, UK.**

Two four-track tapes of 'Apples And Oranges' were entered into the EMI library at the end of October, and it is likely that they originate from these sessions. It is also likely that the band worked on an unknown track – entered into the EMI library as 'Untitled' – over these dates, or those at De Lane Lea. There appear to be five EMI tapes which cannot be attributed reliable recording dates, since they were entered into their archives over the time the band were in the US.

Melody Maker reported on 21 October that the band 'were recording a new single last week in London, which will be released on November 13.'

'Apples and Oranges' was, of course, released on the 18 November, though the quote, if accurate, would be persuasive in arguing that 'Untitled' is another version of 'Paintbox'.

Record Collector 104, reported that EMI had recently located a true stereo mix of 'Apples And Oranges'.[103]

FRIDAY 13

• **The Pavilion, Weymouth, Dorset, UK.**

SATURDAY 14

• **Caesar's Palace, Bedford, Bedfordshire, UK.**

MONDAY 16

• **The Pavilion, Bath, Somerset, UK.**

TUESDAY 17 – FRIDAY 20

• **German TV dates?**

While the *New Musical Express* magazine, UK, reported on 7 October that the Floyd were scheduled to do promotional TV work in Germany on these dates, nothing has appeared to confirm this.

FRIDAY 20 – SATURDAY 21

• **De Lane Lea Studios, London, UK.**

Recording for 'Jugband Blues' and 'Remember A Day'. A mono mix of the tapes was handed over to EMI on the 24th. It has been suggested that 'Remember A Day' is a development of 'Sunshine' an unreleased track, mentioned previously, from the *Piper At The Gates Of Dawn* sessions.

SATURDAY 21

• **University of York, Hesslington, York, Yorkshire, UK.**

• *Piper At The Gates Of Dawn* **released in the USA.**

The track listing is different to the UK and European versions. 'Flaming' and 'Astronomy Domine' were substituted with the band's first two singles 'Arnold Layne' and 'See Emily Play', although some copies only came with the latter. Collectors often seek out 'The Gnome' as it is not joined to 'Interstellar Overdrive'. It is sometimes also suggested that it is a different mix – this is a little hopeful in our opinion.

The Gnome, 2.14

TUESDAY 24

- **'Jugband Blues' and 'Remember A Day' mono versions filed with EMI.**

These would have been recorded at Sound Techniques over the preceding two months.

THURSDAY 26 – SATURDAY 28

- **Fillmore West, San Francisco, California, USA (cancelled).**

These gigs were cancelled due to the band's visas not being sorted out, and while it is generally accepted that the band played these gigs, new evidence has come to light indicating that they were in fact still in the UK.
Mojo magazine in April 1997 quoted Peter Jenner thus:

> I remember that we were booked to play San Francisco around that time but problems with visas meant that we actually didn't play the gig until sometime later – probably around the beginning of November. I recall that Bill Graham really had a go at me because of our failure to get the visas on time.

Graham, the owner of the Fillmore venues, had in fact gone to quite some effort to promote the events, which were advertised by a well-known poster featuring a man in a psychedelic brocade jacket. The poster was reproduced on a smaller scale as a postcard and in still smaller form with differing colour schematics for the tickets. This then standard approach was applied to the Fillmore and Winterland concerts in early November. We would highly recommend *The Art Of Rock* for those who would like to find out more.

The fact that the gigs were cancelled perhaps explains why so many of these tickets are available on the collectors' market.

SATURDAY 28

- **Dunelm Ballroom, University of Durham, Durham, UK.**

Once again we have *Mojo* to thank for this entry, which was obviously hastily scheduled due to the band's problems in gaining entry to the United States. Reader Steve Benson who attended the gig, was also able to provide evidence taken from University newspaper *Palatinate*, confirming the group's appearance.[104]

SUNDAY 29

- **The band fly to the USA in readiness for their first tour outside Europe?**

  Miles suggests that the band flew to the US on the 24th, while *Melody Maker* suggests that they flew on Monday 23.[105] Both are incorrect, given the recently discovered gig above, and the 29th strikes us as being the most likely date.

  The 30 September issue of *Billboard* says that US General Artists Corporation was to handle the group's bookings. Perhaps any Stateside readers may like to contact GAC to confirm the band's bookings at this point.

  Billboard[106] adds unspecified performances in Boston among other 'key cities' to what follows. The article isn't very helpful as to detail.

  Melody Maker on 21 October reported prior to their leaving for the tour that they were due to 'return to Britain on November 13'. Syd was later to comment in *Melody Maker*[107] that the tour had been 'very exciting'.

MONDAY 30

- **KPFA Benefit, Fillmore, San Francisco, California, USA (cancelled).**

  The gig advertisement, which is 'flyer' sized, is a very attractive item and is highly sought after. A copy of it may be found in *The Art Of Rock*.[108]

- **Whisky A-Go-Go, Los Angeles, California, USA.**

TUESDAY 31

- **Pacific West High School, San Jose, California, USA (cancelled).**

- **Whisky A-Go-Go, Los Angeles, California, USA.**

NOVEMBER

WEDNESDAY 1

- **'Apples And Oranges' single master completed.**

  While the Floyd were in America, Norman Smith was working upon the mixes of their last single to feature Syd Barrett. The band had already spent some three days recording the track, and he had reduced their session down to three versions. Logged into the EMI files, but recorded earlier at Sound Techniques, was a version of 'Paintbox', which was to be the B side, and one 'Untitled' track of which there are two versions. Despite the time spent working on the single the band were still unhappy with the final result.

- **Whisky A-Go-Go, Los Angeles, California, USA.**

THURSDAY 2

- **EMI, Studio 3, Abbey Road, London, UK.**

Mixing sessions by Norman Smith. Further work on 'Untitled' and 'Paint-box' – though it would appear that *Relics* is wrong in saying that 'Paintbox' was completed on this day, as the stereo masters for both 'Paintbox' and 'Apples And Oranges' would be completed two weeks later.

- **Fillmore West, San Francisco, California, USA.**

The Floyd were third on the bill to Richie Havens and Big Brother And The Holding Company. Syd and Janis, what a great show!

The poster, postcard and tickets set for this and the following two gigs featured three psychedelic angels in the foreground, with a background of gothic arches over-looked by a hunting bird. One of the figures, with a haunted expression, clasps a rose.

Valid Thursday Only $3.00

FRIDAY 3

- **Winterland, San Francisco, California, USA.**

SATURDAY 4

- **Winterland, San Francisco, California, USA.**

SUNDAY 5

- ***Top Gear*** **broadcast, presented by Pete Drummond and John Peel, BBC Radio 1, London, UK.**

The 5 November broadcast presents us with something of a dilemma. Collectors have often been proven wrong over their vehemently attaching particular dates to recordings. Many will have that which follows listed under 1 October. Such an attribution would seem not to make sense to us on two counts.

First, why is 'Apples and Oranges' present after Ken Garner's very clear comments about its not being broadcast until this day?[109] And second, why is it described as being released in a 'couple of weeks' when it was to be released on 18 November, if this were not the correct date for this copy of the recording. The evidence in these respects seems to us to be conclusive. We are also confident in terms of the continuity of the recording.

To reconcile Garner's comments with the tapes available requires the following; that the broadcast on 1 October featured 'The Gnome', 'Scarecrow', 'Matilda Mother' and 'Flaming' plus 'Set The Controls For The Heart Of The Sun' and 'Reaction In G', with only the latter two tracks surviving on tape, and that on 5 November the first four were repeated, with 'Apples And Oranges' receiving its first playback, in place of 'Set the Controls' and 'Reaction In G'.

13.44, The Gnome, 2.07, Apples And Oranges, 2.52, Scarecrow, 2.01, Matilda Mother, 3.17, Flaming, 2.37

> PD: ... got Pink Floyd once again on *Top Gear*. This is 'Flaming'.

Flaming

> PD: 'Flaming' from the Pink Floyd. Well we haven't heard from James ... >< Ha Ha. Well actually last time I looked it wasn't. It is 17 and a half minutes past 4 on *Top Gear* and in a couple of weeks Pink Floyd have a record out called 'Apples and Oranges', their new single. Here they are to play it for you right now. 'Apples and Oranges' – the Pink Floyd.

Apples And Oranges

> PD: The ethereal surrealistic sound, what did I say then? I don't know ... er anyway it comes from the Pink Floyd, 'Apples and Oranges', title of their new single ... an' realistic I meant, didn't I?

> JP: Yeah, I think you did. Yes Ray Keen just called and said that ... ><

> PD: ... song from the Pink Floyd coming up it's called ... it's a ... this number is actually on the other side of 'See Emily Play'. If you should wish to turn it over you'll find 'The Scarecrow'.

The Scarecrow

The Gnome

PD: 'The G-nome' >< ... other ...

Matilda Mother

PD: Hmm ... the avant-garde music of The Pink Floyd.

There are copies of the session circulating amongst collectors which add additional DJ comments to those we transcribe.

This recording may well document the only attempt at playing 'Apples and Oranges' live. *Top Gear*, it may be useful to note, was aired between 2.00 and 5.00 pm.

As if to complicate matters, an alternative broadcast of 'Apples and Oranges' exists. This variation was probably broadcast sometime in October or November 1967 (before December's *Top Gear* superseded it, and likely as not to promote the single's release):

Apples and Oranges with introduction, 2.55

● ***The Pat Boone Show*, CBS-TV, Los Angeles, California, USA.**

Interviewed on the show, Barrett's reponse was embarrassingly mute. The band also mimed 'See Emily Play', without any help from Syd.

● **Cheetah Club, Venice, Santa Monica, California, USA.**

The poster for this gig is illustrated in *Shine On*.[110] A different ad for the gig was reproduced in *Chapter 24* no. 4. The ad, more woolly, was sourced from *Open City*, a Los Angeles publication.[111]

Nick Schaffner describes the gig, which didn't go too well if his account is to believed:

> Any party atmosphere was rather abruptly dispelled after the Floyd took the Cheetah Club stage, where the silence from Barrett's guitar proved positively resounding. Clutching at it's neck, Syd stared blankly off into farthest space, his right hand dangling inertly by his side. When he also failed to deliver any of his lyrics, Waters and Wright struggled to cover for his vocals.[112]

An (unknown) American reviewer had an altogether more positive perspective on the gig:

> The unbelievable sound of Pink Floyd was first heard through a hurricane of colour, bringing total sensual involvement of audience and performers, each absorbed in the creation of aural/visual experience.

It is known that they played for one hour.[113]

Nick Mason was presumably referring to the same gig, when he commented in *Mojo* magazine:

Syd went mad on that first American tour in the Autumn of '67. He didn't know where he was most of the time. I remember he de-tuned his guitar on stage at Venice, LA, and just stood there rattling the strings, which was a bit weird, even for us. Another time he emptied a can of Brylcreem on his head because he said he didn't like his curly hair.[114]

- **Syd and the gang meet up with Alice Cooper.**[115]

Alice invited them round after the Cheetah Club show; amusing (though not necessarily true!) recollections of this meeting are to be found in *Trouser Press*, 1979.[116]

MONDAY 6

- **Dick Clark's *American Bandstand*, ABC TV, Hollywood, California, USA.**

The show was apparently broadcast on 16 December 1967 at 12.30 pm.
The band performed 'Apples And Oranges' and 'See Emily Play'. Not for the first time, 'Syd wasn't into moving his lips that day'[117] and the rest of the band were forced to mime on his behalf.
'Apples And Oranges' has recently resurfaced, and indeed a section was aired on the BBC 2 TV documentary *Dancing In The Street*.[118] This programme has been released on home video.
The full-length broadcast which is in circulation, complete with a VT editor's counter emblazoned across the bottom of the screen is distinctly longer:

Apples And Oranges, 3.04, video

Introduced by Dick Clark, 'Apples and Oranges, their latest release', the picture quality like the 'official' version is poor.

MONDAY 6

- **Fly back to England?**

WEDNESDAY 8 – SUNDAY 12

- **Belgian TV dates?**

The *New Musical Express* on 7 October reported that the band had booked some dates in Belgium, but no broadcasts appear to have resulted, if ever they did them. Given Syd's ailing state of mind it is unlikely that they ever happened.[119]

THURSDAY 9

• **Fillmore West, San Francisco, California, USA.**

FRIDAY 10 – SATURDAY 11

• **Winterland, San Francisco, California, USA.**

SUNDAY 12

• **Cheetah Club, New York City, New York, USA.**

MONDAY 13

• **Hippy-Happy Fair, Oude-Ahoy Hallen, Rotterdam, Netherlands.**

46.55, Reaction In G Minor, 3.53, Pow R. Toc H., 11.23, An Old Woman With A Casket, 4.25, Set The Controls For The Heart Of The Sun, 8.53, Interstellar Overdrive, 14.03

Reaction In G Minor

Thank you.

Pow R. Toc H.

Thank you. One. This is a song called 'An Old Woman With A Casket'.

An Old Woman With A Casket

One.

Set The Controls For The Heart Of The Sun / Interstellar Overdrive

[Announcer salutes the band in Dutch.]

There have been various rumours about there being a fifty-one-minute tape in existence, but the general consensus is that the said tape contains no extra musical footage. The perpetuators of such rumours tend to rely upon dated timings from multiple-generation, poorly cut copies. It would seem likely that if the tape is genuine it has been recorded at a slightly different speed to that above.

Copies of the recording, like that at the Starclub two months before, are typically pretty poor. The reader, though, should note that where generation loss is evident, its effect is particularly damaging – where the source is reputable, the concert is perfectly listenable. Anecdotal evidence from a still-sane UFO attendee suggests that the barrage of noise occasionally evidenced on the tape is a very true-to-life reflection of how the Floyd often sounded at the time!

The centrepiece of the set is Roger's 'Set The Controls'. Roger sings. It would be easy to get overly romantic about Syd's 'doing everything'.

The show was rescheduled from the 12th, explaining why for so long the tape has been labelled as from this date.

TUESDAY 14

- **The Alchemical Wedding, Royal Albert Hall, Kensington, London, UK.**

The Floyd were featured in a 17-minute slot, opening for Jimi Hendrix in this, the first of Jimi's 16-date tour – an exhausting schedule, there were two gigs a day, a matinee as well as one in the evening. Also on the bill were The Move, The Nice, Amen Corner, The Eire Apparent and The Outer Limits. The shows were compered by Radio 1 DJ Pete Drummond. Syd's unreliability at this time forced Dave O'List, the Nice's guitarist, to join the band on some nights when Syd was absent or unable to play. The set often consisted mostly of instrumentals as they struggled on without a lead vocalist. Some suggest that the band's sets on the Hendrix tour comprised solely a performance of 'Set The Controls For The Heart of The Sun'.

The band's lighting man and roadie, Peter Wynne-Wilson talks about the gig in *Saucerful Of Secrets*. Schaffner comments how 'the scintillating visuals and a sense of event carried the band through their short third-billed set. A credible if undistinguished performance from Barrett proved, however, to be the briefest of remissions'.[120]

Barrett described the gig in an interview with *Melody Maker* in January 1970 as being, 'very much a crescendo' and said he 'felt very good'.[121]

The highly collectable programme for the Hendrix tour – now changing hands at prohibitive prices such that even photocopies are hard to come by, featured two pages on each band: one featuring a picture, the other a biography and history of each group. The Floyd picture, which will be familiar to many, features the four band members, in a state of heightened hilarity, against a background of leaden clouds through which the sun is breaking. The article is hardly earthmoving, though there is one moment of insight on the part of the unnamed author:

> The Pink Floyd remain today both within and yet distinct from the pop scene. A top-five record and a top-three LP have not altered the basic purpose of the group which, on stage, is to aim at a completely free expression of their personalities through the use of light and sound. There are no barriers, there can be no predictions.

WEDNESDAY 15

- **EMI, Studio 3, Abbey Road, London, UK.**

'Apples And Oranges' and 'Paintbox' stereo mixes completed – or at least logged into the EMI library. Whether the band were involved, or if only

Norman Smith worked on these, is unclear. It is perhaps likely that the mixes were only logged after the band had returned from the continent and had a chance to hear them.

- **Winter Gardens, Bournemouth, Dorset, UK (Hendrix tour).**

FRIDAY 17

- **City Hall, Sheffield, Yorkshire, UK (Hendrix Tour).**

SATURDAY 18

- **'Apples and Oranges' / 'Paintbox' single released.**

  This single was only released in the UK and Germany (where it appeared in a colourful, and collectable, picture sleeve).

- **Empire Theatre, Liverpool, Lancashire, UK (Hendrix Tour).**

SUNDAY 19

- **Coventry Theatre, Coventry, Warwickshire, UK (Hendrix Tour).**

WEDNESDAY 22

- **Guildhall, Portsmouth, Hampshire, UK (Hendrix Tour).**

THURSDAY 23

- **Sophia Gardens, Cardiff, South Glamorgan, Wales, UK (Hendrix Tour).**

FRIDAY 24

- **Colston Hall, Bristol, Avon, UK (Hendrix Tour).**

  The gig made the local *Bristol Evening Post* the following day, though not necessarily for the right reasons – 'Over boisterous Welsh teenagers were ejected after incidents in hall bars and the auditorium. In the hall, youths hurled abuse at performers, but the trouble died down as officials brought the shouting minority under control.'[122]

SATURDAY 25

- **An article about Syd Barrett appears in *Melody Maker* newspaper, UK.**

- **The Opera House, Blackpool, Lancashire, UK (Hendrix Tour).**

The Hendrix performance was filmed by Peter Neal for the BBC's *Track Records* show, UK, though it is not known if he filmed the Floyd, or any of the other acts.

Anecdotal evidence confirms that the Floyd supported Jimi Hendrix and Amen Corner amongst others on this date. Both Hendrix and Amen Corner were apparently much better than the Floyd. The source, whose partner (sadly, now deceased) was a casual Floyd fan, recalls a conversation where it was remarked that at least one of several tracks that they played, was on the *Relics* album. (Take your pick). They played very loudly for about twenty minutes and weren't, by all accounts, particularly enjoyable.

A ticket stub from the gig is reproduced in *Chapter 24* no. 3.

SUNDAY 26

- **Palace Theatre, Manchester, Greater Manchester, UK (Hendrix Tour).**

After this gig Syd, along with lighting people Peter Wynne-Wilson and Susie Gawler-Wright, went to visit the poet Neil Oram, one of the English beats.[123]

MONDAY 27

- **Festival '67, Whitla Hall, Queens College, Belfast, County Antrim, Northern Ireland (Hendrix Tour).**

DECEMBER

- **Promotional film for 'Jugband Blues' made.**

A colour film made for the Central Office Of Information. It is also understood that the band were to record a promo of 'Corporal Clegg' sometime in 1968 for the COI, a branch of the UK Civil Service. 'Jugband Blues' would seem to be an unlikely track for the government to finance, after all. We pick up the story again on the 9th.

EARLY

- **'Jugband Blues' recorded, EMI Studios, London, UK.**

It was originally intended that 'Jugband Blues' be released as a single.

Friday 1

- **Central Hall, Chatham, Kent, UK (Hendrix Tour).**

TOP

Chatham Corporation in association with
Harold Davidson Ltd. presents on
Friday, 1 December at 6.15 and 8.45 p.m.

JIMI HENDRIX Experience : THE MOVE
PINK FLOYD : AMEN CORNER

The Nice : Eire Apparent : Outer Limits : Pete Drummond
Seats 10/-. 12/6. 15/-. 17/6. Booking at Bates from Fri. 10 November.

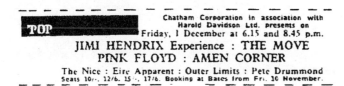

The gig was reviewed in the *Chatham Standard* on 5 December. Apparently there was some confusion about which venue the gig was at – the audience arrived at Central Hall, while the bands were waiting at the Town Hall, some 200 yards up the road! Unfortunately, for the reviewer,

> The Pink Floyd was … the biggest disappointment, because I was expecting so much more. They performed in near darkness for most of the time, played some unrecognisable numbers, and were completely overshadowed by the entertaining antics of a young man in a bear skin jacket whose task seemed to be to leap about the stage adjusting amplifiers, twisting knobs and retrieving the odd cymbal and microphone.[124]

The review provoked a letter from a fan, published on the 12th, who accused the reviewer of getting her facts wrong, telling her to get the album so she'd recognise the songs, and arguing that the light show was only effective in darkness, and that in any case the Floyd hadn't been able to put up their cinema screen. Quite an argument seems to have developed, with the reviewer complaining in her reply to the letter that she'd seen a better lightshow 'on a damp Guy Fawkes night'![125]

The paper, obviously fans of the new psychedelic sounds, despite some of its reviewer's comments, also ran a competition to win tickets for the gig, promising that if the bands 'are not all exhausted by the time they get here on Friday, the Central Hall should be reeling under the pop assault'.[126]

Saturday 2

- **Ally Pally Stuffs, *Bouton Rouge*, French TV, France.**

Most likely mistaken, it is thought that the show repeated the BBC's *Man Alive* footage from the Alexandra Palace Love In, earlier in July.

- **The Dome, Brighton, East Sussex, UK (Hendrix Tour).**

Sunday 3

- **Theatre Royal, Nottingham, Nottinghamshire, UK (Hendrix Tour).**

December 1967

MONDAY 4

- **City Hall, Newcastle, Tyne and Wear, UK (Hendrix Tour).**

D.R. Lamb from Heaton, Newcastle felt moved to write to *Melody Maker* and was published on 30 December:

> I was disgusted by the jeering at the Pink Floyd's show. No groups deserve that when they are only setting out to entertain people.

TUESDAY 5

- **Green's Playhouse, Glasgow, Strathclyde, Scotland, UK (Hendrix Tour).**

Jim Connor from Glasgow was also published in *Melody Maker* on 30 December:

> Glasgow audiences have done it again. At a recent show they clapped the Amen Corner's diabolical act and later had the gall to jeer the Pink Floyd's brilliant performance.

WEDNESDAY 6

- **Royal College of Art, Kensington, London, UK.**

- **Chislehurst Caves, Chislehurst, Kent, UK.**

Now a subterranean tourist attraction, Chislehurst Caves may have the honour of being the most 'underground' of venues frequented by bands in the late sixties.

While the guide may be drawn to recollect the gigs which took place, any evidence was sadly destroyed by overzealous management, who felt that the concert posters which decorated what was once the dressing room, were unsightly, and had them removed in the early 80s.

SATURDAY 9

- **Interviewed for *Oz* magazine, UK.**

We have been unable to find any evidence that this was ever published.

- **'Hits? The Floyd Couldn't Care Less' an article in *Melody Maker*.**

A photo of the band which accompanied the piece was captioned, 'PINK FLOYD: "going through a very confusing stage"'. The paper also reported that the band had made a promotional film of 'Jugband Blues' for the Central

Office Of Information, a branch of the UK government. While the film was
shown to US cinema audiences, it does not appear to have received wider
distribution, and thus remains an intriguing enigma.

• **Middle Earth Club, Covent Garden, London, UK.**

With the closure of the UFO, 'the role of presenting rock and mixed media,
and also that of the freaks' meeting place, passed on to a smaller club,
Middle Earth. Although it was run and staffed by freaks, it was a tighter,
more commercial operation, and the number of dropouts it supported was
only about forty per cent of the number supported by UFO.'[127]
   Previously known as the Electric Garden, Middle Earth had been running
for some months previously, though prior to the closure of UFO it was never
a particularly popular place, a situation not helped by Yoko Ono complaining about the 'bad vibrations' on it's opening night!

TUESDAY 12

• *Bouton Rouge*, **French TV broadcast.**

Repeat of the footage from the BBC's *Man Alive* film, shown earlier in
the UK.

WEDNESDAY 13

• **Flamingo Club, Redruth, Cornwall, UK.**

Dave Bunday of Newquay, Cornwall attended the gig and felt moved to
write to *Melody Maker*. He was published on 30 December:

   If any readers are intending to see the Pink Floyd, my advice is don't.
   They played here recently and were so unbelievably bad the supporting
   group had to be brought back early. It was the opinion of most of the 1,000
   students at our dance that they were the worst group ever to appear in
   Cornwall.

THURSDAY 14

• **Pavilion Ballroom, Bournemouth, Hampshire, UK.**

Robert Plant's Band of Joy also played at this gig.

FRIDAY 15

• **Middle Earth, Covent Garden, London, UK.**

December 1967

SATURDAY 16

- **ABC Television broadcast of Pink Floyd's appearance on Dick Clark's
  *American Bandstand.***

  Their appearance was recorded earlier on 6 November.

- **Ritz Ballroom, Kings Heath, Birmingham, West Midlands, UK.**

- **Saturday Spectacular, The Penthouse, Birmingham, West Midlands, UK.**

SUNDAY 17

- **BBC Studios, London, UK.**

WEDNESDAY 20

- ***Top Gear* recorded at BBC Maida Vale 4, London, UK.**

  The recording was broadcast on the 31st.

THURSDAY 21

- **The Speakeasy, London, UK.**

FRIDAY 22

- **Christmas On Earth Continued, Olympia Exhibition Hall, Kensington,
  London, UK.**

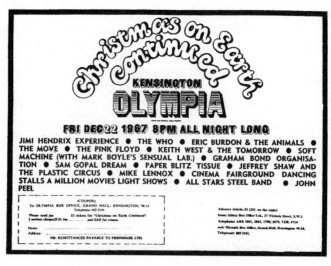

Advertisement in *IT* 22, 15 December 1967

This concert featured Jimi Hendrix, The Who, The Move and others and was the last major Pink Floyd gig with Syd. General comments on the show suggest that it didn't turn out as well as was expected. Tickets cost £1.

The concert was filmed, but never released – the book *Hollywood Rock* describes the film, *Christmas On Earth Continued* as featuring footage of the Jimi Hendrix Experience, The Soft Machine, Pink Floyd, The Who, The Move, Tomorrow, Sam Ghopal's Dream (with Lemmy of Mötorhead!) and others.[128] The Hendrix footage also appeared in the video *Jimi Hendrix: Live In Monterey 1970*.

SATURDAY 30

• **A letter by Peter Jenner and Andrew King appears in *Melody Maker*.**

Jenner and King, clearly incensed by a suggestion in *Melody Maker* on 16 December that 'groups like Pink Floyd are killing pop' were moved to reply. Greater intellect than expected from the average contributor stands out:

> Pop music is a rugged plant and is able to stand up well to the periodic episodes of self torture and internecine warfare which characterise it. Now the Pink Floyd are accused of 'killing pop music' (MM December 16).
>
> No doubt they are about the ninety seventh group to be accused of this, ever since Ida Barr went electric. A lot of people from poor old Engelbert Humperdinck to Ravi Shankar, Dave Clark and John Lennon. If you have a sufficiently closed mind anybody can be seen as a threat.
>
> So yes, the Pink Floyd are killing pop music because there are a large number of people whose minds are too closed to accept what the Pink Floyd do as anything other than a threat to most people's ideas as to what pop music is.
>
> To them all, boring, repetitive, false glitter, the leers, the swinging clothes and rave gear, in other words, the expensive packaging is music and is worth their hard-earned cash and worth protecting and getting excited and hysterical about.
>
> The Floyd are not packaged, they just are. Eighty per cent of Pink Floyd music is improvised. Many people don't seem to realise this and many sets include numbers never played before or since. So the Pink Floyd are largely unpredictable both to the audience and themselves.
>
> They can be sublime. They can be awful. So can audiences and generally the audiences get what they deserve and what they feel.
>
> The Pink Floyd is you. If you feel they are killing something for you, then you are their accomplice. – Peter Jenner and Andrew King (Pink Floyd Management), London w9.

SUNDAY 31

- *Top Gear*, presented by John Peel and Tommy Vance, BBC Radio 1, London, UK.

The recording was made on 20 December and was produced by Bernie Andrews. The identity of the engineer is unknown. It was broadcast between 2.00 and 5.00 pm.

The copy described below is generally circulated under the guise of its being from the original broadcast. Careful listening to varying levels of hiss (!) reveals that it is very likely that it has been derived from several sources and is probably purposefully very finely edited to cut out latter-day DJ comment.

Vegetable Man, 3.14, Scream Thy Last Scream, 3.40, Jugband Blues, 3.39, Pow R. Toc H., 2.55

CHRISTMAS

- **The band decides that Syd is becoming impossible to work with. Over Christmas, they first approach David Gilmour to join the group.**

A sympathetic and well-reasoned collection of accounts of Syd's poor health may be found in *Days In The Life*.[129]

Jeff Beck was considered before David Gilmour as a replacement for Syd, but the band were too in awe of him to ask (according to the *1994 European Tour Programme*). In the same year however, different reasoning was mooted in the May edition of *Mojo* magazine. 'Jeff Beck was considered, but rejected on the grounds that he couldn't sing.'

1968
Beset By Creatures Of The Deep

- 'Flaming' / 'The Gnome' US single released.

  'Flaming' features a distinctly different mix to that which appears on the LP. *Chapter 24* no. 4 pointed out that this may be due to nothing more than the cutting instructions being ignored or misunderstood by the US distributors – in other words, both versions could well be sourced from the same master.

  Flaming, 2.46

- *Tonite Let's All Make Love In London* film released.

  It went on to win the best documentary award in *Films And Filming* magazine January 1969. A detailed description of the film may be found in *Monthly Film Bulletin* magazine February 1968. Those interested in finding out more about the 1960s work of Peter Whitehead would do well to obtain the lengthy piece on him published in the January 1969 issue of *Films And Filming*.
    The original LP sounds nicer than the CD remastering of the album, but is, of course, missing the full length version of 'Interstellar Overdrive'.

  Original LP, 36.23, Interstellar Overdrive, 0.59, Interstellar Overdrive reprise, 0.30, Interstellar Overdrive reprise, 3.05

- **The Arts Council turn down Blackhill Enterprises' request for a grant to further fund their activities.**

  Nick Mason described in *zigzag* 32 how no one knew what it was for: 'I don't think anyone really knew – [to] put on a film or some show, mainly just to keep the finances running, I should think … but the Arts Council aren't into subsidising bands.'

- 'Corporal Clegg' (promo film) for the Central Office Of Information, UK.

  The band were asked to record a promo for this track by the Central Office Of Information, part of the UK's Civil Service. It has never been seen, sadly, and consequently it is impossible to say what it was like.

- 'Let There Be More Light' (promo film) recorded.

  An unusual film of the band miming to 'Let There Be More Light' exists, though it is unknown who or what it was recorded for. The band are seen on a tube train as well as running down an escalator in slow motion!

Let There Be More Light, 1.40, video

- **The future of the band is called into question when Syd decides to add a saxophonist and a banjo player.**

Roger in *zigzag*: 'There was a great plan to expand the group, get in two other geezers, some two freaks that he'd met somewhere or other. One of them played the banjo and the other played the saxophone. We weren't into that at all, and it was obvious that the crunch had come.'

We assume that the above account is correct as it was recorded nearer the time, but Roger recalls Syd's suggestion differently some years later in *Off The Record*:

I remember the final straw, and that was when Syd one day decided that the answer to the band's problems was to introduce two saxophone players and a girl singer. We said , 'Yeah, yeah. Good idea, Syd.'[130]

The former account seems to predominate in pre-80s accounts and the latter mid-80s to present.[131]

- *Tomorrow's World,* **BBC 1 TV broadcast, UK.**

This show was broadcast either on 3 or 10 January 1968, and repeated more recently as part of BBC 1 TV's *Omnibus* documentary.[132] The film was shot at the end of 1967, and focused on the band's old landlord Mike Leonard, and his lighting designs. The band performed an unknown blues-based instrumental, reported in the press as being a Waters / Mason composition, demonstrating his equipment. Barrett appears lucid and contented, contrary to much of the evidence that we and our predecessors present of him around the end of 1967.

Tomorrow's World, repeated on Omnibus, 2.01, two unknown instrumentals with Nick Mason, Mike Leonard and Joe Boyd interviews mixed in.

SATURDAY 6

- **Rehearsals, London, UK.**

It is likely that these rehearsals mark David Gilmour's first time with the band in its expanded five-man form. Sometime during January Syd intro-duced the band to his latest composition, 'Have You Got It Yet'. From Nick's comments below, these rehearsals were probably the occasion for its premiere:

> We were teaching Dave the numbers with the idea that we were going to be a five-piece. But Syd came in with some new material. The song went 'Have You Got It Yet' and he kept changing it so that no one could learn it.[133]

MONDAY 8 – TUESDAY 9

- **Rehearsals, London, UK.**

WEDNESDAY 10 – THURSDAY 11

- **EMI, Studio 3, Abbey Road, London, UK.**

FRIDAY 12

- **Aston University, Birmingham, West Midlands, UK.**

David Gilmour asserted in an interview for *Mojo* magazine, July 1995, that this was the first gig that the band played as a five-piece. Watkinson and Anderson also mention this as the first gig that David Gilmour played at; they say that the band played live as a five-piece for the next five gigs (up to Southampton on the 26th).[134] This would imply that Syd didn't attend any gigs between then and when he left on 1 March, 1968, the date Blackhill was dissolved.

Gilmour addressed the subject again in the 1994 *Omnibus* documentary, recalling that 'Syd seemed to cheer up a little bit when I was there … I think it must have been the sixth one that we would have done together, which I think was at Southampton University … we just never picked him up.'

The observant amongst you will note that Dave is slightly mistaken in asserting that it was the sixth (rather than fifth) gig at which Syd was left behind.

SATURDAY 13

- **Saturday Dance Date, Winter Gardens Pavilion, Weston-super-Mare, Avon, UK.**

Advertisement reproduced in *Chapter 24*, no. 3

January 1968

MONDAY 15 – TUESDAY 16

- **Rehearsals, London, UK.**

WEDNESDAY 17 – THURSDAY 18

- **EMI, Studio 3, Abbey Road, London, UK.**

  'Let There Be More Light' and 'Rhythm Tracks' were recorded during this session.

FRIDAY 19

- **Town Hall, Lewes, Sussex, UK.**

SATURDAY 20

- **Hastings Pier, Hastings, West Sussex, UK.**

WEDNESDAY 24 – THURSDAY 25

- **EMI, Studio 3, Abbey Road, London, UK.**

  'The Most Boring Song I've Ever Heard Bar Two' – recording sessions for the track which was to later become 'See-Saw'!

FRIDAY 26

- **Southampton University, Southampton, Hampshire, UK.**

  The fact that they played at the University is confirmed by Gilmour in the 1994 *Omnibus* documentary.

SATURDAY 27

- **Leicester College of Technology, Leicester, Leicestershire, UK.**

- **David Gilmour joins The Pink Floyd.**

  Somewhat inaccurately, *Melody Maker* reported on 27 January:

  > NEW GUITARIST GILMUR [*sic*] FOR FLOYD
  > A new singer and guitarist has joined the Pink Floyd, increasing their line up to five. He is 21-year-old David Gilmour.
  > A childhood friend of the Floyd's Syd Barrett and Roger Waters, Gilmur [*sic*] has rehearsed with the group for several weeks, and will now join them

on their first European tour which starts on February 18 and includes a performance at the First European International Pop Festival in Rome.

A passport-sized photo of Gilmour accompanies the piece.

WEDNESDAY 31

• **EMI, Studio 3, Abbey Road, London, UK.**

The band continue work on 'The Most Boring Song I've Ever Heard Bar Two' and begin sessions for 'Corporal Clegg'.

FEBRUARY

THURSDAY 1

• **EMI, Studio 3, Abbey Road, London, UK.**

'Corporal Clegg' mix down sessions. It is likely that 'Corporal Clegg' was completed on this date. It was entered into the EMI library on the 7th.

TUESDAY 6

• **Rehearsals, London, UK.**

WEDNESDAY 7

• **Mary Hopkin's TV Show, Paris, France.**

SATURDAY 10

• **The Imperial Ballroom, Nelson, Lancashire, UK.**

SUNDAY 11

• *Top Gear*, **BBC Radio 1, London, UK.**

A rebroadcast of the 31 December, 1967 show.

MONDAY 12

• **EMI, Studio 3, Abbey Road, London, UK.**

12 February was another busy day for the band who managed to get through two versions of 'Doreen's Dream' (later to be retitled 'Julia Dream') and two

titles which most likely ended up as parts of *A Saucerful Of Secrets* – 'The Boppin Sound' and 'Richard's Rave Up'. The band also recorded the first take of 'It Should Be So Nice' (an early title, of course, for their next single).

Richard Wright in *Mojo*, 1994:

> I did the title track and I remember Norman saying, You just can't do this, it's too long. You have to write three minute songs. We were pretty cocky by now and told him, if you don't wanna produce it, just go away. A good attitude I think.

TUESDAY 13

- **'Julia Dream' produced by Norman Smith at Abbey Road Studios.**

This particular entry follows the sleeve notes for *Relics*. Our investigations, particularly having seen Malcolm Jones' research, would indicate that *Relics* is a particularly unreliable source, and the reader may observe that our dates are often in contradiction with the details it gives.

Malcolm Jones notes that the 13th saw recordings of 'Doreen's Dream' and 'Corporal Clegg' as well as mono mix downs for 'The Boppin' Sound', 'It Should Be So Nice' and 'Doreen Dream'.

THURSDAY 15

- **EMI, Studio 3, Abbey Road, London, UK.**

Mono mixes of 'Corporal Clegg' and 'Set The Controls For The Heart Of the Sun'.

FRIDAY 16

- **ICI Fibres Club, Pontypool, Monmouthshire, Wales, UK.**

SATURDAY 17

- **Concertgebouw, Vlissingen, Holland.**

SUNDAY 18

- **The band begin their first European tour.** [135]

It would appear that *Melody Maker*, source of this information, was slightly mistaken regarding the date upon which the tour began.

SUNDAY 18 – MONDAY 19

- **Belgian TV, Brussels, Belgium (recording for later broadcasts).**

The band recorded various promotional films over two days in Brussels. On the 18th David Gilmour was formally declared a full member of the group, so these were probably his first appearances on film with the band.

Seven tracks were recorded, all of which, unusually, have survived the passing of time. 'Astronomy Domine' was performed in the studio and features a liquid light show and spooky girls. 'Scarecrow' and 'See Emily Play' were played in adjacent fields, which both look as though they have the same flyover in the background.

'Apples And Oranges' is promoted by a studio performance. This, and not *Top Of The Pops* (though it may have been shown later in the UK), is the source of the most common 'Apples And Oranges' promo in which Dave is seen 'playing', and Roger seen failing to mime, Syd's parts. So as we're clear that the song is about fruit, a grocer's stall may be seen in the background! The most interesting of the songs is certainly 'Corporal Clegg', which features significant structural differences to the LP version.

17.53, Astronomy Domine, 4.00, The Scarecrow, 2.00, Corporal Clegg, 2.46, Paintbox, 3.26, Apples And Oranges, 2.55, See Emily Play, 2.46, videos

TUESDAY 20

- **ORTF 2 TV Studios, Paris, France (recording for later broadcasts).**

This is the source of the *Bouton Rouge* appearance later in the month, incomplete copies of which exist on video – including a great version of 'Flaming', with a very strange intro on a cuckoo whistle! Also recorded, though not in circulation amongst collectors, was a version of the track 'Set The Controls For The Heart Of The Sun'.

6.00, Astronomy Domine, 3.00, Flaming, 2.38, video

WEDNESDAY 21

- **ORTF 2 TV Studios, Paris, France (recording for later broadcasts).**

The band recorded 'live' studio performances of 'The Scarecrow' and 'Let There Be More Light' for later broadcast on *Discorama* in March.

THURSDAY 22

- **Rij-School, Leuven, Belgium.**

FRIDAY 23

• **Pannenhuis, Antwerp, Belgium.**

SATURDAY 24

• *Bouton Rouge*, **ORTF 2 TV, Paris, France.**

'Set The Controls For The Heart Of The Sun' was broadcast, along with 'Astronomy Domine' and 'Flaming', though the former may actually be the true source of the *All My Loving* clip.

• **Cheetah Club, Brussels, Belgium.**

MONDAY 26

• **Domino Club, Lion Hotel, Cambridge, Cambridgeshire, UK.**

WEDNESDAY 28

• **'Astronomy Domine' featured as the theme for ATV, UK, programme** *The Gamblers.*

Apparently the band were unaware that their song was used, and were never paid!

MARCH

• **Richard Wright is invited to leave the band.**

Robert Sandall in his 1994 *Mojo* magazine article, drew from Wright:

> Peter and Andrew thought Syd and I were the musical brains of the group, and that we should form a break-away band, to try to hold Syd together. He and I were living together in a flat in Richmond at the time. And believe me, I would have left with him like a shot if I had thought Syd could do it.

SATURDAY 2

• **Blackhill Enterprises is dissolved.**

Peter Jenner:

> Basically, the Floyd left us because they thought we'd have no confidence in them without Syd, which was true, even though it was a mistake for us to think like that. We just couldn't conceive how they would be able to make it without

Syd, who put all the creativity into the group … if I'd known then, what I know now, things would have been very different … the Floyd would have made a lot of money much sooner than they did, and I'd be a very rich man.[136]

MONDAY 4

- **Vanessa Redgrave party, London, UK.**[137]

The band probably knew the actress through her appearance in *Tonite Let's All Make Love In London*.

TUESDAY 5

- **EMI, Studio 3, Abbey Road, London, UK.**

'It Would Be So Nice' recording sessions.

SATURDAY 9

- **Manchester Technical College, Manchester, Lancashire, UK.**

TUESDAY 12 – WEDNESDAY 13

- **EMI, Studio 3, Abbey Road, London, UK.**

'It Would Be So Nice' – more sessions.

THURSDAY 14

- **Whitla Hall, Belfast, County Antrim, Northern Ireland.**

FRIDAY 15

- **The Stage Club, Oxford, Oxfordshire, UK.**

SATURDAY 16

- **Crawdaddy, Taggs Island, Hampton Court, London, UK, at 6.30 pm.**

An ad for the gig in *Melody Maker* describes the performance as a 'Sound and Light Show'.[138]

- **Middle Earth Club, London, UK, at 12.30 am.**

Syd turned up to glower at Dave. The original source of this quote is the very readable 'Floyd Joy' article by Chris Welch in *Melody Maker*, 19 May 1973.[139] The Floyd were supported by Juniors Eyes.[140]

Sunday 17

- *Discorama*, ORTF 2 TV, Paris, France.

The band was interviewed to promote the release of *Piper At The Gates Of Dawn*, with the broadcast also including studio footage of the band performing 'The Scarecrow'.

Wednesday 20

- BBC Studios, London, UK.

- New Grafton Rooms, Liverpool, Lancashire, UK.

Thursday 21

- EMI, Studio 3, Abbey Road, London, UK.

Further recording sessions for 'It Would Be So Nice', as well as the production of the final mix.

Friday 22

- Woolwich Polytechnic, Woolwich, London, UK.

Saturday 23

- EMI, Studio 3, Abbey Road, London, UK.

'Julia Dream' finally completed.

Tuesday 26 – Wednesday 27

- BBC Studios, London, UK.

The BBC have not been able to provide any detail on these dates, but it has been suggested that the band took part in a pop music documentary which they were recording at the time.

Friday 29

- EMI Abbey Road Studios, London, UK.

- **'It Would Be So Nice' (promo film) recorded.**

The band are seen miming to the track in the studio at Abbey Road. The best source available seems to be the Knebworth film.

1.03, It Would Be So Nice

- **San Francisco movie soundtrack.**

Interstellar Overdrive (mono), 15.22

As mentioned previously there is little doubt that the recording was made back on 31 October 1966 during the band's first session for Blackhill.

It is unclear quite when Judex Films' *San Francisco* movie was released. *Ink* magazine mentions a showing at the Roundhouse on 30 April 1971, verifying recollections from older fans that it was indeed shown during 1971 and 1972. It seems to be generally accepted that the film was first previewed at this earlier date, however. For those of you who may be interested it toured universities and art theatres, along with numerous other rock and pop shorts from Hendrix's *Experience* to Scaffold's *Lily The Pink*!

The British Film Institute, who helped fund the film, gave a viewing in 1986, and their programme explains something about the film and its intent:

> *San Francisco* examines the characteristics of modern American society through the contrasts in just one city. Using the flash and freeze-frame technique, the film's rapid and closely-cut sequences form a colourful

29 THURSDAY
'Z' (Costa-Gavras, 1968) 3pm, 5.50pm, 8.40pm Hendon Classic, NW2—202 7137 (Hendon Central tube) Tickets 35p, 40p.
THE LEFT HANDED GUN (Penn 1958) 2pm, 5.20pm, 8.45pm Brixton Classic, SW2—274 1649 (Stockwell tube) Tickets 30p.
CREAM (Palmer 1968) 2pm Roundhouse, Chalk Farm, NW3—267 2541 (Chalk Farm tube) Tickets 25p.

30 FRIDAY
'Z'(Costa-Gavras,1968) 3 pm, 5.50 pm, 8.40 pm Hendon Classic, NW2—202 7137 (Hendon Central tube) Tickets 35p, 40p.
THE LEFT HANDED GUN (Penn, 1958) 2pm, 5.20pm, 8.45pm Brixton Classic, SW2—274 1649 (Stockwell tube) Tickets 30p.
MONTEREY POP (Pennebaker 1968) + CREAM (Palmer 1968) 3.30pm, 7pm, 10.30pm Putney Odeon—788 4756 (Putney Bridge tube) Tickets 35p, 50p.
EXPERIENCE (Marshall) with Jimi Hendrix + BE GLAD (Peter Neal) with Incredible String Band + SAN FRANCISCO (Stern) with Pink Floyd 2pm Roundhouse, Chalk Farm, NW3—267 2541 (Chalk Farm tube) Tickets 30p.

Advertisement in *Ink*, 15 May 1971

montage of bizarre images from which emerges a memorable portrait of contemporary city life in all its photogenic glamour and its kooky excesses. It also represents a popular film form of the time; the trick of compressing a day's activities into 15 minutes by using flash and freeze-frame is characteristic of 60s underground film-making, producing a speedy collage of contemporary society with all the confusion of drugs and political violence, and the music that echoed this.

While the majority of the film is comprised of art-house images of San Francisco, the latter part concentrates upon a happening in which a naked woman is wrapped in bacofoil ...

MONDAY 1 – TUESDAY 2

- **EMI, Studio 3, Abbey Road, London, UK.**

FRIDAY 5

- **EMI, Studio 3, Abbey Road, London, UK.**

'Nick's Boogie 1st, 2nd & 3rd Movement' recorded.

SATURDAY 6

- **Syd Barrett's departure is officially announced.**

Syd's presence on *A Saucerful Of Secrets* may be heard on 'Remember A Day', recorded previously for the *Piper At The Gates Of Dawn* album, 'See-Saw', 'Set The Controls For The Heart Of The Sun' and, of course, the poignant 'Jugband Blues'. Dave is also featured on the latter three songs, though who made the greater contribution is a matter for debate.

TUESDAY 9

- *Horrorscope*, **Granada TV, UK.**

Granada used the album version of 'Astronomy Domine' as background music on the show, but 'forgot' to clear it with the band.

WEDNESDAY 10

- **EMI, Studio 3, Abbey Road, London, UK.**

Mono and stereo mixes completed for 'Nick's Boogie 1st, 2nd & 3rd Movement'.

FRIDAY 12

• **'It Would Be So Nice' / 'Julia Dream' released in the UK.**

It is likely that Syd's performance on the above, if any, was minimal.

FRIDAY 12 – SUNDAY 14

• **Recording for Belgian TV, Belgium.**

SATURDAY 20

• **Raven Club, RAF Waddington, Lincolnshire, UK.**

MONDAY 22

• **EMI, Studio 3, Abbey Road, London, UK.**

'The Most Boring Song etc.' mono and stereo mix downs. The title, once again, is after EMI's log sheets – perhaps the band were not only bored with the song, but the title as well!

TUESDAY 23

• **EMI, Studio 3, Abbey Road, London, UK.**

Mixes for 'Set The Controls For The Heart Of The Sun' and 'Let There Be More Light'.

WEDNESDAY 24

• **EMI, Studio 3, Abbey Road, London, UK.**

'Nick's Boogie' transferred from its original tape. This new copy was then edited into the *Saucerful Of Secrets* album master, but since Nick does not receive a sole credit on the album itself, it must have either been part of a larger piece, such as the title track, been credited to another member of the group, or have been eventually dropped from the completed album.

FRIDAY 26

• **EMI, Studio 3, Abbey Road, London, UK.**

The band worked on stereo mixes of 'Set The Controls For The Heart Of The Sun', 'Let There Be More Light' and 'See-Saw', the latter with its final title for the first time.

TUESDAY 30

• **EMI, Studio 3, Abbey Road, London, UK.**

'Corporal Clegg', stereo mix, and remixes / alternative mixes of 'Nick's Boogie' to replace those made on the copied over tape from the 24th. It is likely that these were made on the previous day, and logged with EMI on the 30th.

MAY

• **Big Apple, Munchen, West Germany.**

The band are thought to have played two shows at Big Apple. Perhaps someone would like to look into this?

EARLY

• **Sound Techniques Studios, Chelsea, London, UK.**

Three master tapes were logged with EMI over 5 and 6 May. Since the band were on the Continent over these days it seems likely that the tapes were actually recorded at a Sound Techniques session earlier in the month. It is our contention that certain of these recordings comprise the soundtrack to *The Committee* – the titles logged over two tapes on 5 May were 'In The Beechwoods' (two takes), 'No Title', 'Vegetable Man' and 'Instrumental', while the tape logged on the 6th held only one track, the enigmatically named 'Untitled'.

We make this suggestion for the following reasons – the opening part of *The Committee* is set in a wood, where the 'central figure', John Paul Jones, decapitates 'the victim', Tom Kempinski, before having second thoughts, and reattaching his head. The song which features at this point appears twice in the movie, at the start and the end, in two forms, suggesting two takes. Apart from this piece the film features three other sequences, which could have been reasonably logged as 'No Title', 'Instrumental' and 'Untitled'.

The session recording would not necessarily have been made at EMI since it was not for general release.

• *The Committee* **soundtrack is recorded by the Pink Floyd.**

The movie was premiered at the Cameo Poly, Oxford Circus, London on 26 September 1968. Copies of the soundtrack so far available on bootleg are incomplete and badly edited. However, the tracks and timings listed below are complete and as they appear in the film. Titles are those given by the authors.

17.10, Backwards introduction, 0.34, Fast Theme, 1.05, Rick's Piece, 1.35, Interview Sequence, 6.45 (Part 1 – Interview, 2.30, Part 2 – Other People, 1.40, Part 3 – Open Door, 2.04, Part 4 – Do You Believe, 0.28) Keep Smiling People, 2.37, End Theme, 3.27

It has always been rumoured that a soundtrack album was released in the US on Reprise records, featuring the Floyd and Crazy World of Arthur Brown (who make a cameo appearance during a party in the film). Any reports are mistaken however. Two films entitled *The Committee* were released in 1968 – one in the US and one in the UK. The US guide Films On TV is helpful in this respect, describing the American film as being an amusing cabaret style show featuring a hippie comedy troupe. Investigation has proved that the LP (US Reprise 2023) is actually taken from this movie, and not the one in which the Floyd appeared, which starred the then Manfred Mann singer Paul Jones.

Nick Mason, reproduced in *Through The Eyes Of…* mentions that 'the music had been made in a single morning and, as it was not very convincing, there was no point in releasing it'.[141]

As an aside, any film soundtrack of the Floyd and Arthur Brown taken from the film, would barely fill one side of an LP, let alone be sufficient to justify a whole album. On a truly tangential note, a friend of one of the authors remembers seeing Paul Jones on an early 70s' interview lamenting the film's not being put on general release – he thought it was great!

Stills from the film may be found in the November 1968 issue of *Films And Filming* magazine.[142] Anybody looking for meaning in the film should seek out *Films And Filming* magazine, December 1968 and particularly *Monthly Film Bulletin*, November 1968.

THURSDAY 2

- **EMI, Studio 3, Abbey Road, London, UK.**

'Let There Be More Light' – new stereo mix, replacing that of 26 April 1968 and 'Set The Controls' stereo mix completed in this session.

FRIDAY 3

- **EMI, Studio 3, Abbey Road, London, UK.**

'See-Saw' mono and stereo mixes completed.

- **Westfield College, Hampstead, London, UK.**

An ad for the gig in *Melody Maker* suggests that the band were supported by Grand Union.[143]

May 1968

- **Recording for Belgian TV, Belgium.**

MONDAY 6

- **First European International Pop Festival, Piper Club, Rome, Italy.**

  The festival was moved to the Piper Club because of poor ticket sales. *Melody Maker* first made mention of the festival on 6 January. At the time, it was intended that it take place between 19 and 25 February. The date was then moved back so as it would take place between 4th and 10th at the Palazzo dello Sport,[144] and was finally announced in the press quite late on as being on the 6th.

  It was filmed for ARD TV, West Germany, and the BBC also broadcast excerpts from the concert later, on 18 May. The ARD broadcast of the Floyd showed them playing 'Interstellar Overdrive'. The recording is available in two distinct quality bands: the shorter tends to be of a higher quality.

  While a number of careful listeners detect a second guitarist, suggested to be Davy O'List from the Nice, this is highly unlikely, since Syd had left a month previously, and Dave would have been quite capable of covering for him by this time.

  Interstellar Overdrive, 6.30, 5.29

  Part of the gig was also broadcast on VPRO Radio, Holland.

  14.12, Astronomy Domine, 6.12, Set The Controls For The Heart Of The Sun, 7.49

- **Syd Barrett recording sessions, EMI, Studio 3, Abbey Road, London, UK.**

  This session marks the proper commencement of Syd's solo career. The *Crazy Diamond* box set and the book of the same name contradict one another as to when Barrett's solo career started: the former states that it started on 13 May, 1968 – certainly wrong – and the latter that he started work 'at EMI's Studio Three in early April'.[145] The Floyd were in Studio Three in early April and it is unlikely that the two would share studio time. We would suggest that the book is mistaken.

  'Silas Lang' and 'Late Night' (version 1) recorded with Pete Jenner producing. It is thought that 'Late Night' was erased and then re-recorded on the 21st!

THURSDAY 9

- **EMI logs receipt of a further seven masters, recordings most likely made back in October 1967 at Sound Techniques Studios, Chelsea.**

Malcolm Jones goes into quite some detail in explaining this assertion; that the masters were on half-inch tape – which EMI didn't use, and that while the mono mix of 'Jugband Blues' was received at EMI on the 24 October 1967, the original four-track master was only received at this late date (it was likely that the mono mix was delivered first since it was intended that 'Jugband Blues' be the next single). Recordings received on this date were: 'Remember A Day' (three takes), 'Jugband Blues', 'Jug Band Blues', two takes of 'Vegetable Man' and one of a track called 'John Latham' (bit of a mystery this last one!).
  Two of the reels contained completed mixes of the following tracks: 'Remember A Day' (mono remix – unreleased), 'Jug Band Blues' (mono LP mix), 'Remember A Day' two mono mixes – the final LP version and one which was rejected, 'Jug Band Blues' (stereo mix) and 'Remember A Day' – the final stereo LP mix.
  Those readers interested in the broader history of the counter-culture may be interested to know that John Latham, the subject of one of the songs from this session was instrumental in the first London Happenings – an artist and draughtsman who was involved in the sTigma project at Miles' Better Books in 1965, where he exhibited his 'Skoob Tower', probably his most famous piece, as well as the Royal Albert Hall's poetry reading where he appeared naked, save for a covering of blue paint![146]
  We have a recording of 'Remember A Day' which, it has always been claimed, was recorded on this date in 1967. We can confidently suggest that it wasn't, though it could have been logged by EMI on the 9th.
  One for the reader to have a good listen to, we suggest!

Remember A Day, 4.27, demo

The version on the *A Saucerful Of Secrets* CD times in at 4 min. 33 sec.

SATURDAY 11

- ***Bouton Rouge*, ORTV TV, Paris, France.**

'Set The Controls For The Heart Of The Sun', rebroadcast, first shown on 20 February.

- **Brighton Arts Festival, Thelme House, Brighton, Sussex, UK.**

TUESDAY 14

- **Syd Barrett recording sessions, EMI, Studio 3, Abbey Road, London, UK.**

Produced by Peter Jenner, take 1 (version 1) of 'Golden Hair' was recorded at this session – this was the haunting instrumental backing track which would close the *Opel* compilation some twenty years later. 'Lanky' was also recorded: the song is split into two parts. Take 1 – the only one made – of 'Part One' was finally released on *Opel*. 'Part Two' still remains unissued, and was in any account, simply a seven-minute drum track. Another near legendary track recorded on this date was 'Rhamadan', a twenty-minute instrumental, two minutes of which have recently become available to collectors on bootleg.

Rhamadan, 1.35

The bootlegger's sleeve notes boldly tell us that 'Rhamadan' was recorded on 6 May, and shouldn't be discounted as being incorrect. Conversations with the source of the bootleg leave us with the probability that he picked the date by virtue of its being Syd's 'first' session. The track itself is as repetitive and uninteresting as many of the pre-availability comments suggested. Simply stated, it is nothing more than Syd playing the bongos.

A number of commentators have suggested that Syd is not the player and that one of his friends is. Most notably, Phil Smee commented on 'Rhamadan' and 'Lanky Pt. 2' that they were 'Drumming only. Not very interesting at all really. There's no drumkit used, just a load of tom-toms and bongos and suchlike. "Rhamadan" seems to consist entirely of random thumps on bongos, it sounds a bit like someone trying out a set to see what they sound like.'

The article continues that 'Phil and Brian managed to track down the original engineer, who's still at the studio (he's a producer now). He had a clear recollection that "some weird friends came along to the session".'[147] It may be these 'weird friends' who feature here.

WEDNESDAY 15

- *A Saucerful Of Secrets* mono LP assembled from previous mono mixes.

THURSDAY 16

- *A Saucerful Of Secrets* stereo LP assembled from previous stereo mixes.

FRIDAY 17

- **Middle Earth Club, Covent Garden, London, UK.**

  An ad for the gig in *Melody Maker* suggests that the band were supported by Alexis Korner, Free, Chakara, and DJ Jeff Dexter.[148]

SATURDAY 18

- *Rome Goes Pop*, BBC broadcast of footage from the Rome Pop Festival earlier in the month.

The 18-minute show featured the Floyd performing 'It Would Be So Nice', and was repeated on 3 November. While this show has never to our knowledge been documented, or rebroadcast in recent years, copies have been retained by the BBC, leading the authors to wonder why it was not included on the *Omnibus* documentary in 1994. The show also featured Captain Beefheart, the Nice, the Association and Julie Driscoll with Brian Auger And The Trinity, amongst others.

TUESDAY 21

- **Syd Barrett recording sessions, EMI, Studio 3, Abbey Road, London, UK.**

'Late Night' (version 2) – elements of which were used in the version which appears on *The Madcap Laughs* was recorded on this date, while overdubs were added to 'Silas Lang', recorded a week earlier. Who played on the track, apart from Syd, is a mystery.

THURSDAY 23

- **Paradiso Club, Amsterdam, Holland.**

The Floyd played two shows, it is thought; one 'early' and one 'late'. Recordings have emerged from both. The latter show has, in the numerous copies that we have found, proved to be consistently of superior quality (neither are wonderful). Perhaps the person recording got him or herself better organised in time for the evening performance.

The middle section of 'Interstellar Overdrive' sounds very much like that that may be found on the *San Francisco* soundtrack – the playing is similar, indicating a willingness, or perhaps a need, to look back as far, theoretically, as the end of 1966. Perhaps, as could well be the case at this time of flux, the band were feeling the pressure as they attempted to redefine their sound in the absence of their former leader. It has been written elsewhere that Dave had a tendency to revert back to an overtly Barrettesque style of performance during these early days.

Previous efforts at timing the concert have tended to be woefully inaccurate (even accepting variations in tape speed over multi-generation copies). As the reader will no doubt be aware, the concert has in the past been cut and sliced into all sorts of different running orders, and has been attributed to at least half a dozen different venues and dates. We are confident that our facts are right on this one, not least because our copies of this and of the late performance show no perceptible signs of editing other than that necessary to split the music onto either side of a cassette. All of the tracks on both tapes are complete.

Early, 47.53, Let There Be More Light, 7.10, Interstellar Overdrive, 10.48, Set The Controls For The Heart Of The Sun, 12.04, A Saucerful Of Secrets, 14.43

This is a song called 'Set The ...'. This is a song called 'Let There Be More Light'. Can we have that spotlight out?

Let There Be More Light

Thank you. This is a ... this is an instrumental that is the final track on our first LP and it's called 'Interstellar Overdrive'.

Interstellar Overdrive

We have to step on ... quickly. We're going to do a song now called 'Set The Controls For The Heart Of The Sun'. Then you can all relax.

Set The Controls For The Heart Of The Sun

Thank you, thank you. This is gonna be the last thing we do tonight. It's the title track off the new album we have coming out which this is called 'A Saucerful Of Secrets'. Thanks very much for listening.

A Saucerful Of Secrets

Thank you ... thank you very much, goodnight.

Late, 53.29, Keep Smiling People, 10.13, Let There Be More Light, 8.11, Set The Controls For The Heart Of The Sun, 12.32, Flaming, 4.55, A Saucerful Of Secrets, 12.33

Good Evening ... This is a sort of quiet and er, relaxing thing called 'Keep Smiling People'.

Keep Smiling People

This is called 'Let There Be More Light'.

Let There Be More Light

We didn't really quite manage to ... relax as we meant in that first thing so were going to do a thing called 'S ... Set The Controls For The Heart of The Sun'. Maybe we'll have better luck.

Set The Controls For The Heart Of The Sun

This is called 'Flaming'.

Flaming

Thank you. This is a small argument and a thing called S ... 'A Saucerful Of Secrets One'. And this is it. You'll have to feel this one with us 'cos it's a bit new, a bit strange, and a bit hard to play.

A Saucerful Of Secrets

'Keep Smiling People' would seem to be unavailable elsewhere on tape. It appears in a truncated form on *The Committee* soundtrack.

A snippet of 'A Saucerful Of Secrets' was broadcast by Dutch radio station

VPRO on 12 June 1988 as part of the programme *Erotisch Panorama*. There certainly isn't anything erotic about the excerpt that times in at a distorted twelve seconds.

Roger's quirky comments preceding certain tracks merit further mention, as they have been both a source of confusion regarding which tape is which, and they confirm, to our mind, our earlier assertion that these gigs show a lack of confidence following the departure of Barrett. The fact that both gigs feature similar preoccupations – 'relaxing' and a concern with a spotlight seem to illustrate that Waters had hit upon introductions which he felt happy with, and used them gig to gig with little desire for their alteration. Despite being musical improvisers, Roger in particular would seem awkward in his new role as front man, reverting to a formulaic approach. The same could be said of performances towards the end of 1970, where amusing themes in stage commentary recur night to night. Perhaps, as may seem entirely consistent, it was all part of the show: a 'felt experience'.

FRIDAY 24

- **The Punch Bowl, Lapworth, Warwickshire, UK.**

SATURDAY 25

- **The Belfry Hotel, Sutton Coldfield, West Mildands, UK.**

SUNDAY 26

- **Oz Benefit, Middle Earth Club, Covent Garden, London, UK.**

While the band appear on the poster, we remain doubtful as to whether they actually performed at the gig.

TUESDAY 28

- **Syd Barrett recording sessions, EMI, Studio 3, Abbey Road, London, UK.**

'Late Night' was recorded in this session. To date, two versions of take 2 have been released – the first had overdubs added almost a year later on 11 April and appeared on *The Madcap Laughs*. The original backing track, without vocals, was later released as an extra track on the *Opel* remaster.

Also worked on was 'Swan Lee (Silas Lang)' – additions to the recording made on the 6th. Take 5 has been released on *Opel*, with overdubs recorded on 8 June 1968 and 25 April 1969. Two other instrumental versions have appeared on bootleg – the first with a more pronounced bass and mournful slide guitar, and the other featuring saxophone and banjo! Better copies have Malcolm Jones saying 'Silas Lang ...This is RMI from four track. Take 1' before the tracks start. Five or so months after suggesting that the Floyd bring in a banjo player and a saxophonist, Syd realises his ambition on his own!

Phil Smee: 'The strange slowed-down saxophone sound at the start is half-speed, and … it sounds unintentional. I think this is another one where the faders weren't set properly when it was put on cassette.' [149]

5.35, Swan Lee (Silas Lang) version 1, 2.43, Swan Lee (Silas Lang) version 2, 2.41

Overdubs were also added to take 1 of 'Golden Hair', and 'Rhamadan', both previously recorded on the 14th.

JUNE

* **Alternative mix for 'Jugband Blues', Canadian 7-inch release.**

The version featured on this unique single is the same as that released on the Canadian issue of the *A Saucerful Of Secrets* LP.

SATURDAY 1

* **Lijn 3, Amsterdam, Holland.**

* **Eurobeurs, Apeldoorn, Holland.**

* **De Kentering, Rosmalen, Holland.**

An early morning show, and two evening performances – what a day!

SUNDAY 2

* **Concertgebouw, Vlissingen, Holland.**

MONDAY 3

* **De Pas, Heesch, Holland.**

SATURDAY 8

* **Syd Barrett recording sessions, EMI, Studio 3, Abbey Road, London, UK.**

Overdubs for 'Swan Lee (Silas Lang)' were done during this session. The final mixes were completed over ten months later on 25 April 1969.

'Golden Hair' take 5 continuing overdubs – this version was officially released as a bonus track on *The Madcap Laughs* CD remaster.

- Market Hall, Haverfordwest, Pembrokeshire, Wales, UK.

WEDNESDAY 12

- Kings College, Cambridge, Cambridgeshire, UK.

FRIDAY 14

- Midsummer Ball, University College London, London, UK.

SATURDAY 15

- Magic Village, Manchester, Lancashire, UK.

THURSDAY 20

- Syd Barrett recording sessions, EMI, Studio 3, Abbey Road, London, UK.

  Overdubs added to a number of previous tracks already down on tape, specifically, 'Swan Lee', 'Late Night' (version 2) and 'Golden Hair' (version 1).

FRIDAY 21

- Commemoration Ball, Balliol College, Oxford, Oxfordshire, UK.

- Middle Earth Club, Covent Garden, London, UK.

  Ads for the gig appeared in *Melody Maker* and *IT*.[150] The band were supported by Hurdy Gurdy, Easy Moses and Dexasterous.

June 1968

SATURDAY 22

- **The 1st Holiness Kitch Garden For The Liberation Of Love And Peace In Colours, The Hague, Holland.**

- **University of East Anglia, Norwich, Norfolk, UK.**

TUESDAY 25

- *Top Gear* **recorded at BBC Studios, 201 Piccadilly, London, UK.**

  The show, which was produced by Bernie Andrews and engineered by Dave Tate, was broadcast on 11 August 1968.

WEDNESDAY 26

- **Sheffield Arts Festival, Sheffield University, Sheffield, Yorkshire, UK.**

FRIDAY 28

- **Students Celebration Dance – The End Of It All Ball, Music Hall, Shrewsbury, Shropshire, UK.**

SATURDAY 29

- *A Saucerful Of Secrets* **is released in the UK.**

  David Gilmour in *Mojo*, May 1995:

  > I remember Nick and Roger drawing out *A Saucerful Of Secrets* as an architectural diagram, in dynamic form rather than in any sort of musical form, with peaks and troughs. That's what it was about, it wasn't music for beauty's sake, or for emotion's sake. It never had a story line. Though for years afterwards we used to get letters from people saying what they thought it meant. Scripts for movies sometimes, too.

  The mono and stereo versions of the LP are mixed quite differently. For example, the vocals on 'Jugband Blues' are mixed out halfway through the song, while the guitar features more prominently.
  The Canadian LP featured another slightly different version of 'Jugband Blues', the same as that on the Canadian 45; the difference in this case being a fade at the end of the middle section, prior to Syd's acoustic coda.

- **Midsummer High, Cockpit, Hyde Park, Kensington, London, UK.**

  Hyde Park's first free concert, later to become something of an institution, saw Tyrannosaurus Rex, Jethro Tull and sometime-associate Roy Harper

120

also appearing. The gig was announced in *Melody Maker*'s news section on 15 June, seemingly for the first time, suggesting that it was put together somewhat hurriedly.

The park people built the stage, which was tiny and about six inches off the ground, though it didn't matter as the Cockpit was a natural amphitheatre.

Melody Maker on 6 July reported that 'over 7,000 people turned out to hear Pink Floyd', while John Peel poured praise on the gig during his 11 August *Top Gear* show. Nick Mason, reflecting on the concert in 1974, considered it to mark the band's relaunch after Syd's departure. David Gilmour expressed a similar sentiment in an interview in *Melody Maker* published on 19 May 1973.

Advertisement in *IT* 33, 14 June 1968

Personal recollections of the event indicate that by this point 'Arnold Layne' and 'See Emily Play' had been dropped from the band's live set, and that the concert comprised two parts featuring material from *Piper At The Gates Of Dawn* in the first, performed in the late afternoon, and tracks from *A Saucerful of Secrets* in the second, played as the sun went down.

- **Town Hall, Torquay, Devon, UK.**

SUNDAY 30

- **BBC Studios, London, UK.**

For what reason we don't know.

JULY

THURSDAY 4

- **The band begin their second US Tour.**

The tour was announced in *Melody Maker* on 29 June – 'The Pink Floyd leave for America on July 4 and tour there until August 9 doing concerts in major cities including … [long list, no dates] … They will also do extensive TV and radio work.'

The tour was later extended for another 15 or so days. No radio or TV work is in general circulation and it would be very interesting to know whether any actually exists – the gig schedule doesn't appear to be particularly hectic.

MONDAY 8

• **Kinetic Playground, Chicago, Illinois, USA.**

FRIDAY 12

• **Grande Ballroom, Detroit, Michigan, USA.**

The gig was advertised by a particularly nice 'sword and sorcery' poster.[151]

MONDAY 15 – WEDNESDAY 17

• **Scene Club, New York City, New York, USA.**

FRIDAY 19

• *Tonite Let's All Make Love In London* premiere, New York City, New York, USA.

SATURDAY 20

• **Syd Barrett recording sessions, EMI, Studio 3, Abbey Road, London, UK.**

Syd was to produce this session without the help of Peter Jenner.

This was the initial session for Barrett's 'Clowns and Jugglers' (later re-titled 'Octopus'). Take 1 would appear as a bonus track on the remastered release of *Opel*. Take 2 would also appear on the original issue of *Opel*, complete with overdubs added on 3 May 1969. A further version of take 1 has appeared on bootleg, but features overdubs, made on 3 May 1969 (different to those on take 2) not on the official release.

The Soft Machine overdubs are similar to the usual, but they are, perhaps, a little bit more aggressive and less developed. The four and a half minute recording is probably two overdub takes put together as the Softs appear with the sweep of a pause button. The lyrics go as far as the end of the second verse at which point the track cuts, recommencing four lines from the verse's end with '… the door will always squeak'.

TUESDAY 23

* **Auditorium, Chicago, Illinois, USA.**

Dave's guitar was stolen immediately prior to this gig.

WEDNESDAY 24

* **Summer Music Festival, JFK Stadium, Philadelphia, Pennsylvania, USA.**

FRIDAY 26

* **Shrine Hall, Exposition, Los Angeles, California, USA.**

SATURDAY 27

* *A Saucerful Of Secrets* **is released in the USA.**

* **Shrine Hall, Exposition, Los Angeles, California, USA.**

A small, square postcard was produced to advertise the gig (illustrated in *The Art Of Rock* [152]). The Floyd were supported by Jeff Beck, ironically we think, after their considering him as a replacement for Syd at the beginning of the year. They were second billed to Blue Cheer.

FRIDAY 2 – SUNDAY 4

• **Avalon Ballroom, San Francisco, California, USA.**

The poster, postcard and tickets set for the three gigs at the Avalon ballroom featured virtually indecipherable writing below a black and white psychedelic design, featuring a hand clutching a ball surrounded by speeding globes.

FRIDAY 9

• **Eagles Auditorium, Seattle, Washington, USA.**

SATURDAY 10

• **'Floyd Return To US' entry under 'News' in *Melody Maker*.**

The report was somewhat inaccurate, describing how,

> The Pink Floyd, who complete a six week American tour on 18 August, return to the USA at the end of September. They will play the university circuit and may be accompanied by Tyrannosaurus Rex.
> The Floyd arrive back in Britain and will play concerts in England as well as appearing on TV shows in Britain, Holland, Austria and Sweden.

This latter suggestion cannot at present be substantiated. They did play in Britain and Holland but we have no other mention to hand of their playing TV shows in Austria and Sweden, although it is known that they did do concerts there. As for their being on TV shows in all of the above countries, we can only say with some certainty that they didn't appear on any British programmes.

• **Eagles Auditorium, Seattle, Washington, USA.**

SUNDAY 11

• ***Top Gear*, presented by John Peel, BBC Radio 1, London, UK.**

Of the band's 1960s BBC appearances, this broadcast is the best documented.
The show was recorded on 25 June 1968 and was broadcast on this day between 3.00 and 5.00 pm. The tracks were spread throughout the show, approximately half an hour apart from one another in the following order: 'Murderotic Woman', 'The Massed Gadgets Of Hercules', 'Let There Be More Light' and 'Julia Dream'. The complete timing reflects a few non-Floydian comments by John Peel on our copy, which we have edited for the purposes of our transcription:

21.09, The Murderotic Woman Or Careful With That Axe, Eugene, 3.11, Let There Be More Light, 4.18, Julia Dream, 2.34, The Massed Gadgets Of Hercules, 6.59

JP: The Pink Floyd are in America at the moment, well they're going to be back on August the 18th. Before they went they recorded a rather amazing session for us and er … this is in memory for everybody who was, er, at that thing that they did in the Park a few weeks ago, which is still spinning round in my head somewhere. Their first number is an instrumental called … called 'The Murderotic Woman Or Careful With That Axe, Eugene'. Please yourselves …

The Murderotic Woman Or Careful With That Axe, Eugene

JP: 'The Murderotic Woman Or Careful With That Axe Eugene' by The Pink Floyd, which isn't on their LP *Saucerful of Secrets*, but of course you already knew that 'cos you have the LP already don't you … >< …um … Next number from The Pink Floyd is for everybody who's unhappy this afternoon, because it's such a nice afternoon, least it is down here, that I wish I was out in the park listening to this actually, rather than sitting here whirring away and making mistakes. But um … this is for everyone who's unhappy anyway. It's the next number from The Pink Floyd and it's called 'The Massed Gadgets Of Hercules'.

The Massed Gadgets Of Hercules

JP: Now that is the sort of music that we ought to have coming out of churches and things … it's incredible. Pink Floyd and 'The Massed Gadgets Of Hercules'. >< Next number from The Pink Floyd is also a track on the *Saucerful Of Secrets* LP. It's called 'Let There Be More Light'.

Let There Be More Light

JP: Keep that up and there will be. The Pink Floyd and that was called 'Let There Be More Light' … and I was going to go down to London Airport and scream on the 18th when they come back but I can't 'cos it's next Sunday. I shall be out there screaming mentally though … >< This next thing I'd like to dedicate for a number of people – the mouse in my flat for one, who's been hiding for quite some time, but last night came out and was sporting himself on the beams – possibly herself – and had a good wash. Very unashamed mouse, just standing there on the beams washing while I was watching some ludicrous thing on television, and it's also for Flossie, who's a very small dog who wasn't allowed into Broadcasting House because um … I don't know why, actually, but I'm sure there must be some very sound reason in the regulations for it. And yesterday afternoon I went rowing in Regent's Park, which is something that's quite amazing 'cos you can go and row into little places where nobody can see you and things if you want to do stuff like that … and I did at the time. And er … so it's er … it's nice to go rowing in Regent's Park and when I came off the lake, whatever it is – I don't know what it's called. These people came up and said 'Hello,' called Deborah and Stephanie, so it's for them ... for them as well. It's the last number from The Pink Floyd and it's called 'Julia Dream'.

Julia Dream

JP: It's really so nice that The Pink Floyd have got things together again. That was called 'Julia Dream', and all the things that you heard this afternoon will be repeated on *Top Gear* in a few weeks' time, and they should be well worth hearing twice – and thousands of times more.

'The Murderotic Woman Or Careful With That Axe, Eugene' is an early 'scream-free' version of 'Careful ...'. 'The Massed Gadgets Of Hercules' is a version of 'A Saucerful Of Secrets'. Both were debut appearances. Quite how the title '*Murderistic* Woman' came about is unknown. Ken Garner indicates that 'The Muderotic Woman ...' is the title given on the session sheet at the time, and indeed it is that used by John Peel in this broadcast – perhaps later broadcasters felt it was too much of a mouthful!

Roger Waters was briefly interviewed by Brian Matthews but it was not broadcast at the time. Since Brian Matthews never presented *Top Gear* it is likely that the recording was actually made for broadcast on the BBC's *Top Of The Pops* programme for Transcription Services. This was a programme which the BBC would record for sale to foreign broadcasting organisations around the world. The interview was rebroadcast as part of BBC Radio 1's *Story Of Pop* in 1994.[153]

1.02, Interview with Waters

Legendary BBC Radio DJ Alan Freeman, played 'Julia Dream' with its original lengthy John Peel intro (as above) in a BBC radio programme called *The Sixties At The Beeb* in 1996.[154]

3.30, Julia Dream, with original John Peel intro

- **Eagles Auditorium, Seattle, Washington, USA.**

FRIDAY 16 – SATURDAY 17

- **Sound Factory, Sacramento, California, USA.**

The poster for the above two gigs at the Sound Factory is illustrated in *The Art Of Rock*.[155]

FRIDAY 23 – SATURDAY 24

• **The Bank, Torrance, California, USA.**

An advertisement for the above two gigs is also to be found in *The Art Of Rock*[156] and was gifted to subscribers of *Brain Damage* issue 28.

• **Sky River Rock Festival, and Lighter Than Air Fair, Sultan, Washington, USA.**

SEPTEMBER

SUNDAY 1

• ***Top Gear*, BBC repeat of the session first broadcast on 8 August, again presented by John Peel.**

17.03, Julia Dream, 2.32, The Murderotic Woman Or Careful With That Axe, Eugene, 3.01, Let There Be More Light, 4.12, Massed Gadgets Of Hercules, 6.44

It is interesting to note how different the timings are to those that we have entered under 11 August.

Julia Dream

JP: Written by Roger Waters, the Pink Floyd and that was called 'Julia Dream'. >< ... this isn't recorded either you see, but I hope it will be shortly. It's called 'The Murderotic Woman Or Careful With That Axe, Eugene' – one of those enigmatic titles.

The Murderotic Woman Or Careful With That Axe, Eugene

JP: That's your actual Pink Floyd there, you see, 'The Murderotic Woman Or Careful With That Axe, Eugene'. >< My favourite track on the Pink Floyd LP is 'Saucerful Of Secrets' and after that ... >< Pink Floyd – 'Let There Be More Light'.

Let There Be More Light

JP: I think we ought to play that one again too ... the Pink Floyd, and that was called 'Let There Be More Light'. >< It's time for the last number from the Pink Floyd. This is really amazing so I hope you'll stop and listen to this one as well. The Pink Floyd with the last number of this afternoon called 'Massed Gadgets Of Hercules'.

Massed Gadgets Of Hercules

JP: And that's one of those ... >< ...being hymns to Sunday afternoon. Pink Floyd and 'Massed Gadgets Of Hercules'.

- Oakland Pop Festival, Oakland University, Rochester, Michigan, USA.

WEDNESDAY 4

- Middle Earth Club at Richmond Athletic Club, Richmond, London, UK.

The correct venue is confirmed by an ad in *Melody Maker*.[157]

THURSDAY 5 – SUNDAY 8

- European Tour began in early September, with dates in Holland, Austria, Sweden, Belgium and France.

- Le Bilbouquet, St-Germain-des-Pres, France.

- Psychedelic De La Rue, Ponthieu, France.

- Nancy, France.

- Bordeaux, France.

- Lille, France.

SUNDAY 8

- Le Chatelet, Belgium.

Part of the festival was filmed, but due to problems at customs the band missed the show! Also on the bill were The Kinks, Gilbert Becaud, Nicollette and others. The crowd are reported to have become violent and attacked some of the performers (perhaps it was a good job the band never made it!).

FRIDAY 13

- Mothers, Erdington, Birmingham, West Midlands, UK.

TUESDAY 17

- The band attend the preview of a BBC documentary about them.

Nothing was to come of the film, and the BBC have been unable to provide any further details.

Friday 20

- **Bristol, Avon, UK.**

Saturday 21

- **An interview with David Gilmour and Roger Waters appears in *Record Mirror* newspaper, UK.**[158]

- **Recording for *Samedi Et Compagnie*, ORTF 2 TV, Paris, France.**

  The show was broadcast on 12 October.

Thursday 26

- ***The Committee* opens at the Cameo Poly, Oxford Circus, London, UK.**

  Reviews on the poster suggest that the film should be shown 'everywhere' (it well and truly wasn't!) and that it is a 'chilling fable ... oblique, open ended ... savage narrative' according to Kevin Tynan. The faces of the three lead actors are pictured within the outline of a bird (for a change in Floydian imagery!).

Friday 27

- **Queens Hall, Dunoon, Argyllshire, Scotland, UK.**

October

- **Promo for 'Point Me At the Sky' filmed.**

  The well-known promo showing the band dressed in WW1 airsuits, flying in a biplane.

  Point Me At The Sky, 3.03, video

Tuesday 1

- **The Maryland, Glasgow, Scotland, UK.**

Thursday 3

- ***The Tyrant King*, ITV broadcast, UK.**

  The Tyrant King, a kids' TV show, broadcast nationally, included much contemporary music including tracks by Cream, The Moody Blues and the Nice, although it is unlikely that any new music was recorded for the shows, which have never been rebroadcast.[159]

FRIDAY 4

• **Mothers, Erdington, West Midlands, UK.**

SUNDAY 6

• **Country Club, Hampstead, London, UK.**

TUESDAY 8

• **EMI, Abbey Road Studios, London, UK.**

WEDNESDAY 9

• **EMI, Abbey Road Studios, London, UK.**

THURSDAY 10 – FRIDAY 11

• **Short tour of Holland begins.**

SATURDAY 12

• *Samedi Et Compagnie*, **ORTF 2 TV, Paris, France.**

Copies of this broadcast may be easily distinguished by the fact that the audience clap along out of time.

 3.09, Let There Be More Light, video

Samedie Et Compagnie was a teenage show presented by Albert Raisner and broadcast every Saturday afternoon. It is known that the Floyd did two songs – 'Let There Be More Light' exists on tape, while they also performed 'Flaming', which has yet to make it into general circulation. The show may have been repeated on 21 September. ORTF television's *Point Chaud* repeated the band's appearance on the show in August 1974.

• *A L'affiche Du Monde,* **French TV broadcast.**

This show, a documentary about recent festivals in France, featured footage of the Floyd from their tour earlier in the month.

SATURDAY 12 – SUNDAY 13

* **Tour of Holland continues.**

MONDAY 14 – WEDNESDAY 16

* **EMI, Abbey Road Studios, London, UK.**

WEDNESDAY 16

* **Théâtre Du Huitiéme, Lyon, France.**

  The Floyd appeared with the London Arts Lab collective, contemporaries from their time at the UFO.

SATURDAY 19

* **Salford University, Salford, Lancashire, UK (cancelled).**

  This date was cancelled in favour of further dates in Belgium …

* **Theatre 140, Brussels, Belgium.**

SUNDAY 20

* **Theatre 140, Brussels, Belgium.**

MONDAY 21 – TUESDAY 22

* **West German TV recordings.**

  The press at the time reported that on these dates the band planned to visit Germany to record two TV specials. It is unknown what came of them, or whether the band actually made the trip at all.

  An excerpt of 'Set The Controls For The Heart Of The Sun' from the *All My Loving* broadcast on 3 November is often argued to be from this date.

FRIDAY 25

* **The Boat House, Kew, Berkshire, UK.**

SATURDAY 26

* **Interview with Roger Waters published in *Melody Maker* for the conclusion of a three-part series entitled 'Pop Today And Tomorrow'.**

The article goes some way towards suggesting that Roger had commenced work on 'The Man And The Journey' suite.

> The Floyd are currently working on an entirely new sound system. Says the group's Roger Waters: 'We are working on a 360 degrees stereo system. We want to throw away the old format of the pop show – standing on a square stage at one end of a rectangular room and running through a series of numbers. Our idea is to put the sound all round the audience with ourselves in the middle. Then the performance becomes much more theatrical.
>
> 'And it needs special material – it can include melodrama, literary things, musical things or lights.'
>
> The Floyd plan to unveil their new sound system before the end of this month. Roger describes it as 'like stereo, but 40 times more effective.'
>
> 'The basic format is laid down on four-track tape,' he said. 'The things we do live – songs, movement, etc – are cued by the tape so things run for a set time. Basically, you make a four-way stereo record and play with it.'
>
> '… We are probably not part of the pop scene,' says Roger. 'Though we impinge on the pop market to a certain extent. We are releasing a single, for example. But we don't function in from the usual pop stimuli.
>
> 'We aren't really prepared to compromise over what we are doing – but then I don't think we could even if we wanted to.'

- **Imperial College, Kensington, London, UK.**

- **Middle Earth Club at the Roundhouse, Chalk Farm, London, UK.**

The correct venue for this gig is confirmed by an ad in *Melody Maker*.[160] The band were supported by Gary Farr and July.

WEDNESDAY 30

- **Club Tournee, Paris, France.**

Record Collector no. 187 suggests that the band played this night and that the *Tous En Forme* broadcast was possibly filmed at the Club. Recent evidence would appear to render this suggestion incorrect, however.

THURSDAY 31

- **Recording for *Tous En Forme*, ORTF 2 TV, Paris, France.**

The show was broadcast on 26 November.

- **'A Saucerful Of Quiet Success For The Floyd', an interview with Rick, appears in *Beat Instrumental* magazine, UK.**

  Pop nowadays covers such a wide field that we really need a new name for its various parts. It seems quite probable that in 10, 20 or 100 years' time, groups like the Floyd will be considered classical. Boundaries are being extended almost daily by the Floyd. Long may they continue.[161]

- **EMI, Abbey Road Studios, London, UK.**

  Malcolm Jones asserts that 'work had already begun on what was to become *Ummagumma* (in November) with "Embryo" ...'[162] The track, as most will know, was eventually dropped from the album when it became clear that it was to be split into the four solo parts. It would of course see a later, limited release on Harvest's *Picnic* compilation in 1970, as well as on the US *Works* compilation in the eighties.

  Three 'outtakes' are currently circulating, though careful listening proves the tape to consist of two badly recorded versions (one complete, one edited) of the version on *Picnic* as well as the performance from *Top Gear* in December.

  It could conceivably be the case that 'Embryo' was the germ of an idea which was to become the 'life-cycle' mentioned later in November 1969.

SATURDAY 2

- **Farnborough Technical College, Farnborough, Hampshire, UK.**

SUNDAY 3

- ***Omnibus: All My Loving*, BBC 1 TV broadcast, UK.**

  Notable for its ghastly black and orange colour scheme, this promo appears to have been filmed in a church, and is easily available on private video. *Radio Times* confirms that the show was repeated on 17 April 1973, although it is also known that there have been recent rebroadcasts on the BBC's *Sounds Of The Sixties* in 1991[163] and on a German TV special in 1993.[164]

  UK rebroadcast, Set The Controls For The Heart Of The Sun, 3.21, video

  German rebroadcast, Set The Controls For The Heart Of The Sun, 2.55, video

November 1968

MONDAY 4

- **'Careful With That Axe, Eugene' produced by Norman Smith at Abbey Road Studios.**

  As advised by the *Relics* sleeve-notes; we have no independent confirmation of this date however.

THURSDAY 7

- **Porchester Hall, Bayswater, London, UK.**

FRIDAY 8

- **Fishmonger's Arms, Wood Green, London, UK.**

  The band were supported by Closed Cell Sponge and Stranger Than Yesterday.

SATURDAY 16

- **Restaurant Olten-Hammer, Olten, Switzerland.**

- **Coca-Cola Halle, Abtwil, Switzerland.**

SUNDAY 17

- **2nd Swiss Rhythm and Blues Festival, Zurich, Switzerland.**

FRIDAY 22

- **Crawdaddy, Richmond Athletic Ground, London, UK.**

  Arcadium provided the support.[165]

```
┌─────────────────────────────────────────┐
│            CRAWDADDY                      │
│       RICHMOND ATHLETIC GROUND            │
│              presents                     │
│          PINK FLOYD                       │
│            ARCADIUM                       │
│   Friday, November 22nd, 8 p.m.-Midnight  │
│    10/- Members   Late Licence   12/6 Guests │
│   Fri., Nov. 29th: LED ZEPPELIN           │
│              (formerly YARDBIRDS)         │
└─────────────────────────────────────────┘
```

Advertisement in *Melody Maker*, 23 November 1968

SATURDAY 23

• **Regent Street Polytechnic, Little Titchfield Street, London, UK.**

THE PINK FLOYD
plus
Direct from America
THE GREAT
BOBBY PARKER
THE POLYTECHNIC
Little Titchfield Street, W.1
SATURDAY, 23rd NOVEMBER
7.30 to 11.30

Licensed Bar : Oxford Circus Tube : Admission 10/-

Advertisement in *Melody Maker,* 23 November 1968

SUNDAY 24

• **Country Club, Hampstead, London, UK.**

An ad for the gig appeared in *IT* 44:

COUNTRY CLUB
210a Haverstock Hill
opp Belsize Park Odeon

SUN 17TH NOV
JOHN HISEMAN'S COLOSSEUM
TURQUOISE (DAVID BOWIE ETC)
WED 20TH-NOV
BLONDE ON BLONDE
LINDA & ANDY
SUN 24TH NOV
PINK FLOYD
Tickets in advance from club
or from Simon Stable
WED 27TH NOV
Deviants
Special concessions for students
8.15 ONWARDS

November 1968

TUESDAY 26

- *Tous En Forme*, ORTF 2 TV show, Paris, France.

  Recorded on 31 October, the band performed live versions of 'Let There Be More Light' and 'Flaming' under bright lights in front of a packed and attentive audience. They may well have also performed the single, 'Point Me At The Sky'.

  6.48, Let There Be More Light, 3.42, Flaming, 3.06, video

WEDNESDAY 27

- University of Keele, Newcastle-under-Lyme, Staffordshire, UK.

FRIDAY 29

- Bedford College, Hanover Lodge, Outer Circle, Regent's Park, London, UK.

  An ad in *Melody Maker* suggests that the band were supported by Blonde On Blonde.[166]

SATURDAY 30

- Psychedelic Club, Paris, France.

  The band were recorded performing 'Flaming' and 'Let There Be More Light', for broadcast on the show *Surprise Partie*, on 31 December.

DECEMBER

MONDAY 2

- *Top Gear* recorded at BBC Maida Vale 4, London, UK.

THURSDAY 5

- Bournemouth College Christmas Dance, Royal Arcade Ballrooms, Bournemouth, Hampshire, UK.

SUNDAY 15

- *Top Gear*, presented by John Peel, BBC Radio 1, London, UK.

20.58, Point Me To The Sky, 4.11, Baby Blue Shuffle in D Major, 4.02, Embryo, 3.22, Interstellar Overdrive, 8.35

The show, which was produced by Bernie Andrews, had been recorded on 2 December. *Top Gear* was transmitted between 3.00 and 5.00 pm.

> JP: And this is their current single, and also the first number they did for us this afternoon. It's 'Point Me To The Sky'.

Point Me To The Sky

> JP: You can replace your heads at the count of three. One, two, those were the Pink Floyd >< … bit of a departure for them – it's an acoustic guitar duet called 'Baby Blue Shuffle In D Major'.

Baby Blue Shuffle In D Major

> JP: It is indeed the very excellent Pink Floyd and that was 'Baby Blue Shuffle In D Major'. >< …called, 'The Embryo'.

The Embryo

> JP: 'The Embryo', Pink Floyd there and … er … the Pink Floyd are currently wafting towards Newcastle as I said, and if they're listening I want them to come and visit me at fabled, rambling, gabled Peel Acres sometime during the next week so I can lecture them fairly severely on the advisability of releasing a quadruple LP almost instantly. Anyway … >< 'Interstellar Overdrive'.

Interstellar Overdrive

> JP: I think I'll ask Alan Freeman if he'll run that tape again on *Pick of the Pops*. The Pink Floyd and that was of course 'Interstellar Overdrive' and it was very nice to hear that again.

The transcribed comments about 'The Embryo' assure us that the recording is taken from the original broadcast.

'Point Me At The Sky' has a slight lyric change, and goes by a slightly different title. 'Baby Blue Shuffle In D Major' is an early version of 'The Narrow Way, Part 1'; 'The Embryo' is an early, short version.

• **Newcastle City Hall, Newcastle-upon-Tyne, Tyne & Wear, UK.**

TUESDAY 17

• **'Point Me At The Sky' / 'Careful With That Axe, Eugene' single released in the UK.**

'Careful With That Axe, Eugene': your average Christmas single. It was never to be released in the USA.

December 1968

FRIDAY 20

- *Radio 1 Club*, **live broadcast from the Paris Cinema, Lower Regent Street, London, UK.**

The show was produced by Bev Phillips and was engineered by Pete Ritzema. The live broadcast was between midday and 2.00 pm, and it would seem that nobody taped it at the time. The band played 'Let There Be More Light', 'Set The Controls', 'Point Me At The Sky' and 'Careful with That Axe, Eugene' in that order.[167]

FRIDAY 27

- **Grote Zaal, De Doelen, Rotterdam, Holland.**

SATURDAY 28

- **Margriethal-Jaarbeurs, Utrecht, Holland.**

45.38, Astronomy Domine, 5.44, Careful With That Axe, Eugene, 6.52, Interstellar Overdrive, 11.27, Set The Controls For The Heart Of The Sun, 7.46, A Saucerful Of Secrets, 11.14

'Careful With That Axe, Eugene' cuts and recontinues very near its end, otherwise the tracks are complete. The tape loops briefly part of the way through 'Set The Controls' and suffers again during the closing parts of the 'Celestial Voices' sequence of 'A Saucerful Of Secrets', where it evidently speeds up (possibly so that a person copying it could fit the concert on to one side of a cassette).

Astronomy Domine

… have a look on the B side of our latest single […] called 'Careful With That Axe, Eugene'.

Careful With That Axe, Eugene

This next song's 'Interstellar Overdrive'.

Interstellar Overdrive

One. This is a song on the last LP we released. It's called 'Set The Controls For The Heart Of The Sun'.

Set The Controls For The Heart Of The Sun

This is our final […] title track off the last LP […] It's called 'A Saucerful Of Secrets'. Thank you very much for listening.

A Saucerful Of Secrets

Once again we are indebted to our Dutch friends for having the very good sense to send someone along to record the concert. Readers may like to ponder the fact that it was Dutch fans who were largely responsible for the early recordings which are in circulation – it would not be unreasonable to assume that fans in other countries made recordings which have yet to make it onto the collectors' scene.

The person recording seems to have been situated at the back of the auditorium, and consequently some of the quieter sections are drowned out, while the louder sections take the microphone by surprise. The Floyd, quality concerns aside, exhibit a very heavy and aggressive sound, at times analogous to the unsubtle nature of 'The Nile Song' which was to be recorded a few months later. The tracklist continues to merit a 'Syd' influence, though his subtleties by this stage have been almost entirely sacrificed for a leaden and caustically psychedelicised sound.

All five tracks are power pieces and provide no suggestion of the complexities of the 'Massed Gadgets of Auximenes' which was to debut the following April. Band interviews are very thin on the ground from this, one of several 'lost' periods, and perhaps by their absence, we may find cause to underline the lack of direction that the songs seem to engender. The *Saucerful* LP tends, when it is at its worst, to have the same effect. The 'Celestial Voices' sequence is delivered with passion and metaphorically points, perhaps, to the artistic release and resurgence that was to follow.

TUESDAY 31

- *Surprise Partie*, **ORTF 2 TV, Psychedelic Club, Paris, France.**

The programme, recorded at the club the previous month, featured The Rolling Stones, The Who and Joe Cocker. To the best of our knowledge, copies have not survived – so far all appear to be from the *Samedi Et Compagnie* show from 12 October.

1969
More Furious Madness

- **Belgian TV appearance.**

The BBC's 1994 *Omnibus* documentary[168] went part-way towards confirm-ation of the source of a performance of 'Set The Controls' which had at the time been in circulation on video for several years. The clip may be easily distinguished from others of the period by virtue of the TV station's intro-ducing the band with an oil on slide caption proclaiming the 'Pink Floid' [*sic*]. Waters at one point is seen alone filmed from a low camera angle and lit by a single beam of light from above.

The BBC then caption the piece as being from 'Belgian TV 1969'. Had the piece not been captioned as such, there would not have been any confu-sion amongst collectors as to its true source: the 18/19 February 1968 record-ings. Our 1968 entry details the full length recording.

0.40, Set The Controls, video

- **Promotional film for unknown instrumental recorded.**

Nick Mason's video compilation premiered at the Knebworth Festival in 1990 features a weird and wonderful instrumental, played to psychedelic images of the band performing in the studio. It is possible that the track is a highly improvised version of 'Sysyphus' as the song title is clearly visible in a montage of newspaper cuttings seen in the clip.

0.56, Sysyphus instrumental, video

WEDNESDAY 1

- *Variety* magazine, UK, publishes a feature on *The Committee.*

FRIDAY 10

- **Fishmonger's Arms, Wood Green, London, UK.**

SUNDAY 12

- **Mother's Club, Birmingham, West Midlands, UK.**

FRIDAY 17

- **Royal Albert Hall, Kensington, London, UK.**

  This previously unrecorded concert appearance comes courtesy of the Royal Albert Hall's own records. Unfortunately, no programme has been kept, if indeed there was one, leaving the band's set list at this time an intriguing enigma.

SATURDAY 18

- **London College of Printing, Elephant And Castle, Southwark, London, UK.**

- **Homerton College, Cambridge University, Cambridge, Cambridgeshire, UK.**

- **Turn on The Tap Zap, Middle Earth at the Roundhouse, Chalk Farm, London, UK.**

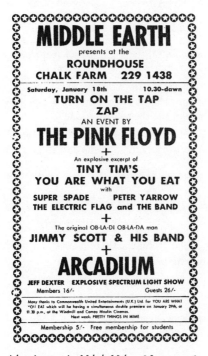

Advertisement in *Melody Maker*, 18 January 1969

January 1969

WEDNESDAY 22

- *Tous En Forme*, ORTF 2 TV broadcast, France.

The band performed 'Careful With That Axe, Eugene'.

- Filming at ORTF 1 TV Studios, Paris, France, for *Samedi Et Compagnie*, broadcast on 15 February.

SATURDAY 25

- 69 Club, Ryde, Isle of Wight, UK.

FEBRUARY

FRIDAY 7

- Hull University, Hull, Yorkshire, UK.

FRIDAY 14

- Warwick University, Coventry, Leicestershire, UK.

SATURDAY 15

- *Samedi Et Compagnie*, ORTF 1 TV broadcast, Paris, France.

This, one of a number of versions of 'Set The Controls' that are available, may be easily distinguished by its French introduction which helpfully introduces it as being from 'le 15 fevrier 1969'.

ORTF-TV's *Point Chaud* showed the footage again in August 1974, and this would appear to be the source of most of the recordings which survive.

Set The Controls For The Heart Of The Sun, with introduction 2.55, video

SUNDAY 16

- 'How The Pink Floyd Defeated Psychedelia' – interview with Nick in *Melody Maker* newspaper, UK.

Nick spoke of the group's early plans for what was to become *Ummagumma*:

Ideally a double album would be the answer, but, says Nick, they are still not sure whether the record company would agree to laying out all that bread. 'There's still hope that we can do one though, which would be really great

142

because we could do our quarters on one album and on the other have one side of straight songs and one side of a major work involving all of us.'

Monday 17

• **Royal Lyceum Theatre, Edinburgh, Lothian, Scotland, UK.**

Premiere of *Pawn to King 5*, a ballet by John Cheesworth of the Ballet Rambert, that featured the music of Pink Floyd.
    It would seem reasonable that the band were not present at the performances – their schedule over the next few days would appear impossible if this were the case.

Tuesday 18

• **Royal Lyceum Theatre, Edinburgh, Lothian, Scotland, UK.**

Performance of *Pawn To King Five*.

• **Manchester University, Manchester, Lancashire, UK.**

Support was provided by Marmalade, Ten Years After, Fairport Convention and Simon Dupree & The Big Sound.[169]

Friday 21

• **Royal Lyceum Theatre, Edinburgh, Lothian, Scotland, UK.**

Performance of *Pawn To King Five*.

• **Alhambra, Bordeaux, France.**

The concert is mentioned in the news section of *Melody Maker* on 15 February. The article also comments that jazz musician Roland Kirk was also scheduled to play.

Saturday 22

• **A reader's question about Barrett and the Floyd appears on the letters page of *Melody Maker*.**

   What has become of Syd Barrett and is there a fan club for the Pink Floyd?
      Syd is working on an LP of his own composition. Pink Floyd fan club is run by Carol Oliver, 1 Randall Drive, Hornchurch, Essex …

Before you think – it's not worth trying!

February 1969

MONDAY 24

- The Dome, Brighton, Sussex, UK.

TUESDAY 25

- Marlowe Theatre, Canterbury, Kent, UK.

Advertisement in *Melody Maker*, 22 February 1969

WEDNESDAY 26

- New Cavendish Ballroom, Edinburgh, Lothian, Scotland, UK.

THURSDAY 27

- Glasgow Arts Lab Benefit, The Maryland, Glasgow, Strathclyde, Scotland, UK.

FRIDAY 28

- Queen Elizabeth College, Camden Hill, London, UK.

MARCH

- Syd Barrett telephones EMI's studio booking office to enquire about starting recording again.

Malcolm Jones, head of Harvest Records and Syd's producer during the following sessions, recalls that 'it all sounded too good for words!'
It was decided that EMI should give Syd a chance to see how he did – 'if it worked, then, OK we'd do an album. If not, we'd call it a day'. Although Jones wanted Norman Smith to work with Syd as producer, it was Syd who made the final decision. 'You do it'.

SATURDAY 1

• **Saturday Night Dance, University College London, Bloomsbury, London, UK.**

The UCL college newspaper, *Pi*, confirms that the Floyd played with support from Playground.[170]

Advertisement in *Melody Maker*, 22 February 1969

MONDAY 3

• **Victoria Rooms, Clifton, Bristol, Avon, UK.**

SATURDAY 8

• **Reading University, Reading, Berkshire, UK.**

Support was provided by the Pretty Things and Gods.[171]

TUESDAY 11

• **Lawns Centre, Cottingham, Yorkshire, UK.**

FRIDAY 14

• **Van Dike Close, Devenport, Plymouth, UK.**

SATURDAY 15

• **Kee Club, Bridgend, Glamorgan, Wales, UK.**

The Kee Club was said at the time, to be the only 'underground club in Wales'.

WEDNESDAY 19

• **University College, Swansea, Glamorgan, Wales, UK.**

FRIDAY 21

- **The Art Ball, Winter Gardens, Blackpool, UK.**

  An amusing interview with the group by a student was recorded on this date.
  Interview, 24.30

THURSDAY 27

- **St James' Hall, Chesterfield, Derbyshire, UK.**

LATE

- **Pye Studios, London, UK.**

  Recording sessions for *More.*
  The band recorded the album over eight days of sessions in late March. As it was a commissioned piece and not a regular Floyd album the band's royalties were higher, but out of these they had to cover their own recording costs, along with the film company. Povey and Russell suggest that the recordings were made in late January and early February. Both accounts are plausible.[172]

APRIL

WEDNESDAY 9

- ***Radio 1 Club*, Paris Theatre, Lower Regent Street, London, UK.**

  The group didn't show up. The show was to have taken place between midday and 2.00 pm. No presenter is listed in Ken Garner's book. UK readers may be interested to realise that the *Radio 1 Club* was a forerunner of the seminal *Radio 1 Roadshows*!

THURSDAY 10

- **Syd Barrett recording sessions, EMI, Studio 3, Abbey Road, London, UK.**

  In the studio again for the first time since July 1968. The booking was from 7.00 pm to 12.30 am, and Syd and Malcolm spent part of it re-appraising the tapes made with Peter Jenner the previous year. Syd also overdubbed guitar and vocal tracks onto the previously instrumental 'Silas Lang (Swan Lee)' and 'experimented with ideas for "Clowns And Jugglers"'. Neither was eventually used, though both agreed that they were an improvement on the previous sessions.

FRIDAY 11

• **Syd Barrett recording sessions, EMI, Studio 3, Abbey Road, London, UK.**

Work was done on 'Love You' in this session, and a grand total of five takes are now available to collectors. Take 1 and take 3 were both added as bonus tracks to the remastered version of *The Madcap Laughs*, while it was take 4, with overdubs recorded on May 5, which was released on the original album. Take 2 and take 5 appeared on bootleg a couple of years ago – the take numbers are calculated guesses made by the authors, based upon the development of the lyrics, which changed slightly as more takes were made – and Malcolm Jones also helps: 'The first was fast, in fact VERY fast (faster than the issued version). The second was very slow! Take 3 was a false start, and take 4 was the one we later overdubbed and issued. All three good takes were perfect, and in fact we weren't sure which take to use. The studio note says "best decided later".'

2.25, Love You take 2, 1.05, Love You take 5, 1.20

Also recorded was the track 'No Good Trying', take 3 of which was released, with overdubs made over May 3 and 4, on *The Madcap Laughs* LP. Take 5, with the slightly longer alternative title 'It's No Good Trying' was released later as an extra track on the CD remaster of the same album. The first take was apparently 'good', while the second was a false start.

'Opel' – take 9 of which appears on the compilation to which it lent its name – was also recorded at this session, take 9 being the first complete take. Recently a second version of this take has appeared on bootleg, and while timing in at less than 30 seconds, it does feature a spoken introduction over the studio talkback!

0.28, Opel with spoken introduction

Two complete takes were made in this session. Phil Smee alluded to the unissued take in the *Chapter 24* fanzine interview, recalling that 'it simply wasn't different enough to justify putting it out.'

Syd also recorded take 1 of 'Terrapin', with vocal double track, onto which overdubs – a guitar solo – were added on May 4. This is the take used on *The Madcap Laughs*.

Syd also overdubbed the vocal and slide guitar for the version of 'Late Night' which was to appear on *The Madcap Laughs*, and transferred the earlier recording of 'Golden Hair' (from May 68) from 4-track to an 8-track master. Two unissued (and unheard) versions were worked on as a result of this, one with a more prominent guitar, the other with an added harmony vocal double track.

• The Massed Gadgets of Auximenes ... More Furious Madness from Pink Floyd, Royal Festival Hall, South Bank, London, UK.

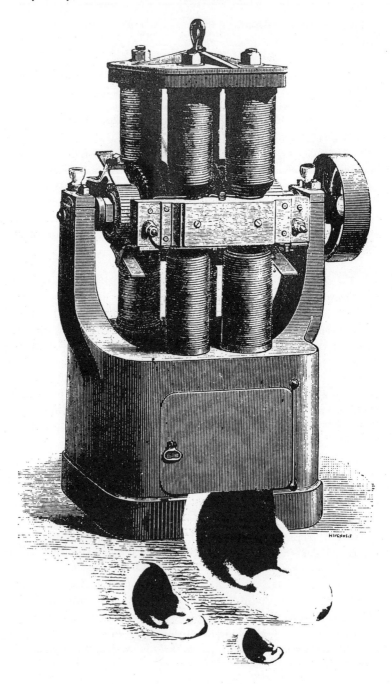

Debut of 'The Man and The Journey' suite. Essentially this, the band's first concept performance, utilised a number of songs which were already part of the band's live repertoire, as well as others which were to be released over 1969 on *More* and *Ummagumma*, along with some compositions which remain unreleased and unique to the piece.

Split into two parts describing an average day and a fantastic journey, the performance comprised *The Man* – 'Daybreak', 'Work', 'Afternoon', 'Doing It', 'Sleeping', 'Nightmare' and 'Daybreak' (reprise) while *The Journey* was made up of 'The Beginning', 'Beset By Creatures Of The Deep', 'The Narrow Way', 'The Pink Jungle', 'The Labyrinths Of Auximenes', 'Behold The Temple of Light' and 'The End of The Beginning'.

'Daybreak' was later released as 'Grantchester Meadows' and 'Afternoon' was retitled 'Biding My Time'.

Some commentators confuse 'Work' and 'Afternoon', suggesting that 'Biding My Time' is 'Work', and that 'Afternoon' was a break during which the band drank tea on stage. If this were necessarily to be the case there would be a forcible cut in the tracklisting below and that of 26 June. There isn't. The performance of the suite here (and later in Manchester and on the Concertgebouw audience tape) has a rhythmic track, complete with taped effects of trains thundering by – perhaps describing the commuter's morning journey – where one would expect to find 'Work'. 'Biding My Time', subjectively more of a laid-back piece, far better suits the title 'Afternoon', particularly considering that it is a song which lyrically recalls work – 'I'll never pine for the sad days and the bad days, when we was working from nine to five ...'

The start of 'Sleeping' is marked by heavy 'quadraphonic' breathing and sounds very much like 'Quicksilver' from the *More* soundtrack. Indeed, evidence from the Royal Festival Hall's own house copy of the programme for the concert features a hand-written note indicating that 'Quicksilver' was used as the piece's title for royalty purposes.

The same programme calls 'Green Is The Colour' 'Stephan's Tit', an amusing reference to the use of the track in the film 'More'. It would be fair to call 'Stephan's Tit' a 'working title'.

'Cymbaline' was performed with the title 'Nightmare', while 'Green Is The Colour' is known as 'The Beginning'. 'Beset By Creatures Of The Deep' is 'Careful With That Axe, Eugene' and 'The Pink Jungle' was their alternative title for 'Pow R. Toc H'. The piece climaxed with 'The End Of The Beginning' – the 'Celestial Voices' movement from 'A Saucerful Of Secrets'.

'Sleeping', 'Daybreak', 'The Labyrinths Of Auximenes' and 'Behold The Temple Of Light' are the only perceptibly unique pieces in the suite, though all of these too, could be comfortably described as either precursors for work that was to come or as reflections of past compositions.

A tape of this concert is available, and is commonly distinguished from the later, more easily obtainable, recording from the Royal Albert Hall in June by virtue of the fact that 'The End Of The Beginning' is featured without either brass or choir. The gigs also featured different encores.

We have a ticket for the concert which informs the bearer that it was due

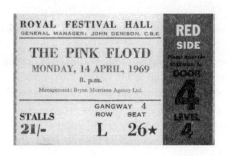

to start at 8 pm. Thanks to the venue's programme for the event, containing notes for the benefit of performing rights submissions, we are able to confirm that the concert started at 8.15 pm and that there was an interval between 8.58 pm and 9.19 pm. The concert finished at 10.13½ pm (!)

This known, 'The Man' must then have lasted 43 minutes and 'The Journey' and 'Interstellar Overdrive' 54 min. 30 sec. The total length of the concert, as timed by the venue, was 97 minutes. It would be too crude to say that our tape, timing in at 89 min. 55 sec. is simply 7 min. 35 sec. short – though you might wish that we had after the complexities that follow!

Side A of our tape lasts 47 min. 13 sec. and Side B, 42 min. 42 sec. 47 min. 13 sec. is the natural point at which a 90-minute tape is forced to cut. The timing of Side B suggests that the person recording had only one tape and wanted to catch the best bits!

The most obvious reasoning for our copy of 'The Man' being approximately five minutes short is that the band *did* play 'Nightmare' ('Cymbaline') and where our tape cuts we miss it in its entirety. Somewhat less likely, it could be the case that the sum of the cut in 'Sleeping' and anything that we might be missing from before 'Daybreak' – taped effects for example – might equally come to five minutes.

89.55, The Man, 37.49 [Daybreak, 6.20, Work, 7.51, Afternoon, 5.34, Doing It!, 5.29, Sleeping, 12.03, Daybreak (reprise), 2.16], The Journey, 30.42 [The Beginning, 4.03, Beset By Creatures Of The Deep, 8.10, The Narrow Way, 4.41, The Pink Jungle, 5.20, The Labyrinths Of Auximenes, 7.34, Behold The Temple Of Light, 6.34, The End Of The Beginning, 4.20], Interstellar Overdrive, 10.21

We adjudged 'Daybreak' to give way to 'Work' when the quadraphonic steam train starts. 'Work' continues through various meanderings and at several points does a good impression of being a variation of 'Up The Khyber' (which is borne out by a note in the house programme). 'Biding My Time' gives way to the noise of heavy breathing marking the commencement of 'Sleeping'. 6 min. 49 sec. in it cuts briefly and 'Daybreak' commences with the sounding of an alarm clock and bird song leaving one with the impression that the track is very much like 'Cirrus Minor'.

'The Beginning' is marked by the cry of seagulls and swirling wind, and then cuts 48 seconds in. A smallish section is lost and the tape cuts to the first line of the lyric. 'The Beginning' and 'Beset By Creatures Of The Deep' segue – we have chosen the point at which Waters' enigmatic bass riff starts to dissect the two pieces as their break point. Some readers might note that this moment is an entirely reliable point of distinction by 1970, but at this point, in the light of the extended 'Green Is The Colour' performed for John Peel in May, the same can't be said in all certainty. 'Beset By Creatures Of The Deep' cuts very nastily and continues with a slight return on side B.

'The Narrow Way' happily gives way to 'The Pink Jungle', 'The Labyrinths Of Auximenes' being marked by footsteps running about the metaphorical labyrinth. The footsteps end and we start upon the mind-expanding 'Behold The Temple Of Light'. This cuts, sadly, after 6 min. 34 sec. and we bump into 'The End Of The Beginning', which is thankfully intact.

'The Journey' was always the shorter of the two halves of the concert but our version here almost certainly accounts for the larger part of the 'lost' music.

'Interstellar Overdrive' is followed by rapturous applause. The version in its context is arguably bettered only by the version from Southampton a month later.

Roger Waters, speaking later in Chris Welch's *Melody Maker* article on 3 May commented that:

> I thought the MM review was a bit over-generous … it was a nerve racking experience for us and probably the audience. A friend of mine who comes to see our normal stage act was very disappointed and felt cheated. He thought it was like paying fifteen bob to see us rehearsing. He was right in a way because we were rehearsing. The people were watching a happening.

Whilst we would recommend this tape, should a copy be found, as *essential* to anyone with an interest in the early Pink Floyd, Roger's comments are fair, and borne out on the recording. Here we have a band evolving before our ears – fumbling somewhat, but defining a conceptual blueprint which would ultimately become their trademark.

The Observer provided a fairly substantial review of the concert on 1 June.

THURSDAY 17

• **Syd Barrett recording sessions, EMI, Studio 2, Abbey Road, London, UK.**

Syd recording 'live' with Jerry Shirley and John Wilson. Syd borrowed Dave's amp – Dave lived in the Old Brompton Road, London, which backed onto the block in which Syd lived, so they were in regular contact.

'Here I Go', take 5 recorded – the version released on *The Madcap Laughs*.[173] Take 5 of 'No Man's Land', also released on Barrett's first solo LP, was also recorded at this session. Three successful takes were made, the last – take 5 – being the best, although it was felt that the bass could be better and this was later re-recorded. Some guitar overdubs (recorded on 4 May) were required to fill the sections where Syd switched from rhythm to lead in the

April 1969

middle of the song. The spoken section was, according to Jones, 'as unintelligible then as it is now!'

An afternoon session, it lasted three hours. After these sessions EMI decided that the pre-mixes they'd heard were good enough to commit themselves to financing a full album.

SATURDAY 19

- ***Pink Floyd Mit Einen Neuen Beat Sound,*** **SDR TV broadcast, Stuttgart, West Germany.**

The show was a broadcast of new material recorded previously; unfortunately very little more has come to light about what must have been a great programme.

TUESDAY 22

- **BBC Studios, London, UK.**

Doing what, we don't know.

WEDNESDAY 23

- **Syd Barrett recording sessions, EMI, Studio 3, Abbey Road, London, UK.**

Sessions working on 'Rhamadan'. This is the famed occasion upon which Syd bought along a tape recorder with a copy of motorbike noises that he wanted to overdub onto the track, which he'd recorded previously with Pete Jenner. The quality of his home-made effects tape was awful, even for a casual listen, let alone a professional recording. It took an hour to wire in Syd's recorder, since it didn't have any studio-standard connectors. 'Even mixed into the conga drums at low level the tape hiss and extraneous noises were unacceptable'. A tape was eventually compiled from the EMI sound effects library, of various motorbike noises. Syd however abandoned the project. As far as is known, this thirty-second effects tape was never mixed into 'Rhamadan', so it would seem that EMI does not hold a copy of the finished item. Of such are legends born!

FRIDAY 25

- **Syd Barrett recording sessions, EMI, Studio 3, Abbey Road, London, UK.**

The recording sheet logged for this date indicates that this session was simply used to mix down some of Syd's previous 4-track tapes onto 8-track, so that

152

overdubs could be added at a later date. Tracks copied over were 'It's No Good Trying' take 4, 'Terrapin' take 3, 'Opel' take 10, 'Clowns And Jugglers' take 3, 'Love You' take 5, 'Golden Hair' take 7, 'Late Night' take 5 and 'Swan Lee' take 6. A note is also made on the sheet that 7 in. stereo copies of 'Terrapin', 'Clowns And Jugglers' and 'Love You' were made and handed to Syd. Due to illness Malcolm Jones was not present at this session, and Syd oversaw the mixes himself.

Syd also carried out some minor overdubs on 'Late Night', though it was not noted what he actually added.

SATURDAY 26

- **Bromley Technical College, Bromley Common, Kent, UK.**

An ad for the gig appears in the 26 April issue of *Melody Maker*. It indicates that the concert was to be 'a LIVE recording session', suggesting that the Floyd may have been recording a number of performances for *Ummagumma* at this point in time – an assertion that is lent weight by Rick's comments that we have reproduced under our 2 May entry. The ad further suggests that it is to be 'a light and sound concert'. Such a description in the ad seems to be thematic: suggesting, perhaps, that around this time a prospective audience might be able to anticipate whether 'The Man and The Journey' were to be performed. Purely conjectural, perhaps!

A LIVE recording session

PINK FLOYD
EAST OF EDEN
& GUESTS

SAT., APRIL 26th, 1969

A LIGHT AND SOUND
CONCERT

BROMLEY TECHNICAL
COLLEGE

Rookery Lane
Bromley Common
Trains: Bromley South
or North

SUNDAY 27

- **Mother's Club, Birmingham, West Midlands, UK.**

There has for some time been debate about when the recordings were actually made for the *Ummagumma* album. The sleeve notes, of course, say that they were made in June, but an advertisement for the above gig, in the *Birmingham Evening Mail* conclusively suggests the above date (though the above entry for the 26th should also be borne in mind).

The band were unhappy with the recordings at Mother's and Rick

April 1969

Advertisement in *Melody Maker*, 26 April 1969

MOTHERS
THE HOME OF GOOD SOUNDS
PRESENTS TONIGHT
THE VERY TALENTED

MOODY BLUES
MOODY BLUES

8 p.m.—Midnight Late, Late Bars!
Admission 12/6.
Plus Erskine with Latest Imports of
Head Sounds.
Next Saturday
THE TASTE

TOMORROW, SUNDAY
MORE FURIOUS MADNESS!!
From The
PINK FLOYD

Recording Tomorrow Night Live at
Mothers.
Get Your Hands Together on this
New L.P.—Compere John Peel.
8 p.m.—Midnight Admission 12/6.

SUNDAY NEXT
PRINCIPAL EDWARDS
MAGIC THEATRE
Plus BLONDE ON BLONDE
MOTHERS
HIGH STREET, ERDINGTON
Phone ERD 5514/4792.
Membership 2/6 yearly.

Wear What You Want.
Two Bars with Pub Prices.
Mothers Posters always available at 2/-.

recalled some months later that 'we felt we'd played really well, but the equipment didn't work so we couldn't use nearly all that one'. The only part of the Mother's gig to eventually end up on *Ummagumma* was a section of 'A Saucerful Of Secrets'.

Advertisement in *Birmingham Evening Mail*, Saturday 26 April 1969

MAY

FRIDAY 2

• **College of Commerce, Manchester, Lancashire, UK.**

This gig was the source of the majority of the recordings for the live set on *Ummagumma*. According to Rick, speaking in *Beat Instrumental* in January 1970 the performance was really bad, 'but as the recording equipment was working well, we had to use it'.

Band friend Roy Harper was also on the bill, as were soon-to-become-better-known Harvest label-mates the Principle Edwards Magic Theatre and Edgar Broughton. Tickets cost 15 shillings.

```
... COLLEGE OF COMMERCE ...
Aytoun Street, MANCHESTER, 1
Friday, May 2nd, 8 p.m.

PINK FLOYD
ROY HARPER
PETE BROWN & HIS BATTERED ORNAMENTS
Principle Edwards Magic Theatre
White Trash • Edgar Broughton
Smokey Rice • The Groundhogs
● LIGHTS BY NOVA EXPRESS
● FAIR GROUND    FILM THEATRE, ETC.

Tickets 15/- from HIME & ADDISON and
ONE STOP RECORDS
```

SATURDAY 3

- **'Chris Welch Finds Out What Britain's Top Overground Group Are Planning'**, *Melody Maker* magazine, UK.

Waters:

> Among the other things we want to do is use an orchestra. We've already had preliminary discussions with the Royal Philharmonic and they are really keen. They really want to do it – huge buzz. We're also in contact with the Boston Philharmonic. It's not that we are such an incredibly successful group, it's just that our name has got about to people who want to do strange things. It's fun – that's what it's all about.

- **Syd Barrett recording sessions, EMI, Studio 2, Abbey Road, London, UK.**

Overdubs for various of the tracks previously recorded by Syd were made at this session by Hugh Hopper (bass), Mike Ratledge (organ) and Robert Wyatt (drums), three members of the Soft Machine (a great band in their own right!). Backing was added to 'Love You', recorded on 10 April and what would appear to be two versions of 'Clowns And Jugglers' recorded on 10 April. One version was later released on the *Opel* compilation and the other has been the subject of an unofficial release.

4.23, Clowns And Jugglers, take 1, with alternative overdub by the Soft Machine

Also overdubbed was 'No Good Trying', recorded on 10 April. Syd's erratic timing, however, resulted in a very difficult track for the Softs to follow. This was the version issued on *The Madcap Laughs*.

155

May 1969

- **Queen Mary College, Mile End, London, UK.**

SAT., MAY 3, 7.45 p.m.
Queen Mary College
Mile End Road, E.1
PINK
FLOYD
+ Watch Us Grow
Tickets: 10/- in advance
12/6 on door : S.U. Cards

Advertisement in *Melody Maker*, 3 May 1969

SUNDAY 4

- **Syd Barrett recording sessions, EMI, Studio 3, Abbey Road, London, UK.**

Continued work on previous tracks. On 'It's No Good Trying' an additional backwards guitar overdub was recorded, while lead guitar tracks were added to 'No Man's Land' and 'Terrapin'.

FRIDAY 9

- **Camden Arts Festival, Parliament Hill Fields, Hampstead, London, UK.**

It is reported that the band played 'Astronomy Domine', 'Set The Controls For The Heart Of The Sun', 'Careful With That Axe, Eugene', and 'A Saucerful Of Secrets'.
    Miles lists this gig has having taken place on the 10th.

- **Southampton University, Hampshire, UK.**

Bi-channel, 52.18, Astronomy Domine, 8.50, Careful With That Axe, Eugene, 8.06, Interstellar Overdrive, 12.03, Green Is The Colour, 8.00, A Saucerful Of Secrets, 12.05

Many copies of Southampton were cut during 'A Saucerful Of Secrets'. If the generation of the copy is low enough the two parts may be almost perfectly segued. We originally found this to be the case through experimentation, and developed our theory significantly when we acquired two separate copies of Southampton that were directly sourced from first generation analogue recordings.
    The first of these copies exhibited a recording in the left channel only. Very nearly all copies in circulation are sourced from this (or an extremely

similar) root. The quality of the recording is better than most, but exhibits a typical semi-murkiness which is exaggerated by low recording level and extensive hiss that buzzes along in the right channel. Sadly also, 'A Saucerful Of Secrets' doesn't continue on side B after it's cut. Most do.

It is worth mentioning at this juncture that the single-channel copy runs consistently faster than the bi-channel. By the end of track one the gain is about thirteen seconds and by track two a further four. The timings listed above reflect the bi-channel copy. The single-channel copy to which we refer, which is rabidly incomplete, times out as follows:

Single-channel, 46.57, Astronomy Domine, 8.36, Careful With That Axe, Eugene, 7.53, Interstellar Overdrive, 11.22, Green Is The Colour, 7.56, A Saucerful Of Secrets, 8.04

The keen of eye will note that this copy's times more closely resemble the calculations of our predecessors, with the notable exception of 'Interstellar Overdrive'.

If we are to accept that this recording is from the master copy (we will from now on), it would be reasonable to assume that the owner of the master did not want his or her copy to circulate in a complete and unspoilt form. The second copy suggests that this would otherwise have been possible in terms of the entirety of 'A Saucerful Of Secrets' but unlikely to ever happen for other reasons which we will go on to explain.

We would not wish to suggest that you are more than likely to obtain a one channel recording. On the contrary, many recorders use splitting devices so as to achieve a bi-channel sound. In terms of putting together your own copy though, we would recommend that you seek out a single-channel copy and enhance it through an EQ and a 'splitter' (or better) yourself, as those that seem to have reached approximately third generation and above, rarely fail to disappoint.

The second copy that we have acquired is of exceptionally good quality. It is bi-channel, bright and at times gives a very good impression of being 'soundboard' (though it definitely isn't). We have carefully examined both copy one and copy two and can say with absolute certainty that they originate from the same master.

It would seem that the second copy was reproduced more recently, using more sophisticated equipment as it would not seem possible to achieve the remarkable quality gain simply through an EQ. Unfortunately, the owner it would seem, is critically aware of his or her treasure, as it has been tampered with at various points.

Both start with 'Astronomy Domine'. It is a good judge of the generation of your copy to note whether Roger's introduction to the track may be heard twice, as his voice is replicated through the on-stage echo unit; the repeat is often lost in the compression and noise of higher generation copies.

'Careful With That Axe, Eugene' is despoiled by a ten-second strike of the master's pause button. The source – judging by the nature of the 'squelch', and its quality – being a reel-to-reel. With the correct editing equipment (or a fast finger!) the edit can be undone. The owner of the master must have wanted to leave an obvious fingerprint; a spiteful one too as the tension builds 1 min. 43 sec. into the piece. Needless to say that on the single channel copy, there is no such edit.

The end of side A is skilfully edited on the bi-channel copy during the band's tuning up. The tape is allowed to repeat a little where it recommences on side B. 'A Saucerful Of Secrets' does blip on side B but not in the same place as it cuts on our first version. Nor for that matter on the third and fourth generation copies which we own (both of these cut and continue). Again, the tension of the piece is blighted by the imposition of another needless edit, on this occasion for a less painful 1 min. 30 sec.

Our single channel 'first gen' copy has a lengthy silent (though noisy) passage after 'Interstellar Overdrive' (there are edits between the majority of the tracks). The passage starts after 29 min. 5 sec. and the concert is then tightly edited for the remaining 23 minutes. This leads us to believe that the master is most likely on a sixty-minute reel-to-reel.

We think it reasonable to assume that the recording is complete in terms of tracklisting and the flow of Roger's comments suggest that the track order hasn't been changed for any reason.

Listen out for a particularly fine 'Interstellar Overdrive', which we would argue is bettered by none from the same period. 'Green Is The Colour', though the subject of many a dropout and warped tape, is equally impressive. 'Green …' is effectively a rehearsal for the *John Peel: Night Ride* session five days later.

The reader will note that on this occasion 'Careful With That Axe, Eugene' is given its ordinary name, so we thought it proper to do the same with 'Green Is The Colour'. It would clearly be incorrect to assume that all of the Floyd's gigs between April and September were to feature 'The Man and The Journey' suite. The same is underlined by our entry for 8 August.

This song's called 'Astronomy Domine'.

Astronomy Domine

Thank you. This is a much newer thing than that one, which is very old, and it's an instrumental, and it's called 'Careful With That Axe, Eugene'. And it's got a very quiet start.

Careful With That Axe, Eugene >< Interstellar Overdrive

Thank you. Thank you ><

Green Is The Colour

Thank you. >< This is gonna be the last thing we do and it's the title track off the last album we released and it's called 'A Saucerful Of Secrets'.

A Saucerful Of Secrets

Thank you.

SATURDAY 10

- Nottingham's 1969 Pop And Blues Festival, Nottingham, Nottinghamshire, UK.

MONDAY 12

- *John Peel: Night Ride* recorded at the Paris Cinema, Lower Regent Street, London, UK.

The recording was broadcast on 14 May 1969.

Meanwhile, the box office opened for tickets to the Royal Albert Hall concert to be held on the 26 June.

TUESDAY 13

- Debut of the film *More* at the Cannes Film Festival, Cannes, France.

The film made its US debut in New York City on the 4 August. The movie lasts a total of 112 minutes and features numerous different takes and mixes of the tracks later released on the album. Most are edited and many appear at more than one point in the film. While it leads to a great deal of detail, it seems worthwhile to list the tracks as they appear on the film, and note where they differ from the LP:

'More' Film Soundtrack, 37.07, Main Theme I (with a different guitar mix), 3.28, Ibiza Bar I (with an improved vocal mix), 1.08, Ibiza Bar II, 0.46, The Nile Song, 1.40, Seabirds (what may be the entire song is featured, though it is edited and looped in order to make a dramatic point), 3.39, Main Theme II (faster than the LP and with additional keyboard jams), 0.41, Cymbaline (a faster version than on the album, with Roger rather than Dave on vocals, and different lyrics at the end of the first verse), 5.05, Embryo (a unique improvised version), 0.36, A Spanish Piece (an instrumental version, different to the backing track used on the album), 1.00, Party Sequence I, 2.20, Party Sequence II, 2.09, Party Sequence III (all three occurrences of this song feature additional improvised guitar overdubs with a broadly Spanish feel), 1.19, Tabla solo (an improvised tabla track, most likely by Nick although we've no evidence to support this), 0.36, Green Is The Colour I, 0.48, Quicksilver I, 2.20, Quicksilver II (different take to the LP), 1.08, Cirrus Minor, 0.45, More Blues (faster take with keyboards, completely unlike the LP), 0.23, Crying Song, 2.10, Up The Khyber (different take to the LP), 1.17, Quicksilver III, 0.42, Main Theme III (faster than the album), 0.47, Dramatic Theme, 0.54, Main Theme IV (faster than the LP), 0.30, Green is The Colour II, 0.44.

WEDNESDAY 14

- *John Peel: Night Ride*, **BBC Radio, London, UK.**

The recording, which had been made two days previously, was produced
by Phil Stannard and engineered by Pete Ritzema. It was broadcast between
8.15 and 9.15 pm. The show was repeated on 1 June 1969.

John Peel: Night Ride should not be confused with *John Peel's Night Ride*
(which ran over the previous year, midnight – 1.00 am on Wednesday nights)
or *Night Ride* (which was a strand running daily from 30 September 1967,
midnight – 2.00 am).

The following recording description and transcription represents the earliest known broadcast to be in general circulation. It couldn't possibly be from
1969 and is very probably from the early 70s judging by John Peel's comments.

*18.39, Daybreak, 3.36, Nightmare, 3.28, The Beginning / Beset By Creatures of
The Deep, 6.38, The Narrow Way, 4.49*

A song called 'Daybreak'.

Daybreak

And complete with BBC-Sessions songbirds, those were the Pink Floyd from
their *Ummagumma* period.

Nightmare >< The Beginning / Beset By Creatures From The Deep

... Floyd. In session with the Pink Floyd.

The Narrow Way

Now you have proof that they've always been fond of the old wind machine;
those old time film-makers the Pink Floyd, and that's 'The Narrow Way'.

THURSDAY 15

- **The band embark upon their first organised UK tour since 1967.**

Dates were scheduled and advertised in the tour programme and national
music press up to and including 26 June. The concerts, which were to be
directed by Peter Bowyer, boasted the 'azimuth co-ordinator' which provided
a full 360 degree quadraphonic sound system. The tour was to be vigorously
advertised in the national music press weekly from 10 May to its conclusion.

The artwork in the tour programme may have been (unconsciously)
inspired by the cover of *IT* 9.[174]

- **It's A Drag, City of Coventry College of Art May Ball, Locarno Ballroom,
Coventry, Leicestershire, UK.**

The Floyd were supported by Spooky Tooth and Wellington Kitch.

FRIDAY 16

- **Leeds Town Hall, Leeds, Yorkshire, UK.**

The extremely desirable Hypnosis handbill which was produced to advertise the concert was reproduced in the 1994 European Tour programme. The same illustration was used for concerts on 8 and 25 June.

SATURDAY 17

- **Paradiso, Amsterdam, Holland.**

SUNDAY 18

- **Concertzaal de Jong, Groningen, Holland.**

SATURDAY 24

- **City Hall, Sheffield, Yorkshire, UK.**

Advertisement in *Melody Maker*, 24 May 1969

SUNDAY 25

- **Benefit for The Fairport Convention, Roundhouse, Chalk Farm, London, UK.**

Two members of Fairport had recently died after their van crashed; the Floyd and others played to help the band out.

FRIDAY 30

- **Fairfield Halls, Croydon, Surrey, UK.**

Syd came along to see the band. He decides to ask Roger and Dave to produce the final part of his album, and they agree.

SATURDAY 31

- **Pembroke College, Oxford, Oxfordshire, UK.**

JUNE

SUNDAY 1

- *Top Gear*, **BBC Radio 1, London, UK.**

A rebroadcast of the *John Peel: Night Ride* show, previously aired on 14 May,
presented again by John Peel.

SATURDAY 7

- **Barrett reply on letters page of *Melody Maker*.**

A small comment is produced in reply to a letter regarding an enquiry about
Barrett's involvement in *A Saucerful of Secrets*. He (allegedly) confirms that
he played on 'See-Saw' and another Richard Wright composition which he
recalls had steel guitar on it – though he doesn't mention its title. Factually,
it would seem unsound: it would be easy to fake a reply from a person who
would have other things on their mind.

SUNDAY 8

- **The Rex Cinema, Cambridge, Cambridgeshire, UK.**

The concert kicked off at 2.30 pm (being a Sunday) and was advertised
with a flyer by Hypnosis, the Floyd's LP sleeve designers, who were also
responsible for the tour programme.

TUESDAY 10

- *Laying Down Tracks*, **BBC Radio 3 documentary, UK.**
  6.03 / 5.57, dialogue and excerpts from Cirrus Minor

We have been unable to track down any evidence of this programme's date and content – *Radio Times* on this date lists nothing which would confirm the show. It is possible that there was more Floyd on it than has survived.

It is also very possible that the programme's title has been made up after one of the narrator's comments. The segment that we have sounds like it was recorded off television. Radio 3 is, and was, unlikely to broadcast anything to do with popular music: it is the BBC's 'serious music' station and tends to concentrate on classical and jazz music. The source programme is evidently the third in a series.

• **Ulster Hall, Belfast, Northern Ireland, UK.**

THURSDAY 12

• **Syd Barrett recording sessions, EMI, Studio 3, Abbey Road, London, UK.**

Produced by Dave and Roger – their first studio session with Syd since his leaving the band in 1968.

'Remakes' of 'Golden Hair' were recorded on this date. Two versions of 'Golden Hair' have been released: take 6, an instrumental backing track which appeared on *Opel*, and take 11, the final version released on *The Madcap Laughs*. Take 7 was 'more or less completed', while takes 8–10 were all false starts! The vocal was overdubbed onto take 11, with which they were most happy, later on in the session, the original takes having been instrumental. Dave and Roger provided the backing of organ, cymbals and vibes, although it is rumoured that Rick made an appearance and may have taken part in this recording.

'Octopus', as it was now known, was also given another chance at this session. Quite a number of takes were attempted, and three have been released – take 11 (of the remake!) as the single, and on the *The Madcap Laughs* LP. Takes 1 and 2 were issued as extra tracks when the album was remastered for CD in the early 90s.

FRIDAY 13

• **Soundtrack from the film *More* released in the UK.**

Melody Maker reported as follows on 14 June:

> Pink Floyd's new album *More* consisting of soundtrack music they wrote for the film, is due for release on Columbia tomorrow (Friday).

The 14th was a Saturday, so presumably, if we were to accept the accuracy of this article, the album was released on Friday 13 June. Perhaps this report should be measured against the accuracy of the report on the release date of *Ummagumma*.[175]

The actual film was never to be released in the UK.

- **Syd Barrett recording sessions, EMI, Studio 3, Abbey Road, London, UK.**

  This, the penultimate session as far as *The Madcap Laughs* went, was entirely given over to recording overdubs, with Syd and Dave producing (Roger was not mentioned on the original recording sheet).

  'Dark Globe' – Syd completed the song satisfactorily on the second take, the version issued on *The Madcap Laughs*, but Dave decided to go back to it at the end of the session. The track was mixed on 5 August, and it would appear that this is the source of the false recording date given on the sleeve of *The Madcap Laughs* CD reissue. The third take is 3 min. 15 sec. long, compared with 1 min. 57 sec. for the issued version (the album lists it as 2 min. 10 sec. however the actual track is some 13 seconds shorter – perhaps a false start was excluded at the last minute?). 'Long Gone' was also worked on in this session, though the result was two unsuccessful attempts, and the song was abandoned until later, when it was re-recorded for the LP on 26 July.

  The bass, guitar and drum parts of *The Madcap Laughs* version of 'Octopus' were also added during this session.

- **Van Dike, Devonport, Plymouth, Devon, UK.**

SATURDAY 14

- **Colston Hall, Bristol, Avon, UK.**

SUNDAY 15

- **Guildhall, Portsmouth, Hampshire, UK.**

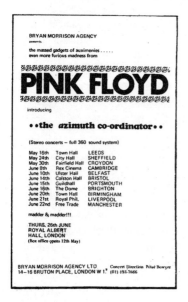

Advertisement in *IT* 56, 9 May 1969

MONDAY 16

- **The Dome, Brighton, Sussex, UK.**

An early version of the tour programme (which was updated as the schedule continued) has the Floyd as being in France on this date.

- *Soirée Dim Dam Dom* **TV show, Abbaye De Royaumont, ORTF TV, France.**

2.56, Cymbaline

We understand that this was recorded live some time earlier in either the UK or France but the above entry should be borne in mind.

TUESDAY 17

- **EMI, Studio 2, Abbey Road, London, UK.**

Mixing took place for David Gilmour's studio part of *Ummagumma* at this session. Nick and Rick had already recorded their parts in March, 1969. The recordings were made on 8-track, even though 16-track had just become an available technology. Dave Gilmour was at the meeting to discuss which format to get and suggested going for 16-track, a move which would have put Abbey Road and EMI at the forefront of recording technology. His opinion was ultimately overridden by EMI who felt this would be both too expensive and too risky.

WEDNESDAY 18

- **Den Haag, Holland. TV show.**

An early copy of the 1969 UK tour programme confirms that the band were in Holland on this date.

FRIDAY 20

- **Town Hall, Birmingham, West Midlands, UK.**

Advertisement in *Birmingham Evening Mail,*
19 June 1969

June 1969

- **Royal Philharmonic, Liverpool, Lancashire, UK.**

- **Free Trade Hall, Manchester, Lancashire, UK.**

  62.55, The Man, 22.41 [Daybreak, 2.51, Work, 1.05, Afternoon, 3.39 Doing It, 2.01, Sleeping, 5.20, Nightmare, 7.25] The Journey, 28.53 [The Beginning, 5.37, Beset By Creatures of the Deep, 7.13, The Narrow Way, 5.25, Behold The Temple Light, 1.51, The End of The Beginning, 8.02], Set The Controls For The Heart Of The Sun, 11.06

The above timing represents a suggested version of the tape following the method set out below. The collector is likely to receive a 65 min. 7 sec. copy. The extra few minutes reflect duplicated music. Manchester was either recorded by a nervous recorder or – more likely – one with a dodgy tape player. Alternatively, we suppose it could be the case that there is a more complete master.

The person recording hits the pause button during 'Daybreak' 2 min. 11 sec. in, and again after 2 min. 36 sec. The track then cuts and continues at 2 min. 51 sec. … Oops!

'Work' also cuts (after 1 min. 5 sec.) – sadly, as it is a unique recording. Starting with an explosion, it proceeds through Schoenbergian percussion which was evidently panned through the Azimuth Coordinator.

'Afternoon' also highlights the band's quadraphonics, but sadly joins its predecessors by cutting after 2 min. 41 sec., then continuing for a further 58 seconds. Before the cut we have the pastoral, after, quadraphonic mayhem – with no idea of how the two were juxtaposed. Distortion becomes particularly noticeable during 'Afternoon' and rarely departs altogether for the rest of the tape.

In the first of several reactions the observer seems to turn his or her recording level down part way through the track and there is another nervous pause after 2 min. 22 sec.

'Doing It!' sadly cuts after 26 seconds and a radio DJ is heard saying 'now it's news time' (not part of the concert, kids!). It then continues for a further 1 min. 35 sec. but is blighted by an intermittently wandering tape azimuth. There then follows another semi-silent cut of 16 seconds, during which radio music can be heard from the same radio programme. Most likely the person recording the concert was re-using an old tape, and this effect is a consequence of the incomplete erasure of the original recording.

'Sleeping' is complete (except perhaps for a few bars of breathing), the tape azimuth has recovered; the distortion subsides, and it segues unblemished into 'Nightmare'. Is the recording blight to be over?

No, sadly. 'Nightmare' breaks after 4 min. 54 sec. for a few seconds and then again after a further 2 min. 26 sec., never to return. The three-second break cannot be rejoined as it occurs during an instrumental section and resumes mid-chorus. 'Nightmare's' healthy start gives way to heavy distortion.

The total time for 'The Man' is 22 min. 41 sec., representing tape time elapsed. We are inclined to remove the poor edits leaving us with 22 min. 22 sec.

As 'Nightmare' cuts we immediately jump to well-balanced seagull effects, marking the opening of 'The Beginning'. The recording progresses happily through 'The Beginning', into 'Beset By Creatures Of The Deep' and off into 'The Narrow Way' only to be undone when this quietens distinctly and cuts after 5 min. 25 sec.

After a two-second break, we hear the final 1 min. 51 sec. of 'Behold The Temple Of Light'. It is a matter for interpretation, but some might perceive that 'Behold' is only about a minute and a half long, meaning that we have a very small segment of 'The Labyrinths Of Auximenes'. 'The End Of The Beginning' only lasts for an unhappy 42 seconds before side A ends.

Side B duplicates 'Behold The Temple Of Light', and is followed by a far more distinguished – almost complete – 'End Of The Beginning'. This cuts (for want of a surprise) and after a couple of seconds a rousing encore of 'Set The Controls For The Heart Of The Sun' ends the tape on a high. The only (legitimate!) dialogue on the tape then follows amidst rapturous applause:

ROGER: Thank you, thank you. Bye-bye.

'The Journey' minus very sensible edits lasts 38 min. 53 sec. (including duplication). The extent of edits on this recording is perhaps best seen as an attempt by the person recording to gain maximum highlights when taping onto a 60-minute reel.

The quality of compact-cassette recorders at the time was truly terrible – that of a Dictaphone. The quality of this recording suggests the use of a reel-to-reel. Perhaps it is too easy to forget the problems facing a would-be archivist at the time. The equipment was portable in that it could fit into a handbag or bag, and due to the limited size of a compact machine, any single reel would have been limited to 60 minutes – or less; it is likely that our Mancunian friend had one (used!) tape, and so was forced to be selective in their efforts.

MONDAY 23

* **EMI, Studio 2, Abbey Road, London, UK.**

Mixing took place for Roger Waters' part of *Ummagumma*.

TUESDAY 24

* **Queen's College, Oxford, Oxfordshire, UK.**

June 1969

- **Pink Floyd feature in a programme of pop films shown at the Open Space Theatre in Tottenham Court Road, London.**

The *Observer* newspaper reported on 22 June as follows:

> Jimi Hendrix – Pink Floyd: Programme of pop films (Open Space Theatre, Tottenham Court Road, w1. Tuesday, 24 June to Saturday, 28 June, 6.30. Admission 8s).

We have no idea what the Floyd film(s) were, but would speculate that since Hendrix was also on the bill, this could have been a showing of the *Christmas On Earth Continued* concert footage from 1967.

- **Royal Albert Hall, Kensington, London, UK.**

It has long been rumoured that two recordings of this show exist. Our analysis proves this to be mistaken, however.

Long recording, 80.29, The Man, 25.11 [Afternoon, 5.34, Doing It!, 4.00, Sleeping, 5.03, Nightmare, 9.48, Daybreak (reprise), 0.44], The Journey, 42.19 [The Beginning, 4.30, Beset By Creatures Of The Deep, 5.52, The Narrow Way, 5.16, The Pink Jungle, 5.36, The Labyrinths Of Auximenes, 8.04, Behold The Temple Of Light, 4.10, The End Of The Beginning (with choir), 8.58], Set The Controls For The Heart Of The Sun, 9.33

> **The Man and The Journey** ><
>
> Thank you. Thank you […] so I'll just thank you very much, and we're off, and thank you. This is called 'Set The Controls For The Heart Of The Sun'. >< [Tuning.]
>
> **Set The Controls For The Heart Of The Sun**

There is also a 70-minute version in circulation which doesn't feature the encore (and for that matter, the stage comments detailed above). It has also been suggested that this shorter version may have been recorded nearer the stage; that one recording – the shorter – was made from the 'floor' and one from the 'balcony' – that above. Both versions however derive from the same master although both have evidently – in a similar way to that which you will note under 17 September 1969 – had very different lives.

Short recording, 70.08, The Man, 26.23 [Afternoon, 5.35, Doing It!, 4.05, Sleeping, 5.10, Nightmare, 10.44, Daybreak (reprise), 0.44], The Journey, 42.59 [The Beginning, 4.32, Beset By Creatures Of The Deep, 5.58, The Narrow Way,

5.18, The Pink Jungle, 5.41, The Labyrinths Of Auximenes, 8.07, Behold The Temple Of Light, 4.14, The End Of The Beginning (with choir), 9.10]

The footsteps sequence of 'Labyrinths' is much louder on the above and it is at this point the case for there being two copies is at its strongest. The footsteps are punctuated by a woman's laugh (pre-recorded); on the short version it jumps out of the speakers and on the long it is reasonably difficult to discern. Convincing perhaps, but – here's where our thoroughness goes into overdrive – the audience 'whooper' at the end of the footsteps is evidently the same person on both tapes. The Albert Hall is a big place! We shouldn't go on.

Elsewhere in the tape, the shorter version is far more prone to distortion, over-saturation, and compression. What was probably a reel-to-reel has been put through an equaliser (perhaps), ostensibly dropping the high frequencies and boosting the mid-range and the lows. The longer version strikes us as being largely unspoilt, with the major exception of 'The Pink Jungle'.

This unhappy combination does though allow the listener to feel closer to the stage. Take for example, 'The Beginning', a pop can be heard on the stage during the first few moments of the seabird and surf effects; on the shorter version it is more of a bang.

The opening of 'Work' on the longer version features some nine or so seconds more 'fiddling' before Dave's repeating guitar phrase. This is an omission/error on the part of the source. Had we had two different master sources, the chances are that one of them would have recorded at least part of 'Daybreak'.

The obvious reaction to the applause at the beginning of the seventy-minute version is that it may mark the end of 'Daybreak'. It doesn't. The applause has been edited in from the end of 'The Journey'. The careful listener will hear a 'thank you' by Roger. If the editor had left the recorder running a little longer the seventy-minute copy would have started with the encore – novel indeed!

'Afternoon' is sung by Waters; his voice carries better to the recorder than Gilmour's which is often virtually lost beneath guitar, bass and keyboard later in the recording. Perhaps this was literally the case, reflecting Waters' sometimes-quoted greater confidence in the suite.

'Afternoon' segues into 'Doing It!' which seems to largely exist as a vehicle for showing off the 'sound in the round'. All of the tracks segue and 'Sleeping', which segues into 'Nightmare', is no exception. 'Sleeping' is clearly the focal point of the first half of the concert and the group seem to settle into its more regular form of expression as against the companion pieces.

The attentive reader may wonder why the shorter version features a version of 'Nightmare' that is substantially longer than the long, especially since it ostensibly cuts exactly eight minutes in! Far too much time spent comparing versions proves that where it cuts and resumes, approximately 40 seconds of music is repeated – a perfectly unnecessary despoilment to an otherwise fine master copy.

The beginning of 'Daybreak (reprise)' is barely detectable – we have

!! TONIGHT !!
THE FINAL LUNACY !!
ROYAL ALBERT HALL
Some more musical callisthenics
PINK FLOYD
with the
AZIMUTH CO-ORDINATOR
(Only 7/6 and 10/6 left)

Advertisement in *Melody Maker*, 28 June 1969

perceived it to be at a point where the music stops and the tape effect begins. 'Daybreak' seems to be largely represented by an extended quadraphonic ticking clock, preceded by the ringing of the clock's alarm bell. The alarm on the shorter version sounds more like a buzz than a shrill. Impressed by either the quadraphonics or the first section's ending, the audience applaud at length.

The taper has at some point reasonably skilfully segued 'The Man' to 'The Journey'. It would have been helpful to have been as well informed as we are with regard to the 14 April concert, nevertheless the rise in the applause suggests that the group left the stage at the end of 'The Man'.

'The Beginning' – much the same as on *Top Gear* in May and the 14 April concert, opens with swirling wind and squawking seagulls. Wright and Gilmour (not Waters, who is by some accounts tone deaf anyway!) use the chance to tune up for about a minute. Unfortunately, 'The Beginning' distorts heavily at times, particularly, as one might expect, on the shorter version. Perhaps there had been some adjustment to amps or recorder during the interval.

While 'The Pink Jungle' is split on both tapes, for those who are able to make a seamless edit when making a continuous recording, 'The Pink Jungle's' continuation on side B may be rejoined on the longer version.

'The Labyrinth Of Auximenes' on the short version cuts 16 seconds in but no music is lost. We have started the timing for 'Behold The Temple Of Light' where Gilmour's tranquil guitar line enters at the end of the 'footsteps sequence', as we did for the purposes of the Royal Festival Hall on 14 April.

Reports at the time described someone in a gorilla suit wandering through the audience during the interval and the band sawing wood on stage. The orchestra, conducted by the group's producer, Norman Smith, comprised part of the Royal Philharmonic.

SUNDAY 29

- **Winter Gardens, Weston-super-Mare, Somerset, UK.**

MONDAY 30

- **Top Rank, Cardiff, Glamorgan, Wales, UK.**

JULY

FRIDAY 4

- **Selby Arts Festival, Selby, Yorkshire, UK.**

  John Hiseman (of Coliseum fame) and Eire Apparent were also on the bill.[176]

WEDNESDAY 9

- **EMI, Studio 3, Abbey Road, London, UK.**

  'Biding My Time' produced by Norman Smith.

THURSDAY 10

- **Recording date for Moonhead, commissioned by the BBC for its coverage of the first moon landing.**

  The programme was broadcast on 20 July.

- **The band commence a tour of Holland.**

SUNDAY 13

- **The band return from their mini tour of Holland.**

  It is not known what they got up to while they were there.[177]

MID

- **The Floyd's jetting off for their tour of Holland necessitates Syd's sessions being put on hold.**

  He gets fed up waiting for Dave and Roger to return and goes on holiday to Ibiza.[178]

July 1969

SUNDAY 20

- *Omnibus: So What If It's Just Green Cheese*, BBC 1 TV, UK, shown at 10.00 – 11.00 p.m.

   An entertainment for moon-night. The *Radio Times* listing magazine describes the Floyd's contribution as 'a new number', while also featured in the show were actors Judi Dench, Ian McKellen, Michael Hordern, comedian Dudley Moore and Tamas Vasary playing Debussy![179] The band were seen performing the song, an improvisation, 'live' in the studio. It is believed that more music was performed than has been saved by collectors. Unfortunately our investigations indicate that the BBC is no longer in possession of the show – another victim of their arbitrary archive policies during the 70s.
   Introduced by Judi Dench, 'Oh moon, when I look on thy beautiful face'.

   5.51, Moonhead, 1.01, Moonhead (reprise), 4.44

TUESDAY 22

- SDR TV, Stuttgart, West Germany.

   Further recording sessions, this time for the show *P-1*, broadcast on 21 September.

THURSDAY 24

- Recording for *Apollo 11 – Een Man Op De Maan*, Nederland 1 TV, Amsterdam, Holland.

   It is unknown whether or not this recording was ever broadcast, or what material the band actually recorded.

SATURDAY 26

- Syd Barrett recording sessions, EMI, Studio 3, Abbey Road, London, UK.

   Syd recorded take 1 of 'Wouldn't You Miss Me' at this session – this would be officially released on *Opel*. However, a version of the same take which appears to have a different vocal double track has appeared on bootleg.

   Wouldn't You Miss Me, 2.57

   'Long Gone' was also recorded, and organ overdubs added, and three takes are available to collectors. Take 1 was the official version released on *The Madcap Laughs*. Take 2 has found release on bootleg, while another, unknown take featuring guitar and vocal only has also made its way onto the bootleg market. This unknown take unfortunately fades very abruptly.

Long Gone take 2, 1.42, Long Gone (guitar and vocal), 1.47

Syd was also to record 'She Took A Long Cold Look' on this date. Takes 4 and 5 have been released – the latter on *The Madcap Laughs*, the former, under the slightly longer title 'She Took A Long Cold Look At Me' was released only as a bonus track when *Madcap* was remastered for CD.

'Feel' and 'If It's In You' were also recorded on this date – take 5 of the latter would be released on *The Madcap Laughs* – (note that the sleeve notes to *The Madcap Laughs* CD reissue are incorrect on this point), while take 1 of 'Feel' was also that which was included on *The Madcap Laughs* LP. Quite why the false starts were left in 'If It's In You' and 'She Took A Long Cold Look' is unknown, as it is obvious that better takes existed, at least of the former. It seems regrettable that better editorial control was not exercised by Roger and Dave on this occasion.

AUGUST

• **Soundtrack from the film *More* released in the USA.**

FRIDAY 1

• **Van Dike, Devonport, Plymouth, Devon, UK.**

TUESDAY 5

• **Syd Barrett recording sessions, EMI, Studio 3, Abbey Road, London, UK.**

Dave and Roger worked on the mixes for the album in two three-hour sessions, one in the morning and one in the afternoon. In the morning they completed 'Octopus', 'Long Gone', 'Feel', 'If It's In You' and 'She Took A Long Cold Look', while the afternoon session saw the mixing of 'Golden Hair', 'Terrapin' and 'Dark Globe' (perhaps this is the source of the assertion that it was recorded on this date).

FRIDAY 8

• **Ninth National Jazz And Blues Festival, NJF Festival, Plumpton Race Track, Streat, Sussex, UK.**

The poster for this gig is illustrated in *The Art of Rock*.[180] A black and white copy of the programme is in *Le Livre Du Pink Floyd*.[181] The Floyd topped the bill, following the Soft Machine. Two years after their appearances at UFO they were still seen together, but how they had both changed.

9ᵀᴴ NATIONAL
JAZZ · POP · BALLADS &
BLUES FESTIVAL

Previously at Windsor and Sunbury

An NJF/MARQUEE presentation

AUGUST 8 - 9 - 10

WEST DRAYTON
near London Airport

Friday 8th August
Tickets 15/-   8 - 11.30 p m

PINK FLOYD · SOFT MACHINE
EAST OF EDEN · BLOSSOM TOES

Keith Tippett Jazz Group
JUNIORS EYES · THE VILLAGE

TRAVEL: By road only 15 miles from Central London. M4 Motorway to Heathrow Airport Exit. Underground to Uxbridge or Hounslow West then BUS. Western Region Trains. SPECIAL LATE SERVICE back to Paddington.

Saturday 9th August   [ ] 2 Sessions

[ ] Afternoon
2 - 5.30 p m   **BONZO DOG BAND**
Tickets 10/-   **Roy Harper**
THE STRAWBS · JO-ANN KELLY
MARTIN CARTHY and DAVE SWARBRICK

For advice on
TENT HIRE
and details of camping facilities
contact NJF Camp Secretary
at 01-437 6603

[ ] Evening   7 - 11.30 p m   Tickets £1   *The Jazz Sound of*

THE WHO · CHICKEN SHACK · FAT MATTRESS · JOHN SURMAN
AYNSLEY DUNBAR · YES! · The Spirit of JOHN MORGAN
GROUNDHOGS · KING CRIMSON · IDLE RACE · BREAKTHRU'
Introducing from Holland CUBY'S BLUES BAND

Sunday 10th August   [ ] 2 Sessions

[ ] Afternoon
2 - 5.30 p m   **THE PENTANGLE**
Tickets 10/-   **Long John Baldry**
RON GEESIN
MAGNA CARTA · NOEL MURPHY

For Special
PARTY RATES
and all enquiries contact the NJF
Secretary at the MARQUEE. 01-437-2375

[ ] Evening   7 - 11.30 p m   Tickets £1   *The Blues Sound of*

THE NICE · THE FAMILY · London Cast of 'HAIR' · CHRIS BARBER
KEEF HARTLEY · ECLECTION · Mick Abraham's BLODWYN PIG
JIGSAW · CIRCUS · HARD MEAT · STEAMHAMMER · BABYLON
Introducing from Greece APHRODITE'S CHILDREN

FESTIVAL VILLAGE — — — — Open all day to Ticketholders

An advertisement in *Melody Maker* before the venue was changed

Melody Maker had previously announced in its 5 July issue that the three-day festival was to be retitled the London Jazz, Blues And Pop Festival and that it was to be held at West Drayton, Middlesex on 15 August. Adverts were to appear to this effect in the national press, including the *Melody Maker*, on 12 July. The older title was later (on or about 26th) reinstated but reversed so as to properly reflect the festival's content and the venue was changed to Plumpton on the 8th.

Melody Maker's review of the gig shortly after the 8th was negative and brief – suggesting that both the band and the audience were bored with the sonic trickery and the music as a whole.

IT 63 was equally non-committal, complaining about how the festival 'had a smell' (whatever that means!) and at how the power blew twice during the Soft Machine's set, after which most of the audience went to sleep, much to the relief of the organisers and despite some eager hustling from DJ Andy Dunkly with some inaudible records.

The Floyd finally appeared at 11, very cool and unconcerned by it all, starting with a cautious sounding 'Heart Of The Sun'. Their sound was as nicely balanced as it's ever been outdoors but there was a controlling restraint that went through the first part of their set which was unfortunate under the circumstances, as already there were hang-ups with the last train.

Apart from their first two songs their set was made up of the second half of their concert programme – 'The Journey', and it wasn't until mid way through this that they really moved the audience and by that time it was too late.[182]

Generation loss tends to badly affect this recording. We have acquired a distinctly better copy than that which seems ordinarily available. Bootleggers have frequently reproduced excerpts from the 85 minutes worth of original recordings which are available. The reader should note that there is some duplication in the recordings.

Some collectors say that the shorter excerpt from 'The Journey' is merely a part of the longer recording. It may be distinguished by its having different background chatter, more fumbly mics (!) and different recording qualities – it's basically less clear sounding.

34.22, Set The Controls For The Heart Of The Sun, 8.55, Cymbaline, 8.53, The Journey, 14.36 [The Beginning, 3.06, Beset By Creatures Of The Deep, 5.56, The Narrow Way, 5.07]

ANNOUNCER: Welcome to The Pink Floyd!

RW: One, one-two, one-two, one, one, two. This is a song called 'Set The Controls For The Heart Of The Sun'.

Set The Controls For The Heart Of The Sun

RW: Thank you. This is a much newer song and it's called 'Cymbaline'.

Cymbaline

RW: Some of you may have seen we did a kind of concert thing around the country a bit earlier this year, and this, which is what we're gonna do now 'til we finish, is the second half of that concert. It's called the … it's called 'The Journey'.

The Journey [Cuts, fumbling mics.]

50.04, The Journey, 39.33 [The Beginning, 3.14, Beset By Creatures Of The Deep, 6.06, The Narrow Way, 5.17, The Pink Jungle, 5.50, The Labyrinths Of Auximenes, 8.15, Behold The Temple Of Light, 3.28, The End Of The Beginning, 6.23], Interstellar Overdrive, 10.07

RW: Some of you may have seen we did a kind of concert thing around the country a bit earlier this year, and this, which is what we're gonna do now 'til we finish, is the second half of that concert. It's called the … it's called 'The Journey'.

The Journey

RW: Thank you.

ANNOUNCER: The Pink Floyd … Let's hear it now – The Pink Floyd. [Probably edited on from the end.] ><

Interstellar Overdrive<

ANNOUNCER: Pink Floyd – let's hear it now, The Pink Floyd!

SATURDAY 9

- **Paradiso, Amsterdam, Holland.**

SEPTEMBER

SATURDAY 13

- **Rugby Rag's Blues Festival, Rugby, Warwickshire, UK.**

TUESDAY 16

- **David Gilmour mixes for *The Madcap Laughs*, EMI, Abbey Road Studio 3, London, UK.**

Dave spent the day mixing Malcolm Jones' productions, 'No Good Trying', 'Love You', 'No Man's Land', 'Here I Go' and 'Late Night'.

WEDNESDAY 17

- **The Floyd arrive in Amsterdam for the commencement of a Continental tour.**

Melody Maker reported on 30 August 1969 that 'Floyd start a 12-day Continental tour on 17 September, visiting Holland, France and Belgium.'

If we accept the accuracy of this report, it would seem that the tour was at some point extended to include some German dates. The French dates are accounted for but with no particular certainty – we strongly suspect that our knowledge is lacking in this respect.

- **Concertgebouw, Amsterdam, Holland.**

This show was, there is no doubt, broadcast by VPRO Radio, Holland, but there is some debate as to whether it was first broadcast on the 17th, sometime in September, or perhaps even in October 1969.

There are at least two collectors we are aware of who claim to have two-hour versions from the VPRO archives. One collector is English and one Dutch. We understand that the 'two-hour version' contains the complete concert, which has recently become available in all its glory for the first time in the best part of 30 years, and interviews with the band from the day before. Presumably, if we could locate these 'interviews', we might go some way to conclusively discovering the message behind the suite, if indeed there is one!

VPRO rebroadcast the vast majority of the concert over two dates in late 1997 and early 1998. On 26 November 1997 they started with the 'introductions' and carried on through 'The Man', missing out on 'The Labyrinths of Auximines' (preferring a very quick fade, unfortunately), whilst adding introductions and lengthier music elsewhere. On 17 February 1998 'The Journey' was broadcast and, thankfully, only adds to the original copy in circulation.

VPRO 1997 & 1998, 69.21, Introductions, 1.31, The Man, 28.42, [Daybreak, 7.26, Work / Afternoon, 5.12, Doing It!, 1.19, Sleeping, 4.27, Nightmare, 7.39, Daybreak (reprise), 1.06], DJ's narrative, 0.17, Seagulls and tuning, 0.58, The Journey, 38.03, [The Beginning / Beset By Creatures Of The Deep, 9.48, The Narrow Way, 5.11, The Pink Jungle, 4.51, The Labyrinths Of Auximenes, 6.21, Behold The Temple Of Light, 5.30, The End Of The Beginning, 5.49]

We have two copies of the original radio broadcast which evidently were originally sourced from the same master. The first, obtained some years back, is superior in terms of content but is in many ways inferior in terms of sound quality. There's little point in detailing the differences in this respect, save to say that the second isn't consistently better than the first, but where it is it *leaps* out. Its strengths are mainly concentrated in the first half hour. The only real point in having the second copy is to enjoy its sound quality, which for many we appreciate will be the deciding factor.

VPRO Radio original broadcast, 60.50, Introduction, 0.23, The Man, 23.03, [Daybreak, 6.39, Work / Afternoon, 4.50, Doing It!, 1.17, DJ's narrative, 1.22, Sleeping, 3.00, Nightmare, 7.39, Daybreak (reprise), 0.58], DJ's narrative, 0.17 The Labyrinths Of Auximenes, 2.56, DJ's narrative, 0.14, Introduction, 0.21, The Journey, 27.24, [The Beginning / Beset By Creatures Of The Deep, 8.48, The Narrow Way, 4.39, VPRO Station ident, 0.07, The Pink Jungle, 4.31, The Labyrinths Of Auximenes, 3.23 Behold The Temple Of Light, 3.21, The End Of The Beginning, 5.25]

Evidently, a good deal of effort has gone into bootlegging the concert over the years which has now been overwhelmingly superseded by the rebroadcast. We have heard all the bootlegs and none of them add to the audio tape of the original broadcast in circulation, either in terms of musical content or additional DJ narrative. They are all shorter than the audio cassette and where they include the DJ (they often don't) it is nearly always edited down. Two CDs produced in recent years do, though, distinctly improve upon both of our taped sources' sound quality. In all then, the enthusiastic collector might like to seek out roughly five copies of the concert broadcast.

For those interested in the original broadcast, it may be worth our going into a little more detail about what's available on audio tape. In terms of content, our tape one is, as we have said, superior. To begin with, the DJ's introduction to 'Daybreak' is twice as long, providing the listener with additional background music. The DJ narrative during 'Labyrinth' on the second copy has been badly edited (it cuts where tape one continues), and we again consequently lose a small portion of music.

Tape one has been edited so it fits onto a sixty-minute cassette and version two for a ninety. The first side of the former ends with a reasonable edit during the 'footsteps sequence' – the latter continues, of course, but an audible cut may also be heard at the exact same point. Side A on tape two ends with the VPRO ident and an audible cut may be heard at the same point on side B on tape one. Following?

Slightly more interestingly, on tape two 'The Pink Jungle' does not segue into 'The Labyrinths Of Auximenes' (it omits it completely). However on tape one it does. The bootlegs that don't savage the piece altogether cut (reasonably skilfully) in the same way as that which may be observed on tape two. Before this tape cuts we hear half a note of 'The Labyrinths Of Auximenes', adding to the argument that version one is genuine – complete – and intended. This is followed by 'Behold The Temple Of Light' rather than 'The Labyrinths Of Auximenes'.

'The Labyrinths Of Auximenes' on tape one cuts at its end and we then hear 'Behold The Temple Of Light'. It would seem that an element of fluctuating standards or intentional despoilment has entered into our original source's recording process. This is not uncommon, as the reader will note elsewhere.

The complete spoil at the end of our second tape is that it cuts during the 'Celestial Voices' sequence. Our first version continues unblemished to the audience appreciation, which fades.

Also in circulation is an audience recording, excellent content:

Audience recording, 36.58, Announcer 0.13, The Man, 36.45, [Daybreak, 6.50, Work, 3.30, Afternoon, 4.39, Doing It!, 3.32, Sleeping, 4.16, Nightmare, 7.42, Daybreak (reprise), 1.25]

FRIDAY 19

- ***Samedi Et Compagnie*, ORTF 2 TV, France.**

Further recording sessions. This could be a rebroadcast of the *Soirée Dim Dam Dom* shown on 16 June. If *Melody Maker*'s report entered under the 17th is accurate, it would suggest that the Floyd *were* in France at around this time.

Cymbaline, 2.56, video

This video and audio tape is very likely to be a misnamed copy of the 16 June broadcast. Of this we are at present uncertain.

• **Grote Zaal, De Doelen, Rotterdam, Holland.**

SUNDAY 21

• **Het Kolpinghuis, Nijmegen, Holland.**

One of the more difficult venues to pronounce (for those not too good at Dutch).

MONDAY 22 – TUESDAY 23

• **RTBF Studios, Brussels, Belgium.**

Recording sessions for Belgian television.

THURSDAY 25

• **Stadsschouwburg, Maastricht, Holland.**

FRIDAY 26 – SUNDAY 28

• **Theatre 140, Brussels, Belgium.**

OCTOBER

• **Live take of 'Interstellar Overdrive' pressed up as an EMIdisc acetate but not given a general release.**

It was intended that it appear on *Ummagumma*, but was cut due to lack of space. A copy of the acetate was given to John Peel (who probably didn't play it or we'd have a copy!), but it was stolen sometime later ...
    Roger Waters in an interview with Richard Williams published in *Melody Maker* said when discussing *Ummagumma*:

> Only one song is missing: the famous 'Interstellar Overdrive', which, says Roger, 'we don't dig very much.'
>   But there are plans to produce 2,000 acetates of the 'live' version of this song, which was left off the album, and distribute to the many people who have shown an interest in it.

'We gave one to John Peel and he really liked it, so we may make up these acetates for people.'[183]

FRIDAY 3

• **Birmingham University, Birmingham, West Midlands, UK.**

SATURDAY 4

• **Reading University, Reading, Berkshire, UK.**

MONDAY 6

• **Syd Barrett's *The Madcap Laughs* is assembled into its final running order.**

Syd and Dave put the final album master together. It had taken two months from the completion of mixing to get the album compiled. Malcolm Jones: 'Syd was a bit pissed off with the delay, as I was!'

FRIDAY 10

• **Loughborough University, Loughborough, Leicestershire, UK.**

SATURDAY 11

• **Internationales Essener Pop And Blues Festival, Grugahalle, Essen, West Germany.**

The band performed on the third day of the festival, and were second on the bill to the Nice. Also appearing on the 11th were Deep Purple, Aynsley Dunbar Retaliation, Taste, Keef Hartley, Hardin And York, Amon Duul II and Cuby's Blues Band (later to achieve fame as Cuby And The Blizzards).

27.27, Astronomy Domine, 8.47, Green Is The Colour / Careful With That Axe, Eugene, 10.09, Interstellar Overdrive, 5.45

'Interstellar Overdrive' cuts during a quiet passage. While most tapes in circulation appear to have been recorded in a toilet somewhere at the back of the site, if collectors wish to work hard for it, low generation tapes are of very good quality.

ANNOUNCER: ... The Pink Floyd ><

RW: ... 'cos our equipment was so late arriving you'll have to bear with us while we tune up. >< This is a song called 'Astronomy Domine'.

Astronomy Domine

RW: Thank you. This is two things here, one of which is quite a new song called 'Green Is The Colour', and the other is an instrumental which is called 'Careful With That Axe, Eugene'.

Green Is The Colour / Careful With That Axe, Eugene

RW: Thank you. This is an instrumental, and it's ... this is obviously ... it's called 'Interstellar Overdrive'.

Interstellar Overdrive

SATURDAY 18

• **University College London, London, UK.**

WEDNESDAY 22

• **Nottingham University, Nottingham, Nottinghamshire, UK.**

FRIDAY 24

• **Fillmore North, Locarno Ballroom, Sunderland, UK.**

SATURDAY 25

• **Actuel Festival, Mont de l'Enclus, Amougies, Belgium.**

The festival was to last five days and the Floyd would top a bill of ten bands on its second and main night, Saturday – a measure of their stature. The poster for the gig may be found in the 18 October issue of *Melody Maker*.

14.03, Green Is The Colour / Careful With That Axe, Eugene

It is generally agreed that this recording is taken from the *Music Power* soundtrack. Video copies of this film have yet to become available. We are presently sceptical that it is in fact sourced from the film soundtrack.

If the recording is from the movie it must have been recorded in a cinema or some other public place as audience chatter disrupts the recording and Roger's scream massively distorts. On balance, it would seem more likely that this recording is bogus but contemporary (though this should be informed by Roger's 'some time ago' comment, which he repeatedly makes in much later recordings). It also seems peculiar that the two parts of the recording are from different sources, and unavailable as a whole.

Listen out for Roger's repeatedly muttering 'careful ...' before the scream and Dave's interesting guitar work towards the end.

JEAN GEORGAKARAKOS AND JEAN LUC YOUNG
PRESENT
THE FIRST PARIS MUSIC FESTIVAL
actuel
ORGANIZED BY
BYG
RECORDS
AND
RICARD
ANISETTE

OCT. 24/28 · 60 HOURS OF MUSIC · 60 FRANCS

**INTRODUCED BY FRANK ZAPPA
& PIERRE LATTES**

FRI 24 (NIGHT)
POP MUSIC
TEN YEARS AFTER
COLOSSEUM
AYNSLEY DUNBAR RETALIATION
ALAN JACK CIVILIZATION
FREE JAZZ
ART ENSEMBLE OF CHICAGO
SUNNY MURRAY
BURTON GREENE
360 DEGREE MUSIC EXPERIENCE
NEW MUSIC
FREE MUSIC GROUP

SAT 25 (NIGHT)
POP MUSIC
PINK FLOYD
FREEDOM
KEITH RELF'S RENAISSANCE
ALEXIS KORNER & THE NEW CHURCH
BLUES CONVENTION
FREE JAZZ
GRACHAN MONCUR III
ARTHUR JONES
JOACHIM KUHN
DON CHERRY

SUN 26 (AFTERNOON)
FRENCH POP GROUPS
MARTIN CIRCUS
ALAN JACK CIVILIZATION
TRIANGLE
WE FREE
CRUCIFERIUS
INDESCRIPTIBLE CHAOS RAMPANT

AMPLIFICATION BY STANDEL
(INTERIM SPECTACLE:
MAX AUER & CLAUDIA SAUMADE)

ENVIRONMENTAL DIRECTION :
JACQUES CHERIX

COORDINATION : BRIGITTE GUICHARD

SUN 26 (NIGHT)
POP MUSIC
NICE
CARAVAN
BLOSSOM TOES
AME SON
FREE JAZZ
ARCHIE SHEPP
KENNETH TERROADE
ANTHONY BRAXTON
NEW MUSIC
GERM (P.MARIETAN)

MON 27 (NIGHT)
POP MUSIC
YES
PRETTY THINGS
CHICKEN SHACK
SAM APPLE PIE
FROGEATERS
DAVID ALLEN GROUP
KEITH TIPPETT GROUP
FREE JAZZ
PHAROAH SANDERS
DAVE BURRELL
JOHN SURMAN
CLIFFORD THORNTON
SONNY SHARROCK
NEW MUSIC
ACTING TRIO

TUE 28 (NIGHT)
POP MUSIC
SOFT MACHINE
CAPTAIN BEEFHEART
EAST OF EDEN
FAT MATTRESS
ZOO
FREE JAZZ
ALAN SILVA
ROBIN KENYATTA
CHRIS MACGREGOR
STEVE LACEY
DAVE BURRELL BIG BAND
NEW MUSIC
MUSICA ELETTRONICA VIVA

SPONSORED BY RADIO-TÉLÉ-LUXEMBOURG (PARIS)
TICKETS AND INFORMATIONS:
BYG RECORDS, 6 NEW COMPTON STREET LONDON WC 2, TEL : 01-836 81 71/2
29 AVENUE DE FRIEDLAND PARIS 8°, TEL : ELY 66-03 / 48-22
P.S. THANKS FRANK & HERB !

Advertisement in *Melody Maker*, 18 October 1969

The next two things we're gonna do we're gonna do together, and one of them is a song off the soundtrack of a film called *More*, and it's called 'Green Is The Colour', and the other thing is an instrumental we did some time ago and it's called 'Careful With That Axe, Eugene'.

Green Is The Colour / Careful With That Axe, Eugene

There is also a separately sourced tape which was apparently recorded in a cinema in Amsterdam in 1975/6.

5.10, Set The Controls For The Heart Of The Sun

Set The Controls For The Heart Of The Sun

Thank you.

FRIDAY 31

- **Pink Floyd are reported as travelling from Detroit to London to attend a Science Fiction and Voodoo Festival.**

Unlikely. Rick does however recall in January 1970 that 'While we were in America we were asked to play at a voodoo convention. Sadly we couldn't make it because the American Musician's Union wouldn't let us play. It would have been marvellous. All the voodoo cults from all over the world meeting up with all the science-fiction writers.'[184]

NOVEMBER

SATURDAY 1

- *Ummagumma* **released in the UK.**

Melody Maker were a month early with their release date: on 30 August they reported that it would be issued 'at the end of September'.
   If you have the equipment, try slowing down 'Several Species' to half speed.

- **A 'major' band interview by Richard Williams is published in** *Melody Maker.*

Perhaps the most interesting comment by Waters in the interview was that 'we'll be in the studios for ten days in December. I don't know exactly what we'll be doing, but it will probably be a life-cycle thing of some kind.'
   It is known, of course, that the Floyd worked on *Rollo* and *Zabriskie Point* in December. It would seem reasonable to suggest that the band had a vague

or general intent at the time to make a recording of something like 'The Man and The Journey' suite. Looking at their December schedule, there was clearly time enough to at least have begun recording such a project. The 'ten days' are certainly possible. It might, however, be the case that the intended project, whatever it might have been, was superseded by *Zabriskie Point* (which was recorded in Rome, of course) or the studio time could have been cancelled.

Finally, it might be the case that the time was dedicated to putting together the embryonic form of *The Amazing Pudding*. Roger did spend some time at the end of November, into December, working with Ron Geesin on *The Body* – perhaps this was what he was referring to … suggestions abound!

Mentions may also be found about the 'Interstellar Overdrive acetate' and the '*Rollo* project'; quotes are used elsewhere.

- **Radio Lille, Amougies, France.**

Details at this point are somewhat sketchy. A local radio station is said to have interviewed the band for broadcast on this date. It is probable that the interview was recorded in mid-September.[185]

- **Manchester University, Manchester, Lancashire, UK.**

FRIDAY 7

- **Waltham Forest Technical College, London, UK.**

SATURDAY 8

- **Leeds University, Leeds, Yorkshire, UK.**

SUNDAY 16

- **Recording for *Zabriskie Point* soundtrack, Rome, Italy.**

We are indebted to David Fricke's excellent accompanying notes to the remastered double soundtrack album, released in October 1997, for clarifying the previously vague facts surrounding the recording of the music for *Zabriskie Point*.

The 16th saw the successful recording of 'Love Scene – Version 4' and 'Love Scene – Version 6', which appeared on the above mentioned album, but probably doesn't mark the beginning of the *Zabriskie* sessions.

The band's schedule suggests that any earlier studio time could have taken place anywhere between the 11th and 25th, and is also reasonably evidenced by virtue of their already having completed at least three other pieces of music by this date (if, as seems reasonable the 'Versions' were titled in chronological order), and Fricke's later reference to an 'even earlier take'. Apparently the band tried 'damn near everything' to fulfil Antonioni's wants for a musical backdrop to his surreal love scene.

That 'even earlier take', judging by Fricke's description, is extremely likely to be the same track that bootleggers have since referred to as 'Oneone'.

SATURDAY 22

- **An interview with David Gilmour is published in *Disc & Music Echo*.**

He talks in broad terms about the Floyd's music and their direction.[186]

WEDNESDAY 26

- **Friar's, Civic Hall, Dunstable, Bedfordshire, UK.**

Advertisement in *Melody Maker*, 15 November 1969

The usual venue given for this gig is Friar's, Aylesbury, Buckinghamshire. However on this occasion Friar's, 'the progressive rock organisation', were operating in Dunstable. The confusion may have arisen due to tickets being available from the Aylesbury address.

THURSDAY 27

- **Liverpool University, Liverpool, Merseyside, UK.**

November 1969

FRIDAY 28

- **Refectory Building, Brunel University, Uxbridge, Middlesex, UK.**

An advert for the same appeared in *Melody Maker* on 22 November and again on the 29th. The band were supported by Gracious and Pongo's Litter amongst others.

Advertisement in *Melody Maker*, 29 November 1969

SUNDAY 30

- **Sundays at the Lyceum, The Lyceum, The Strand, London, UK.**

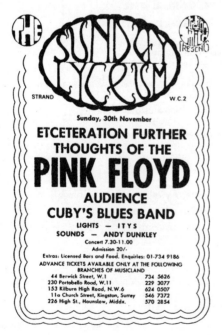

Advertisement in *Melody Maker*, 29 November 1969

- **Roger Waters and Ron Geesin recording for *The Body* at Geesin's home studio.**

Ron Geesin would remix the sessions for the album following the completion of the *Atom Heart Mother* album in July 1970.

- **'Octopus' / 'Golden Hair' single by Syd Barrett released in the UK and Europe only.**

Syd was asked in an interview in *Melody Maker* on 31 January 1970, how well the single was doing – 'I haven't noticed ... I don't think it was necessarily a good idea to do a single, but it was done.'

- **'Point Me At The Sky' promotional film, Belgian TV.**

Some collectors are quite sure that an alternative to the standard 'biplane' promotional film exists which was originally sourced from, or made by, Belgian television. We have not come across it.

- **Recording for *Zabriskie Point* film soundtrack, Rome, Italy.**

Recording, which had begun in early November, continued in earnest, returning to certain tracks which were also laid down, as evidenced by the dates recently attributed to 'Heart Beat, Pig Meat', 'Crumbling Land' and 'Come In Number 51, Your Time Is Up'.

Rick, interviewed for *Beat Instrumental* in January 1970 was asked how the band approached the recordings:

> It's all improvised, but nonetheless it was really hard work. We had each piece of music and we did about, say, six takes of each, and he'd choose the best. Antonioni's not hard to work with ... but he's a perfectionist. He was with us in the studios every night for two weeks from nine in the evening until eight in the next morning ... every night for two weeks to get 20 minutes of music, it was hard, but it was worth it.

Nick Mason, reproduced in *Through The Eyes Of ...* – 'It was a terrible experience. Antonioni was a right bastard.'

The result of the sessions which are available to the collector were three tracks included on the original album, supplemented recently by four more on the reissued version; four outtakes, which while unreleased, are available on bootleg; and the three tracks included on the movie soundtrack, which again differ from the other versions available.[187]

Tantalisingly, David Fricke, author of the notes included with the 1997 reissue, refers to at least 50 minutes of unissued pieces which remained in the 'vault' before he issued his 25 minutes.

Our calculators suggest that the outtakes listed below, Fricke's 25, and the alternate versions in the film itself add up to 53 min. 42 sec. worth of music (in crude terms) – make of it what you will!

Unreleased outtakes from 'Zabriskie Point', 21.39, Love Song – Early Version (Oneone), 7.05, Fingal's Cave, 1.50, Crumbling Land (variation), 6.28, Unknown Song (variation, also known as Rain In The Country), 6.13

The outtake of 'Crumbling Land' features an extended outro not found on the album version. It is likely that the outtake variation on 'Unknown Song' was recorded on December 6, at the same time as the version which was eventually released officially.

The versions of the songs featured in the movie are not those included on the album or other sources – in detail the film's music consisted of:

7.04, Heart Beat, Pig Meat (a different mix, most notably without the fanfare following the reference to 'New York dry-cleaners'), 2.46, Crumbling Land (edited, with only one verse and chorus featured; a more 'laid-back' take, with different, harmonised 'lazy' vocals), 0.34, Come In Number 51, Your Time Is Up (different lead guitar and a less bass heavy mix, snared drums – far clearer than the album), 3.27, Come In Number 51, Your Time Is Up reprise, 0.37.

Also mentioned on the Floyd's recording sheets for the end of 1969 was 'Highway Song', which could well be the proper title for 'Rain In the Country', as well as the unknown track 'Jews Harp And Windchimes'. To these, Fricke adds the existence of 'a six-minute hymn played by Rick Wright', known previously to many collectors of live performances as 'The Violent Sequence', giving it the alternative, perhaps original, title 'Riot Scene'.

SATURDAY 6

- **Recording for *Zabriskie Point* film soundtrack, Rome, Italy.**

The sleevenotes to the reissued *Zabriskie Point* soundtrack give the 6th as the date upon which 'Unknown Song' was recorded.

While this may appear to make one or other of the events on this day impossible, it is reconcilable given the fact that recordings are often listed by the date upon which they are logged into a tape library, rather than the actual date of completion.

- **Afan Festival of Progressive Music, Afan Lido Indoor Sports Centre, Port Talbot, South Wales, UK.**

A copy of the advert for the gig may be found in *Le Livre Du Pink Floyd*.[188]

```
┌─────────────────────────────────────────────┐
│           J.C. PROMOTIONS LTD.                │
│      (Wales' Leading Agency)   present        │
│     AFAN FESTIVAL PROGRESSIVE MUSIC           │
│            SOUTH WALES                         │
│           PENTANGLE                            │
│ TERRY COX, BERT JANSCH, JACQUI McSHEE, JOHN RENBOURN, DANNY THOMPSON │
│           PINK FLOYD                           │
│   EAST OF EDEN      SAM APPLE PIE              │
│   SAMSON        DADDY LONG LEGS                │
│              (On Tour From America)            │
│           SOLID STATE                         │
│ on SAT., 6th DECEMBER, 1969—Doors open 5, commence 6.30-12 approx. │
│   At AFAN LIDO INDOOR SPORTS CENTRE, PORT TALBOT │
│              Seats: 25/-, 20/-, 15/-          │
│ For tickets, send P.O. and S.A.E. to J.C. Promotions (Tickets), 1 Kee Club │
│   Lane, Bridgend, Glam., or direct from Kee Club or Afan Lido. │
└─────────────────────────────────────────────┘
```

Advertisement in *Melody Maker*, 29 November 1969

The Floyd were to be second billed, for a change, to Pentangle.

FRIDAY 12

• **Recording for *Zabriskie Point* film soundtrack, Rome, Italy.**

'Country Song', later released on the 'deluxe' edition of the soundtrack album, is listed as having been recorded on this date – our comments above should however be borne in mind.

LATE

• **The Floyd worked on the music for a cartoon series by Alan Aldridge called *Rollo*.**

A pilot for the series of seventeen 30-minute shows was completed, but the project never seems to have seen the light of day. Miles provides a very detailed description, after *zigzag* 32.

The first recorded reference to the project seems to have been in Richard Williams' *Melody Maker* interview on 1 November.

We're now going to do the music for an Alan Aldridge TV cartoon series, called *Rollo*, which will be in 26 half-hour instalments. It's being put together by a private company for sale to the States, and I [Waters] saw the pilot pro-gramme recently – it's rather Yellow Submarine-ish, about a little boy in space.

We're not going to sit down and tape 13 hours of music, of course. What we'll probably do is record a four-hour 'kit' of music, which can be fitted to the film – like there'll be so many take-offs, so many landings, so many impacts, and so forth.

We'll be doing the dubbing ourselves, and that takes a hell of a long time.

Rick spoke about the *Rollo* project in *Beat Instrumental* a month later.[189] The magazine reported on the show as having been sold all over the States on the strength of the pilot. 'It's really incredible,' said Rick, 'You know what Aldridge's drawings are like. It's about a boy, Rollo, who goes around space with Professor Creator ... I think that's his name ... who collects galactic animals for his zoo.'

- *Music Power*, **a film directed by Jerome Laperrousaz, released.**

Previously mentioned, the film documents the Actuel Festival, Belgium, on 25 October 1969. It is often noted that it included footage of Frank Zappa jamming with the band on 'Interstellar Overdrive'. If this were the case, how come all recordings purporting to be from the soundtrack omit this, the most interesting sequence?

1970
Are The Controls Set?

- *European Music Revolution*, documentary directed by Jerome Laperrousaz, released.

Apparently the film featured footage of the band, but no actual music.

- 'Pink Floyd Progressing, But Starting At The Top Again'. A lengthy interview with Rick appears in *Beat Instrumental* magazine, UK.

> I'm very happy in what I'm doing, but I would like to try lots of other things. Sometimes I feel like leaving the business completely. Doing something else … but always connected with music.[190]

- *The Madcap Laughs* by Syd Barrett released in the UK.

- EMI Studio outtake recorded with Kevin Ayres and Syd Barrett.

Religious Experience, 2.37

The track is incomplete and cuts abruptly.

'Religious Experience' has appeared on a number of bootleg compilations and is often known by its official release title, 'Singing A Song In The Morning' – a lift from the lyrics. We also understand that an even more prominent 'Syd Mix' exists only on an EMI 10-inch acetate which is in somebody's collection. Syd was effectively mixed out, apparently, for the official release, which may be found on Ayres' *Odd Ditties* compilation and the *Art School Dancing* Harvest compilation LP. Perhaps we're perpetuating a myth. There isn't any 'official' biographical evidence confirming its existence, though Bernard White is confident that it is genuine.

Phil Smee added to the argument in the fanzine *Chapter 24*. Smee had been responsible for putting together a Kevin Ayres compilation for EMI and looked into its authenticity at the time:

> We went right back through the archive to the original multi-track tape and only the take used on the single was recorded at the session. No alternative or unreleased versions exist and the tape box and notes helpfully give no clues as to the identity of the lead guitarist.
> I once heard an acetate of this that had a slightly different mix with a louder

guitar sound. I didn't notice any Syd vocals though. Perhaps it was this version that lead to the rumours of an alternate take.[191]

Stylistically, the copy that is in general circulation should be taken seriously: it could very well be the Madcap about 1969 (the date that some give it) who runs up and down the scales in the guitar solo, though we can't find any discernible evidence that he does the backing vocals as well, as some suggest. The rest of the song could not be said to be similar to any other Barrett work: those who are familiar with Kevin Ayres, would say that it is reasonably typical of his. Perhaps, on the downside, it's like 'Bananamour'[192] – simply a tribute.

SATURDAY 10

- *Melody Maker*, UK, publishes a 'Blind Date' with Roger Waters.[193]

In a 'blind' listening Roger gave his opinion on 'Let's Work Together' by Canned Heat, 'Hold On' by The Rascals, Flaming Youth's 'Guide Me, Orion', 'I'm Too Busy' by the New York Rock And Roll Ensemble (!), 'For As Long As You Need Me' by The Art Movement, The Kenny Clarke – Francy Boland Big Band's 'Solarisation', 'Evil Woman' by Black Sabbath, as well as Barrett's 'Terrapin'.

- **University of Nottingham, Nottingham, Nottinghamshire, UK.**

SATURDAY 17

- **Lawns Centre, Cottingham, Yorkshire, UK.**

SUNDAY 18

- **Fairfield Halls, Croydon, Surrey, UK.**

It is generally agreed that this concert marked the premiere of 'The Amazing Pudding' – sadly it cuts seconds before its climax.

119.15, Astronomy Domine, 9.04, The Violent Sequence, 15.12 [Heart Beat, Pig Meat, 7.55, The Violent Sequence, 7.17], Set The Controls For The Heart Of The Sun, 14.02, Biding My Time, 5.53, The Amazing Pudding, 25.21, Careful With That Axe, Eugene, 10.58, The Embryo, 9.39, Main Theme From More, 12.54, A Saucerful Of Secrets, 16.32

A second (older in collecting terms) source also exists:

128.00, Astronomy Domine, 9.33, The Violent Sequence, 15.35, Set The Controls For The Heart Of The Sun, 14.23, Careful With That Axe, Eugene, 11.15, The Embryo, 11.39, Main Theme From More, 13.15, Biding My Time, 5.57, A Saucerful Of Secrets, 16.48

There's not a lot of point in having the older source as the quality is significantly worse (the new version could hardly be described to be brilliant). This set, seemingly, is the lengthiest effort so far that an illicit taper felt able to record. Both this and the quality suggest that it was the first recording now in circulation to be made on compact-cassette equipment, which after some twenty years' development in terms of fidelity, most of us still use today.

MONDAY 19

* **The Dome, Brighton, East Sussex, UK.**

FRIDAY 23

* **Théâtre des Champs-Elysées, Paris, France.**

This concert was broadcast by ORTF Radio, France.

Cameron Watson, a friend of the band who used to work for Bryan Morrison's Agency, recalled the reaction to this gig:

> The audience couldn't believe their ears; you could hear the sound going round the room from behind. I was sitting on the stage on Dave's side. When they began to play the first bars of the 'Main Theme from *More*', the audience became almost hysterical. Dave looked round and asked me, 'Hey, what's up?' I said, 'Well, you're like gods here, you know!' – and the concert got better and better …'[194]

The complete ORTF Radio Broadcast (edited), 62.04, Green Is The Colour / Careful With That Axe, Eugene, 8.55, The Violent Sequence, 4.23, Biding My Time, 5.10, The Amazing Pudding, 18.07, Daybreak, 6.24, Doing It!, 6.04, Sleeping, 6.07, Main Theme From More, 6.40

>Green Is The Colour / Careful With That Axe, Eugene /
The Violent Sequence >< Biding My Time >< [Birdsong intro into]
The Amazing Pudding

Thank you. ><

Daybreak / Doing It! / Sleeping >< Main Theme

Edited copy off vinyl, 37.17, Green Is The Colour / Careful With That Axe, Eugene, 8.55, The Violent Sequence, 4.23, Biding My Time, 5.16, The Amazing Pudding, 18.41

An excerpt was broadcast on *Tout Peut Arriver*, Europa 1 Radio 1 May 1982, with comments from Nick and Dave.

Tout Peut Arriver, 4.47, Doing It!, 2.58

January 1970

An excerpt from the concert was also rebroadcast on Europa 1 radio, France on 30 April 1995. The quality of this recording makes it essential of course, and is a 'must-have' item. We believe that more than the following two tracks were broadcast, but few people seem to have made recordings.

Europa 1 rebroadcast, 20.06, The Amazing Pudding, 15.36, The Violent Sequence, 3.30

> [Dave chats in French.] We only wrote this last week!
>
> **The Amazing Pudding**
>
> Thank you. ><
> Le Pink Floyd, Hotel de Champs Elysées a Paris >< le 23.01.70.
>
> **The Violent Sequence**

SATURDAY 24

- **Théâtre des Champs-Elysées, Paris, France.**

SATURDAY 31

- **'Confusion And Mr Barrett', an interview with Syd appears in *Melody Maker* newspaper, UK.**

Syd commented that there were a few plans for him to do some appearances and there were 'vague ideas' about a group, but there was 'nothing positive enough to talk about'.

FEBRUARY

MONDAY 2

- **Palais des Sports, Lyon, France.**

It may have been the case that excerpts from this concert were broadcast on Europa 1 Radio.

THURSDAY 5

- **Cardiff Arts Centre Benefit Event, Sophia Gardens Pavilion, Cardiff, South Glamorgan, Wales, UK.**

A copy of the ad for the gig may be found in *Le Livre Du Pink Floyd*.[195] The band were supported on this occasion by Quintessence and Daddy Longlegs.

SATURDAY 7

- **Royal Albert Hall, Kensington, London, UK.**

The advertisement for the concert, featuring the sun rising over the ocean between two tall cliffs, recalls the artwork from the 'Massed Gadgets Of Auximenes' 1969 tour programme.

A highly interesting programme was produced to promote the concert (and perhaps those others at the time). It features a two-page article written by Rick Sanders, who was later to pen the first full-length biography of the group, along with two otherwise unpublished photographs of the band who are seen alternately in the burnt remains of a garden shed (!) and an alleyway reminiscent of that featured on the cover of The Doors' *Strange Days* LP. As usual Sanders' writing is fine and insightful, particularly so, as it is rare to find early accounts of the band's beginnings.

Of the Floyd at the time he writes that:

> They have also moved on to the stage where their work is beginning to attract attention from 'serious' musicians – which isn't to say that they don't consider themselves serious, however. They do; but they see no reason to be glum and sombre about it. Plans are afoot for the group to work in collaboration with the Royal Philharmonic Orchestra on writing and performing, and they are going to be doing the music for a forthcoming production of the National Theatre.

Too bad this didn't come off!

Melody Maker's review, published on the 14th, describes their set as comprising 'Sysyphus', 'A Saucerful Of Secrets', 'The Embryo', 'Main Theme From More', 'Careful With That Axe, Eugene', and 'Set The Controls For The Heart Of The Sun'. As bad reviews go, it's very good! Richard Williams complains that 'Richard Wright's 'Sysyphus' for instance, had it's opening and closing theme statements almost ruined by David Gilmour's slipshod pitching, and an apparently unconscious disagreement over time between Roger Waters, Nick Mason and Wright, all of whose downbeats arrived separately like raindrops in the barrel.'

SUNDAY 8

- **Manchester Opera House, Manchester, Lancashire, UK.**

WEDNESDAY 11

- **Town Hall, Birmingham, West Midlands, UK.**

Tape source, 111.44, The Embryo, 11.51, Main Theme From More, 11.48, Careful With That Axe, Eugene, 10.18, Sysyphus, 8.34, The Violent Sequence, 26.08 [Heart Beat, Pig Meat, 6.11, Sleeping, 6.43, The Labyrinths Of Auximenes, 4.36, The Violent Sequence, 8.38], Set The Controls For The Heart Of The Sun, 13.24, The Amazing Pudding, 23.36

... new song and its called 'The Embryo'.

The Embryo

Thank you. This is 'Main Theme' from a film called *More*, shortly released ... [Drowned out by crowd.]

Main Theme

[Tune ups.]

Careful With That Axe, Eugene

Thank you. >< Those of you, anybody's got *Ummagumma*, well [...] by Rick called 'Sysyphus' [...] not quite like the record.

Sysyphus< The Violent Sequence

Thank you. >< This is an oldie an' its called 'Set The Controls For The Heart Of The Sun'.

Set The Controls For The Heart Of The Sun<

[Tune ups.] ><

The Amazing Pudding<

An edited version featuring all of the tracks except 'Set The Controls For The Heart Of The Sun', has been pressed onto vinyl, and while not wonderful, it is of slightly higher quality. It's a serious shame that the available recording of the concert is of such dodgy quality, as the middle section, which is largely improvised, is extremely interesting.

Vinyl source, 86.28, The Embryo, 10.30, Main Theme From More, 10.10, Careful With That Axe, Eugene, 8.51, Sysyphus, 10.21, The Violent Sequence, 22.13 [Heart Beat, Pig Meat, 5.32, Sleeping, 5.55, The Labyrinths Of Auximenes, 3.59, The Violent Sequence, 6.47], The Amazing Pudding, 21.49

SATURDAY 14

- **King's Hall, The Town Hall, Stoke-on-Trent, Staffordshire, UK.**

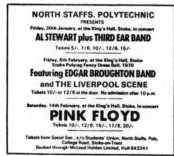

The show was promoted by an advertisement which appeared in *Melody Maker*, 7 February 1970.

SUNDAY 15
_____

- The Liverpool Empire, Liverpool, Merseyside, UK.

TUESDAY 17
_____

- City Hall, Newcastle, Tyne & Wear, UK.

SUNDAY 22
_____

- The Electric Garden, Glasgow, Lanarkshire, Scotland, UK.

MONDAY 23
_____

- University of Edinburgh, Edinburgh, Scotland, UK.

TUESDAY 24
_____

- **Syd Barrett records his first session for John Peel's *Top Gear* programme at BBC Maida Vale 4, London, UK.**

The session was produced by John Walters and engineered by Tony Wilson. Tracks from the show were first broadcast on 14 March.

THURSDAY 26
_____

- **Syd Barrett recording session, EMI, Abbey Road Studios, London, UK.**

Take 1 of 'Baby Lemonade', guitar and vocal double track was recorded. This was to appear as one of the bonus tracks on *Barrett* when it was remastered for CD. The same version was embellished and appeared on the original album.

Also completed on this date was 'Maisie', take 2 of which was released on the *Barrett* LP. Take 1 was a false start and both versions appeared on bootleg vinyl in 1996. Take 1 came complete with studio announcements, while the version of take 2 on bootleg was mixed quite differently to the *Barrett* version and contains a couple of extra lines that were evidently mixed out on the LP.

3.31, Maisie take 1, 0.10, Maisie take 2, 2.45

At some point during these sessions it is supposed that Syd recorded four versions (some of which were probably false starts or were unfinished) of 'Bob Dylan Blues'. Phil Smee commented in *Chapter 24* that 'I heard a tape of this a long time ago. It was about 4–5 minutes long and Syd played it in a sort of "Bob Dylan" style, similar to the sort of mid-range performance of "Long Gone".'

The tape, which was a demo for Syd's second album, was at some point taken away by David Gilmour, and most assume that he still has it. It also included another lost piece called 'Living Alone'. It has been suggested that two versions of this track exist, one being a solo demo and the other with the *Barrett* LP band backing him.

Syd also attempted a recording of 'Millionaire', sometimes known as 'She Was A Millionaire', a track that he first recorded and played when he was with the Floyd in 1967. Phil Smee doesn't comment on the solo version's similarity or otherwise:

> This is a backing track only. It isn't really a releasable recording as such, just a rough run-through. The trouble was it was so vague; there wasn't a strong enough chord structure you could hang a tune on. To be honest it would have been too boring to include it [in the *Crazy Diamond* box set].[196]

FRIDAY 27

• **Syd Barrett recording session, EMI, Abbey Road Studios, London, UK.**

Recording sessions for 'Baby Lemonade'. Evidently this was quite a tough song to get right as at least 15 takes were attempted. Take 9 was released as a bonus track on the remastered *Opel* CD, while take 15 was that used on the *Barrett* LP, with overdubs added on 2 April.

Also recorded on this date was 'I Never Lied To You'. Two versions of take 1 have been released officially. The first, featuring guitar and vocal only, is found as a bonus track on the *Barrett* remaster, while the second was that selected for the original *Barrett* LP. This second version has overdubs and a new vocal, both recorded later on 2 April.

Another track recorded on this date was 'Waving My Arms In The Air', take 1 of which appeared, with overdubs recorded on 2 April, on the *Barrett* LP. A sparser version, without overdubs features as a bonus track on the *Barrett* CD remaster.

SATURDAY 28

• **Leeds University, Leeds, Yorkshire, UK.**

MARCH

SUNDAY 1 – THURSDAY 5

• **EMI, Studio 2, Abbey Road, London, UK.**

It is likely that this is the date upon which the band began work on the *Atom Heart Mother* album (though they may have been in the studio slightly earlier, at the end of February). The first track which they recorded was the as-yet-untitled title track. During March and early April they would record a rudimentary backing track, with drums, bass and guitar, the results of which they handed over to Ron Geesin for further work while they were on tour in the States. Nothing however was done while they were away as Geesin felt he needed them around, and the result was that it was rushed upon their return.

Ron Geesin would later describe how the band at the time 'were creatively exhausted, simply because of the pressure on them to constantly perform concerts and create albums to justify the huge outlay EMI had made on them. They were getting popular but they just couldn't come up with this next thing. There was no other reason why they would have asked me to get involved if they couldn't have come up with the goods themselves.' [197]

FRIDAY 6

* **Imperial College, London, UK.**

An advert in *Melody Maker* shows the support act as Juicy Lucy.[198]

SATURDAY 7

* **University of Bristol Arts Festival, Colston Hall, Bristol, Avon, UK.**

SUNDAY 8

* **Mother's, Birmingham, West Midlands, UK.**

MONDAY 9

* **City (Oval) Hall, Sheffield, Yorkshire, UK.**

WEDNESDAY 11 – TUESDAY 24

* **European Tour: West Germany, Sweden and possibly elsewhere.**

WEDNESDAY 11

* **Stadthalle, Offenbach, West Germany.**

THURSDAY 12

* **Auditorium Maximum, Hamburg Universität, Hamburg, West Germany.**

Sourced from vinyl, the recording of this gig should be viewed with a healthy dose of suspicion. Often mislabelled as being from Hyde Park 1970, it would have been helpful to have had comments from Waters, as we have for the next three concerts, which all closely resemble one another, allowing comparisons to be made.

39.43, The Embryo, 8.31, Interstellar Overdrive, 11.38, The Amazing Pudding, 19.25

FRIDAY 13

- **Konzert Saal, Technische Universität, West Berlin, West Germany.**

117.45, Astronomy Domine, 10.21, Careful With That Axe, Eugene, 9.27, Cymbaline, 8.56, A Saucerful Of Secrets, 15.52, The Embryo, 9.32, Interstellar Overdrive, 15.12, Set The Controls For The Heart Of The Sun, 16.14, Atom Heart Mother, 19.46, Blues, 5.42

OK. This is called [German translation?] This is called 'Astronomy Domine'.

Astronomy Domine

Thank you. >< ... off our last LP *Ummagumma*, and it's called 'Careful With That Axe, Eugene'.

Careful With That Axe, Eugene

[Roger 'shushes' the audience about ten seconds in.] Thank you. >< This is a song we recorded for a French film called *More* an' it's called 'Cymbaline'.

Cymbaline

Thank you. ><

A Saucerful Of Secrets

>< ... another new song and it's about an embryo.

The Embryo

Thank you. >< This is another instrumental number an' it's off the first LP we made an' it's called 'Interstellar Overdrive'. ><

Interstellar Overdrive

Thank you. >< This is another song. It's called 'Set The Controls For The Heart Of The Sun'.

Set The Controls For The Heart Of The Sun

>< And it's gonna be ... and it's, and ... an' it's ... and. And it's gonna be on our next album. Are you nearly ready, Rick? Richard? RICHARD?! [whispers] Richard ... are you ready? You ready?! Are you ready? Rick. Richard. Richard. Richard, are you ready? [Someone laughs heartily and the audience claps excitedly.] OK.

The Amazing Pudding

Thank you. [...] ><

>Blues<

- **Syd Barrett on John Peel's *Top Gear* show, BBC Radio 1, London, UK.**

Broadcast between 3.00 and 5.00 pm, the show was recorded on 24 February. Four out of the five recordings made on the 24th were broadcast on this date; the fifth, 'Two Of A Kind', was aired later on 30 May. The entry in the 'A–Z' section of *Through The Eyes Of ...* suggests that 'Two Of A Kind' was written by Rick Wright.

The band featured Syd Barrett (guitar, vocals), David Gilmour (organ, bass, guitar), Jerry Shirley (drums) and possibly Alan Styles (guitar). Styles was not listed on the session contract, and is only rumoured to have been present. The complete session was officially released by Strange Fruit records in June 1988.

- **Meisteringer Halle, Nuremberg, West Germany.**

The same set as the 13th, bar the absence of 'Blues'. It is interesting to note how some tracks have become shorter (which could of course just be down to tape speed), whereas others are longer. The pieces are consistently and distinctly shorter on the 17th.

110.12, Astronomy Domine, 9.07, Careful With That Axe, Eugene, 9.09, Cymbaline, 10.27, A Saucerful Of Secrets, 16.16, The Embryo, 9.44, Interstellar Overdrive, 14.28, Set The Controls For The Heart Of The Sun, 12.41, The Amazing Pudding, 21.37

Astronomy Domine

K'you. This next thing is a track ... a track off our last album, *Ummagumma*, and it's called 'Careful With That Axe, Eugene'.

Careful With That Axe, Eugene

Thank you.

Cymbaline ><

This is going to be the last thing we do in this half of the concert. It's off our LP before last an' it's the title track and it's called 'A Saucerful Of Secrets'.

A Saucerful Of Secrets

Thank you. See you ... >< ... new song called 'The Embryo'.

The Embryo >< Interstellar Overdrive ><
Set The Controls For The Heart Of The Sun ><

[...] new tonight ... song called [...]

The Amazing Pudding

Thank you. >< [Guy recording the concert gives the date in German.]
[Mics seem to be malfunctioning throughout the recording.]

SUNDAY 15

- **Niedersachsenhalle, Hannover, West Germany.**

85.31, Set The Controls For The Heart Of The Sun, 11.20, Careful With That Axe, Eugene, 7.48, Cymbaline, 8.16, A Saucerful Of Secrets, 14.00, The Embryo, 9.10, Interstellar Overdrive, 13.10, The Amazing Pudding, 19.01

Set The Controls

Thank you. This next number appears on the live half of our album *Ummagumma*, it's called 'Careful With That Axe, Eugene'.

Careful With That Axe, Eugene

Thank you. A song that we recorded for a French film called *More*.

Cymbaline

Thank you. We're going to finish the first half now with a number; with the title track of the album *A Saucerful Of Secrets*.

A Saucerful Of Secrets

We'll be back soon. ><

The Embryo

Fine. This is called 'Interstellar Overdrive'.

Interstellar Overdrive

Thank you. This next thing is going to be the last thing we do and it's, erm, it's something we're recording at the moment for our next LP and consequently … [TAP immediately starts – enigmatic intro!]

The Amazing Pudding

THURSDAY 19 – SUNDAY 22

- **Scandinavian Tour.**

THURSDAY 19

- **Konserthuset, Stockholm, Sweden.**

So far nothing has come to our attention which pins this appearance down with certainty to this date; perhaps a Swedish reader would like to investigate further.

FRIDAY 20

• **Akademiska Föreningens Stora Sal, Olympen, Lund, Sweden.**

91.32, Astronomy Domine, 7.18, Careful With That Axe, Eugene, 9.21, Cymbaline, 9.00, A Saucerful Of Secrets, 12.55, The Embryo, 8.39, Set The Controls For The Heart Of The Sun, 11.07, Interstellar Overdrive, 13.11, The Amazing Pudding, 18.58

Astronomy Domine

Thank you. ><

Careful With That Axe, Eugene

Thank you. K'you … ><

Cymbaline

Thank you. ><

A Saucerful Of Secrets >< **The Embryo** >< **Interstellar Overdrive** >< **Set The Controls For The Heart Of The Sun** ><

… and it's a new thing we're in the process of recording at the moment for our next album.

The Amazing Pudding

Copies in circulation all seem to derive from vinyl or CD bootlegs.

SATURDAY 21

• **Tivolis Koncertsal, Copenhagen, Denmark.**

WEDNESDAY 25

• **EMI, Studio 2, Abbey Road, London, UK.**

Further work on *Atom Heart Mother*.
    According to Nick Schaffner, Syd and Geoff Motlow dropped in to watch the sessions at some point.[199]

MONDAY 30

• **Le Festival Musique Evolution, Hall des Expositions, Bourget, France.**

This concert was filmed for a French TV special on the festival, featuring the Floyd and others, broadcast on 16 April. A French RTL radio broadcast may also have been made, although this is unconfirmed.

APRIL

FRIDAY 3

- **Syd Barrett recording sessions, EMI, Abbey Road Studios, London, UK.**

  Recording 'Wolfpack', take 2 of which was used for the *Barrett* LP. 'Wolfpack' was reputedly Barrett's favourite track from the album.

TUESDAY 7

- **EMI, Studio 2, Abbey Road, London, UK.**

WEDNESDAY 8

- **The band embark upon their third American tour.**

THURSDAY 9

- **Fillmore East, Manhattan, New York City, New York, USA.**

  The band hired Fillmore's East and West themselves as the owner, Bill Graham, only offered them a forty-minute spot with three other groups.

FRIDAY 10

- **Aragon Ballroom, Chicago, Illinois, USA.**

SATURDAY 11

- **'Floyd In The Pink', an interview with Dave and Rick appears in** *Melody Maker* **magazine, UK.**

  Chris Welch wrote of how the band were soon to start work on music for the *Rollo* cartoon, which was clearly still in production at this point. Rick commented: It'll be a lot of work but we'll give them a stock of music to draw from for each episode.' Elsewhere in the article he complains that:

  > Our only real problem is the time factor. We just don't have enough time to do all the things we want. We are working too hard – incredibly hard since last November.[200]

- **State University of New York (SUNY), Stony Brook, Long Island, New York, USA.**

  68.23, Astronomy Domine, 9.56, Careful With That Axe, Eugene, 11.36,

Cymbaline, 11.55, The Amazing Pudding, 14.04, Set The Controls For The Heart Of The Sun, 14.24, A Saucerful Of Secrets, 5.03

'A Saucerful Of Secrets' as recorded at this concert is incomplete, with a convincing edit into the version commercially available on the *Ummagumma* LP. The timings above have been adjusted to account for this fact.

Right. This is called 'Astronomy Domine'.

Astronomy Domine

Thank you. ><

Careful With That Axe, Eugene

[Guy taping it tries to get it together with the girl he's next to with little luck.] ><

Cymbaline

Thank you. ><

The Amazing Pudding< [Girl almost switches tape off at the start.]
Set The Controls For The Heart Of The Sun

Thank you. >< This is going to be the last piece we play and it's off the album before last, before last. It's the title track and it's called 'A Saucerful Of Secrets'.

A Saucerful Of Secrets< [Continual audience chatter during quiet segments.]

THURSDAY 16

* *A L'affiche Du Monde*, **French TV, France.**

Recorded at Le Festival Musique Evolution on 30 March.

* **Fillmore East, New York City, New York, USA.**

FRIDAY 17 + SATURDAY 18

* **Electric Factory, Philadelphia, Pennsylvania, USA.**

SATURDAY 18

* *Zabriskie Point* **film soundtrack LP released in the USA.**

The film premiered in the US on 5 February.

WEDNESDAY 22

* **Capitol Theater, Port Chester, New York, USA.**

April 1970

- **East Town Theater, Detroit, Michigan, USA.**

WEDNESDAY 29

- **KQED Studios, San Francisco, California, USA.**

The show was directed by John Coney and produced by Coney and Jim Farber for the Bay Area Educational Television Association. It was broadcast on KQED, a Public Broadcasting Service (PBS) station later that year. (The show lists 'Atom Heart Mother' in the closing credits, indicating it must have followed the album's release – at this point the track was still commonly known as 'The Amazing Pudding'.)

The concert was later broadcast, sometime in the 70s, on WNEW–FM, New York City. This is the most likely source of the CD copies in circulation, which are of reasonable quality. Generation spotters will however be interested to hear that a copy of the complete radio broadcast, including the novelty song 'Here Comes Santa', is available in surprisingly high quality – comparable with top-quality copies of the Paris Cinema sessions.

KQED PBS broadcast, 57.25, Instrumental introduction, 0.06, The Amazing Pudding, 16.16, Cymbaline, 8.33, Grantchester Meadows, 7.20, Green Is The Colour / Careful With That Axe, Eugene, 12.20, Set The Controls For The Heart Of The Sun, 11.32, introduction to following programme, 0.12, video

WNEW FM broadcast, 57.32, The Amazing Pudding, 16.44, Cymbaline, 8.45, Here Comes Santa, 0.13, Grantchester Meadows, 7.21, Green Is The Colour / Careful With That Axe, Eugene, 12.43, Set The Controls For The Heart Of The Sun, 11.43

- **Fillmore West, San Francisco, California, USA.**

Soundboard, 92.49, Grantchester Meadows, 6.40 Astronomy Domine, 9.08 Cymbaline, 9.06, The Amazing Pudding, 19.59, The Embryo, 11.23, Green Is The Colour / Careful With That Axe, Eugene, 14.56, Set The Controls For The Heart Of The Sun, 9.31, A Saucerful Of Secrets, 6.24

A ticket for the concert is illustrated in Hypnosis' *Shine On* book and reflects the rear cover of *Ummagumma*.[201] The poster, which is identical except for the small print, is illustrated in *The Art Of Rock*.[202]

Grantchester Meadows / Astronomy Domine

Thank you. If I could remember what it was that we were going to play next I'd tell you, but I can't, so I won't. OK. I've been reminded. This is a song that we recorded for a French film all about drugs and sex, like all the films we're asked to do film music for. I dunno why it is, but it always seems to turn out like that. Anyway, this is called 'Cymbaline' and it's about a nightmare ... three, four.

Cymbaline

Thank you. Thank you. [Imitates American accent.] Terriffic! When we're in England, we're making a new album at the moment, and this next thing that we're going to play is going to be one side of it. Also, we're taking a break when we finish this – it seems to have gone very quickly this evening, maybe we've been playing really fast. Anyway, we are, so don't go away, when we leave the stage we are coming back. Won't be very long. OK. Ha ha. OK.

The Amazing Pudding

>< One ... Whew! ... called 'The Embryo'. Altogether – one ... one, two, three, four.

The Embryo

Thank you. We're gonna do two things cunningly run together now, the first of which is the song called 'Green Is The Colour', which is about being on Ibiza, and the second is an instrumental off of ... of, er ... our last album, *Ummagumma*, which is called 'Careful With That Axe, Eugene'.

Green Is The Colour / Careful With That Axe, Eugene

Thank you.

>Set The Controls For The Heart Of The Sun

Thank you. OK? OK. This is the last tune we're going to play, if you can call it a tune, and it's er ... the title track off the last album before last, before last, and it's called 'A Saucerful Of Secrets'. Thanks. Last thing we're gonna play and thanks very much for coming and listening.

A Saucerful Of Secrets<

It has been suggested that the concert was recorded for later use in the KQED broadcast. Although it is clear that this was not eventually used in the TV special, it does explain why a soundboard recording is available. The extent of Roger's comments between tracks would also indicate that this concert was in some way special – he is rarely this talkative!

Collectors should avoid being misled by the double CD sets circulating of the concert – the most complete recording we have come across is from older vinyl copies, which while not adding anything further to the musical record, do feature additional commentary, most notably from Nick Mason (a rare treat!).

MAY

- **Sound On Film: Zabriskie – What's the Point?, WBAI–FM, New York City, USA.**

A radio discussion programme about the film and the issues it raised. The hour-long show included some of the Floyd's tracks from the movie, but none of the members are involved in the discussion. The show is available on a US radio promo LP (*MGM Sound On Film no. 5*).

Sound On Film no. 5, 53.26, discussion with music

Anyone particularly interested in the film might care to seek out a detailed review in *Movie* magazine no. 18, published in the UK in the winter of 1970–71. Alternatively, *Films And Filming* magazine's March 1970 issue features an attractive set of stills from the film, as well as a set of stills from *More*.

- *Picnic – A Breath Of Fresh Air*, **Harvest sampler released.**

The album features Pink Floyd's 'Embryo' and Syd Barrett's 'Terrapin'. As most will be aware, 'Embryo' was a demo, and its release was not sanctioned by the band. Consequently, the album was promptly withdrawn. Copies are easy to come by, however, and the track is, of course, now available on the US *Works* compilation.

FRIDAY 1

- **Santa Monica Civic Center, Santa Monica, Los Angeles, California, USA.**

  83.38, Astronomy Domine, 9.30, Cymbaline., 11.21, The Amazing Pudding, 20.16, Embryo, 11.39, Set The Controls For The Heart Of The Sun, 13.33, Interstellar Overdrive, 13.41

  [Birdsong segue from 'Grantchester Meadows' into …]

  Astronomy Domine

  Thank you. >< [Dave seems to have a couple of problems.] […] we're going to do a song called 'Cymbaline'.

  Cymbaline ><

  Alright then! This is something we're recording at the moment for our next album. When we finish this, we're going to take a break, but we will be coming back so don't go away.

  The Amazing Pudding

  Thank you – back soon. Thank you, see you in about twenty minutes. ><

  The Embryo

  Thank you. ><

  Set The Controls For The Heart Of The Sun

  Thank you. >< OK. Right. We've been doing this one since we were teenagers, which is a long time, and it's called 'Interstellar Overdrive'.

  Interstellar Overdrive

WEDNESDAY 6

- **University of California Los Angeles (UCLA), Los Angeles, California, USA.**

  Melody Maker covered the concert in an article by Chris Welch under the headline 'Floyd's Bit For Peace', published in the newspaper on the 16th.
  The band are reported to have put on a free concert for 10,000 students

at the California University, Los Angeles, California, as part of an attempt to quell a near-riot situation, amidst a stand off between students and the National Guard.[203]

SATURDAY 9

- **San Diego, California, USA.**

Billboard magazine's tour announcement lists this show as having taken place on 9 May, but doubts have been expressed about whether it was replaced by the Salt Lake City show below, or whether it took place on a different date.

- **Terrace Ballroom, Salt Lake City, Utah, USA.**

TUESDAY 12

- **Municipal Auditorium, Atlanta, Georgia, USA.**

SATURDAY 16

- **The Warehouse, New Orleans, Louisiana, USA.**

The Floyd were supported by Country Funk and The Allman Brothers.
The band opened with 'Grantchester Meadows', played by Roger and Dave, alone on the stage. 'Grantchester' was segued into 'Astronomy Domine' and the rest of the set featured tracks then available on the *Ummagumma* live set as well as others, undocumented.
Talking a month later to *Melody Maker* Roger complained how:

> We found that New Orleans was the worst music scene in the world. It's just full of strip joints and there was no jazz at all, just drunks. All the jazzmen have split.

The band had a truck containing all their equipment stolen while they were there. It 'was nearly a total disaster. We sat down at our hotel thinking – well that's it. It's all over. We were pouring out our troubles to a girl who worked at the hotel and she said her father worked for the FBI. The police hadn't helped us much, but the FBI got to work and four hours later it was found – £15,000 worth.' The band also made appeals on TV and radio for the return of their equipment.
By all accounts this gig did not go smoothly. Not only did the band have their kit stolen, but the gig was marred by technical problems when their quad sound system broke down.

FRIDAY 22

- **Houston Music Theater, Houston, Texas, USA.**

SATURDAY 23

- **State Fair Music Hall, Dallas, Texas, USA.**

The Floyd opened for Grand Funk Railroad on 22 and 23 May.

SUNDAY 24

- **Kansas City, Missouri, USA.**

FRIDAY 29

- **Chicago, Illinois, USA.**

SATURDAY 30

- ***Zabriskie Point* film soundtrack LP released in the UK.**

The film was available briefly on video in the UK in the mid-80s and was given an airing on BBC 2 TV, UK, on 26 January 1997. One may assume that its original release was concurrent with the UK album release. It is presently available on video in Italy, though readers should be wary of the dubbed version – Italian dialogue rather spoils it. The film is also available with Italian subtitles.

- **Syd Barrett on *Top Gear*, presented by John Peel, BBC Radio 1, London, UK.**

Top Gear was broadcast between 3.00 and 5.00 pm. The final track from the recording made by Barrett on 24 February – 'Two Of A Kind' – was given its first airing. It is likely that the other tracks from his session recorded on the 24 February were also repeated.[204]

- **Chicago, Illinois, USA.**

The dates on the 24th, 29th and 30th are unconfirmed, and taken from *Billboard*.

JUNE

- **Ludlow Garage, Cincinnati, Ohio, USA.**

Billboard magazine advises that the band played here on the 5th and 6th, though it is generally thought that the band were in the UK on these dates.

- **EMI, Studio 2, Abbey Road, London, UK.**

Geesin finally gave up, exhausted by the difficulties with the recording of
'Atom Heart Mother'. John Aldiss would take over, and see the track through
to its completion at the end of the month.

FRIDAY 5

- **Syd Barrett recording sessions, EMI, Abbey Road Studios, London, UK.**

These sessions saw the recording of 'Birdy Hop', a two-track demo (released
on *Opel*). This same track has appeared on bootleg complete with the spoken
intro where it is introduced as take 1. The title is said to refer to UFO co-
founder John 'Hoppy' Hopkins. 'Rats' was also recorded on this date – the
version on *Barrett* is a demo version with overdubs added on 7 May (this
date may prove to be incorrect). The second version – another two-track
demo – which appears on *Opel* is this same take, but without the overdubs.
    Syd also recorded a two-track demo of 'Wined And Dined', which can be
found on the *Opel* compilation.

SATURDAY 6

- **Extravaganza '70, Music and Fashion Festival, Olympia, London.**

Syd Barrett appeared with David Gilmour and Jerry Shirley.

*15.50, Terrapin, 3.26, Gigolo Aunt, 4.08, Effervescing Elephant, 0.41, Octopus,
4.24*

Melody Maker announced the festival line-up on 28 March. Promoter Bryan
Morrison was quoted as saying 'In addition to the pop and fashion attrac-
tions, record companies and all ventures allied to the record business will be
taking part. There will be film shows and high divers. £10,000 in rent has
already been spent so far'. Also appearing at the festival were Simon Dee And
The Tremeloes on 30 May, Matthews Southern Comfort and compere Pete
Drummond on 1 June, Bo Diddley on 3 June, Tyrannosaurus Rex and compere John Peel on 4 June and Fairport Convention on the 5th.[205]

SUNDAY 7

- **Syd Barrett recording sessions, EMI, Abbey Road Studios, London, UK.**

The version of 'Milky Way' which was released on the *Opel* compilation –
take 5 – was recorded at this session. *Opel*, the then-current Syd Barrett
magazine back in 1985 added (on the strength of a phone call to EMI)
'She Was A Millionaire' and 'Rats'.
    Syd wasn't to record at EMI again until late 1974.

SATURDAY 27

- **'Easy Riding With The Pink Floyd', interview with Nick and Roger,** *Melody Maker,* **UK.**

Roger and Nick talked about the US tour from which they'd just returned. 'They were both laughing about their memories of the Fats Domino band they chanced upon in a night club during their travels, when they entered the MM boozer. "They had the greatest brass section in the world – until they played together" said Nick'. High praise indeed!

- **Bath Festival of Blues And Progressive Music,** **Bath and West Showground, Shepton Mallet, Somerset, UK.**

Two tapes are available, both from the same master, but of varying quality. The first, available for some time, is incomplete, while the second more recent copy features 'The Amazing Pudding' with orchestra for the first time, and is of improved quality.

First source, 32.58, Green Is The Colour / Careful With That Axe, Eugene, 13.47, A Saucerful Of Secrets, 18.51

Second source, 69.36, Green Is The Colour / Careful With That Axe, Eugene, 13.07, A Saucerful Of Secrets, 17.51, Set The Controls For The Heart Of The Sun, 13.16, The Amazing Pudding, 24.05

>Green Is The Colour / Careful With That Axe, Eugene >< A Saucerful Of Secrets ><

[GUY IN AUDIENCE: Good, that's two my, two mine two favourite songs that there, is good. Oh fantastic, they'll do this much better.]

Set The Controls For The Heart Of The Sun

>< ... together it's going to be one whole side on our next album, and it has a tentative working title which is 'The Amazing Pudding'.

The Amazing Pudding

A copy of the poster for this gig may be found in *Le Livre Du Pink Floyd.*[206]

SUNDAY 28

- **Kralingen Pop Festival, Kraalingse Bos, Rotterdam, Holland.**

This was the opening gig of a short two-week European Tour.
    There are two different tapes purporting to be from this show in cir-culation. The shorter version is actually from the Open Air Pop Festival, Reiterstadion Soers, Aachen later the following month. We understand the

details below to be roughly correct, though the reader should note that we have been unable to verify the content of the recording.

100.00, Astronomy Domine, 8.32, Green Is The Colour / Careful With That Axe, Eugene, 12.15, Set The Controls For The Heart Of The Sun, 11.30, A Saucerful Of Secrets, 19.30, Interstellar Overdrive, 12.00, The Amazing Pudding, 18.30

Footage from this show also appears in the *Stamping Ground* film which was released in Denmark in 1971 under the title *Love And Music.* More recently the Floyd footage was released in the UK in early 1996 on a video entitled *Psychomania – The Best Of Psychedelic Rock.*

Stamping Ground, 10.02, Set The Controls For The Heart Of The Sun, 3.47, A Saucerful Of Secrets, 6.04

JULY

- *The Best Of Pink Floyd* European-only compilation LP released by Pathé Marconi.

Better known by the name given to its 1974 re-release – *Masters Of Rock.* This album was to tread much the same ground as *Relics* in the following year. As would be the case with *Relics*, a number of the tracks would be treated to give a fake-stereo effect – 'Arnold Layne', 'Candy And A Currant Bun', 'See Emily Play' and 'It Would Be So Nice'. 'Paintbox', 'Julia Dream' and 'Apples And Oranges' were included as true-stereo mixes. Further background on the differences between the original singles and subsequent compilation releases are to be found later when we examine *Relics*. Any rumours regarding differences between the version of 'Julia Dream' here, and that on *Relics*, however, are to our minds mistaken.

- **Hamburg, West Germany.**

- **Munster, West Germany.**

- **Frankfurt, West Germany.**

- **Berlin, West Germany.**

SUNDAY 12

- **1st Open Air Pop Festival, Reiterstadion Soers, Aachen, West Germany.**

83.40, Astronomy Domine, 2.32, Green Is The Colour / Careful With That Axe, Eugene, 13.47, The Amazing Pudding, 20.14, Set The Controls For The Heart Of The Sun, 13.42, A Saucerful Of Secrets, 17.08, Interstellar Overdrive, 12.32

>Astronomy Domine

Thank you. One two one two. One. One two. One. One two. >< [Dave false-starts the opening bars, then tries again.]

Green Is The Colour / Careful With That Axe, Eugene

Thank you >< [...] is the one side on our next album which should be out in August [...]

The Amazing Pudding >< Set The Controls For The Heart Of The Sun

Thank you ><

>A Saucerful Of Secrets ><

One. [Banging mics.] One. OK. This ... really is the last one and this is called 'Interstellar Overdrive'.

Interstellar Overdrive

TUESDAY 14

- **Syd Barrett recording sessions, EMI, Abbey Road Studios, London, UK**

Take 1 of 'Dolly Rocker' – that released on *Opel* – was recorded at this session, along with three takes of 'Dominoes'. Take 3 was that which was released on *Barrett*, while takes 1 and 2 have appeared on the remastered *Barrett* CD. On the subject of take 1 (presumably) David Gilmour has said that 'The song just ended after Syd had finished singing and I wanted a gradual fade so I added that [final] section myself. I played drums on that by the way.'[207]

A number of takes of 'Effervescing Elephant' were also recorded – take 2 would appear as a bonus track on the *Opel* remaster, while take 9 was eventually selected as the one released on *Barrett*.

Also recorded on this date were take 1 of 'Let's Split' – the version found on the *Opel* compilation, and take 1 of 'Love Song'. Two versions of this take are available on official releases. The first – with overdubs added on the 17th – was released on *Barrett*, while the second, unembellished recording, was released as an extra track on the *Barrett* remaster. Also released on the *Barrett* LP was a version of 'Wined And Dined' – take 10 for those of you who wish to know!

MID

- **EMI, Studio 2, Abbey Road, London, UK.**

Recording sessions for 'Summer 68', with the Abbey Road Pops Orchestra brass section. The band also completed the final mix for 'Atom Heart Mother'.

THURSDAY 16

- *Pink Floyd In Concert With John Peel* recorded at the Paris Cinema, London, UK.

The concert was broadcast on 19 July.

FRIDAY 17

- Syd Barrett recording sessions, EMI, Abbey Road Studios, London, UK.

These sessions saw the recording of 'It Is Obvious', and four takes are currently available on official releases. Take 1, with overdubs added on the 20th, was released on *Barrett*. Take 2 (electric guitar and vocal only) where Syd's voice growls in a Captain Beefheartian fashion, was released as a bonus track on the remastered CD of that album. Takes 3 (electric guitar and vocal) and 5 (acoustic guitar and vocal) appeared as extra tracks on the remastered CD version of *Opel*. Also recorded on this date was 'Word Song', take 1 – this track of course, also appeared on *Opel*.

SATURDAY 18

- *Disc* magazine, UK, publishes an article: 'Floyd With A Choir'.

A feature previewing the *Atom Heart Mother* album, to be released in September. The article also reported that 'Floyd have also been asked to write the music for a film being made by an island owner in the Canaries. He has a rough idea of what the film project is about, but he wants the group to just arrive, wander round the island and write music from their impressions, to see if they coincide with his.'
Was anything to come of this? Frankly, we have no idea!

- Blackhill's Garden Party, Hyde Park, Kensington, London, UK.

A free five-hour concert from 1 pm – 6 pm which 100,000 people attended. The show was filmed privately by a group of art students, but never received an official airing. Their film was, however, screened publicly on two occasions, and advertised in *Melody Maker*. The footage has not entered general circulation.
The band were supported by Formerly Fat Harry, Kevin Ayers And The Whole World (with guest drummer Robert Wyatt, from Ayers' previous band, the Soft Machine), the Edgar Broughton Band and Roy Harper (who replaced The Third Ear Band, who had to pull out).
The Floyd performed 'Green Is The Colour', 'Careful With That Axe, Eugene', 'Set The Controls For The Heart Of The Sun' and 'The Amazing Pudding'.

The highlight of the concert is said to have been 'The Embryo' during which the audience were thoroughly freaked out by a sound effect of a child crying, which appeared to be circling the park.

SUNDAY 19

* ***Pink Floyd In Concert With John Peel* broadcast, BBC Radio 1, London, UK.**[208]

The concert had been recorded on the 16 July. The show was produced by Jeff Griffin and broadcast at 4.00 pm (on Radio 1's medium wave frequencies). *Radio Times*' Dick Lawson previewed the show on 16 July:

> From the early days of English 'psychedelia' the Floyd (along with the Soft Machine) have preserved their musical integrity in quiet isolation, and developed their techniques and use of electronics to a high degree of perfection. After their last album *Ummagumma*, the film score for the French film *More*, and a successful tour of America, they are beginning to receive the acclaim they deserve.

61.30, Embryo, 9.37, Fat Old Sun, 5.10, Green Is The Colour / Careful With That Axe, Eugene, 10.49, If, 4.25, Atom Heart Mother, 24.53

The concert has been rebroadcast many times in many countries since but most times minus the (probable) debut of 'Fat Old Sun'. The source for many of the broadcasts has been BBC Transcription Services, who must have seen fit to leave the song off due to the restrictions of the vinyl format. 'If', you will note, is unavailable as a live piece (bar Roger's solo performances) on any other recording, and it is likely that this was the band's only attempt at the song.

An insert was prepared to accompany the 1976 issue of the vinyl – '46 (i & ii)' – to whatever radio station it would end up at. The insert confirms that the original recording was made in mono:

> In 1970, before we began the regular fortnightly issue of stereo 'Pop Spectacular' programmes, a number of 'In Concert' recordings were made in mono. They were not issued by Transcription Services at the time but fortunately tapes of the outstanding concerts were retained. We are now issuing some of these in simulated stereo, using every technique at our disposal to create an acceptable stereo effect, while retaining a good mono sound.

A mono recording of the whole concert (most recently rebroadcast in the UK during the early 80s) together with Peel's comments has been retained by the BBC. Tapers have copies from the original broadcast, which though not of particularly good quality, serve to underline the above. The writers have had the pleasure of listening to the BBC's ¼-inch master copy.

Reaching a total timing for the concert has been difficult. Pressings on CD and vinyl have slightly altered the speed of playback over the years. On what was a one-off opportunity to listen to the original reels, our stopwatch failed during 'Embryo' – the total timing of 61 min. 30 sec. partially reflects a substituted timing of a reliable copy of 'Embryo'. Our experience with the rest of the timing suggests that if the BBC were ever to replay the whole show again, it would approximate about 61 min. 45 sec.

Hello and welcome to a rather special Sunday-repeated-on-Wednesday programme, and this is one that, er, I, and I hope you have been looking forward to for several weeks ever since it was going to happen. We have The Pink Floyd.

Embryo

Nicest thing about The Pink Floyd's music is that it always makes me at least feel very hopeful, it's optimistic music and that was no excer ... exception. Called 'Embryo' an' it's written by Roger Waters. This next one which is written by Dave Gilmour, is 'Fat Old Sun'.

Fat Old Sun

Excellent – yeah, it's really beautiful. That's 'Fat Old Sun', a Dave Gilmour composition. Is that going to be on the next LP, is it? [DAVE: Mmm Hmm.] It is? Great, good. These, er, next two things are going to ... have already been, in fact, recorded and you doubtless have the records already. They are 'Green Is The Colour' and that's going to be followed with 'Careful With That Axe, Eugene'.

Green Is The Colour / Careful With That Axe, Eugene

And that was 'Green Is The Colour' and 'Careful With That Axe, Eugene', an' if any there be who don't know who The Pink Floyd are they're er ... Roger Waters, bass and vocals, Nick Mason, percussion, Dave Gilmour, guitars and vocals, and Rick Wright, keyboards and vocals. And this next thing, which, er, in fact Roger will be playing acoustic guitar on, and Rick is going to play organ and bass simultaneously, so I'm told, which should be well worth watching and hearing. It's called 'If'.

If

That was another Roger Waters' composition, called 'If'. And next week on this programme, we've got rather a lot of people actually. We have Mungo Jerry, Joanne Kelly with Bob Hall, Simon and Steve, and Brett Marvin And The Thunderbolts. And this programme has been produced by Jeff Griffin, sound balanced by Chris Lycett, and leaping about this week by Bob Conduct. And now, we're going to hear the music that was the high point of the recent and much discussed Bath Festival, and, er, it's working title is 'The Atom Heart Mother', and it will appear under some title on the next Pink Floyd LP, due in September or thereabouts. And Pink Floyd will be accompanied by The Philips Jones Brass Ensemble, and the John Alldiss Choir, and the arrangements are written by The Floyd in conjunction with Ron Geesin. So, 'The Atom Heart Mother'.

The Atom Heart Mother

WEDNESDAY 22

- *Sounds of the 70s*, presented by John Peel, BBC Radio 1, London, UK.[209]

Repeat of the show first broadcast on the 19th. This was aired at 6.00 pm, again on the station's AM frequency. Both original broadcasts were in mono.

- University of Essex, Colchester, UK.

SATURDAY 25

- 'Playing In The Park', full page review of the Hyde Park concert on July 18 is published in *Disc & Music Echo*.

  The Pink Floyd gave an hour of beautifully mature music, soothing and inspiring to listen to. They kept the numbers short, apart from the finale, and carefully restrained. With the sun glinting on Nick Mason's drums and the clouds breaking up overhead, it seemed as if the sounds were dropping from the sky itself.[210]

- *Melody Maker*, UK 'Good Music, Bad Vibes And Free Hyde Park' review published.

Mark Plummer reviewed the concert, complaining that:

  the Hell's Angels brought their usual brand of violence with them. Acting as unofficial policemen they hit anyone whom they thought was getting in their way, and took great delight in riding their bikes through the crowd. Back stage the vibes were bad too. The stewards would let no one sit in the enclosure at the front of the stage, and one man in a leather hat took great delight in pushing people around …
  … Bill-topping Pink Floyd went on stage last, but the beauty of their music was lost to the birds and the trees. Using their usual stereo and complex sound system they played some oldies like 'Green Is The Colour', and 'Set The Controls For The Heart Of The Sun,' which came over well, even though half the sounds just disappeared.

Coincidentally, *Melody Maker* also featured a letter from a fan asking what equipment the band was using at the time – Peter Watts, the Floyd's road manager was obliging in his response, listing:

  Richard Wright: Hammond M102 and farfisa Double Duo, played through a Binson echo unit and two 100-watt Hiwatt amplifiers, with the Hammond augmented by a Leslie 147 speaker, put through a WEM PA with four 4 x 12 WEM speaker cabinets and a second Binsen echo unit.
  Roger Waters: Fender Precision Bass with two 100-watt WEM valve

amplifiers and four 2 x 15 WEM reflex bass cabinets.

Nick Mason: Ludwig double kit comprising 22-in. and 24-in. bass drums, 12-in. x 14-in. mounted tom-toms, 14-in. x 16-in. floor tom-toms, 14-in. snare drum, and 16-in., 18-in., 20-in. and 22-in. Zildjian cymbals and a 12-in. hi-hat.

Anyone interested in the band's technical history at this time should seek out the UK magazines *Sound On Stage* (March 1997), *Musician* (September 1989) and *Total Guitar* (September 1996). The former in particular is an extremely interesting and well-researched piece, with the following three issues covering the tours from 1975 to 1994.

SUNDAY 26

- **Syd Barrett recording sessions, EMI, Abbey Road Studios, London, UK.**

'Feel' take 1 recorded – this version was that released on *The Madcap Laughs.*

- **XI Festival International de Jazz, Antibes, Juan-les-Pins, France.**

Excerpts from this show were shown on ORTF television on 22 August.

AUGUST

- **EMI, Studio 2, Abbey Road, London, UK.**

The sessions at Studio 2, Abbey Road during August saw 'If' and 'Alan's Psychedelic Breakfast' completed.

- **EMI, Studio 3, Abbey Road, London, UK.**

Recording sessions for 'Fat Old Sun'.

SATURDAY 1

- ***Melody Maker* publishes a letter from a fan discussing 'The Amazing Pudding' and 'Atom Heart Mother'.**

Not particularly useful, though they do publish a rather nice photograph of Nick on drums at Hyde Park on 18 July.

- **Festival d'Aix-en-Provence, Aix-en-Provence, France.**

WEDNESDAY 5

- **Festival Maudit de Biot, Le Biot, France.**

FRIDAY 7

- **Popanalia Music Festival, Nice, France.**

The Floyd were due to play at this festival on its second day, but were unable to after the festival was abandoned when members of a clique hippie cult called *Les Compagnons De La Route*, egged on by a young left wing political element, vandalised the stage and equipment.

'Thus, through sheer irresponsibility', *Melody Maker* wrote on 15 August, '… was abruptly halted a determined attempt to change the French government's attitude not only to the whole phenomena of pop and festivals, but of mass conventions of young people in France.'

SATURDAY 8

- **'Waters In The Pink', *Disc & Music Echo*, UK, publishes an extensive interview with Roger.**

Caroline Boucher's article was lengthy, and, like many from around this time, showed a maturity and thoughtfulness which was to set the tone for the band's work over the next decade – not to mention the themes which were to become central as the basis for the conceptual pieces which were to come:

Roger's main aim at the moment is to continue the struggle of finding the best means of communication. 'I wonder if there's anything to say which I'm capable of articulating. There's words, obviously, but unless you know someone very well so you're not at all frightened of them, it's very hard to communicate with words. But we don't say what we mean half the time, we say either what sounds right, or what the other person wants to hear, or any number of things.'

How long the Floyd will last Roger can't envisage. Certainly at the moment they have a very good work relationship, and he sees no reason why they shouldn't get together when they're 40 if something interests them, and there's enough of interest to them at the moment to keep them together for a very long time.

- **St Tropez Music Festival, Les Arenes, St Tropez, France.**

Extracts of the performance were broadcast on *Pop 2*, ORTF TV, France, on 10 October, and repeated on the 24th.

Pop 2, 26.23, soundcheck jams I, 0.26, soundcheck jams II, 0.31, Cymbaline I, 0.43, Cymbaline II, 0.39, The Embryo, 10.04, Atom Heart Mother, 12.50

[Keyboards soundcheck, Nick hams it badly in French, French narrator's introductions, guitars soundcheck.]

Cymbaline

Sort it out, Pete – PA's far too loud. One. One. You've probably got it a bit too much now … start, Dave, and we'll come in with you.

Cymbaline

[French narrator.] This is called 'The Embryo'.

The Embryo

[French narrator.]

Atom Heart Mother

[French narrator to end.]

WEDNESDAY 12

- **Fête de Saint Raphaël, Les Arénas, St Raphaël, France.**

SATURDAY 15

- **Yorkshire Folk, Blues and Jazz Festival, Krumlin, Barkisland, Near Halifax, Yorkshire, UK.**

  The Floyd were booked to top the bill on this three-day event which began on Friday 14. Their appearance was cancelled however, due to the typical Yorkshire weather. The promoters had advertised the show as being their 'final festival appearance until 1971'.[211]

SATURDAY 22

- **ORTF TV broadcast of the XI Festival International de Jazz, Antibes from 26 July.**

SEPTEMBER

SATURDAY 12

- *Melody Maker* **newspaper, UK, announces that the Floyd are to write music for French ballet producer Roland Petit.**

- **Fête de L'Humanité, Grand Scéne, Bois de Vincennes, Paris, France.**

  The show was filmed for French TV, but never broadcast. An audio tape of the show is in circulation, taken from the film. There were about 45,000 people at the festival.

37.56, Astronomy Domine, 8.53, Green Is The Colour / Careful With That Axe, Eugene, 14.49, Set The Controls For The Heart Of The Sun, 14.57

Astronomy Domine

Thank you. ><

Green Is The Colour / Careful With That Axe, Eugene

Thank you. ><

Set The Controls For The Heart Of The Sun<

'Atom Heart Mother', which doesn't appear on this tape, was performed with the Voices of East Harlem Choir. Dave would later comment in an interview with *Melody Maker* that he 'wasn't all that impressed [with Voices of East Harlem]. I think they could be a really amazing band, if they were handled right – with all those voices. But they are handled rather unimaginatively'.[212]

SUNDAY 20

- **The group flies to America to begin their US *Atom Heart Mother* tour, which would last from 26 September to 25 October.**

SATURDAY 26

- **'The Floyd On Rock Today ...', interview with Rick, *Melody Maker* newspaper, UK.**

Michael Watts spoke to Rick about their recent commission by Roland Petit to work on his ballet project, then scheduled for performance at the Grand Palais, Champs Elysées, Paris from 1 June to 10 June 1971 (these dates were later scrubbed). Rick also comments upon film music, the *Atom Heart Mother* album – soon to be released, and their search for the ultimate in hi-fi sound.

> We want to really perfect the sound live, and then release it on a 4-track tape, and hopefully get EMI to sell 4-track tape recorders for home use. This might not be so far in the future as you might think, because in America it is happening now. In terms of playing live on stage, all of us want to get a superb hi-fi sound, although we do not have those thousands of boxes of tricks that people fondly imagine we do.

- **Electric Factory, Philadelphia, Pennsylvania, USA.**

SUNDAY 27

• **Fillmore East, New York City, New York, USA.**

Two shows were played – one at 6.00 pm and one at 9.00 pm. Both included
brass and choir on 'Atom Heart Mother' performed by the Roger Wagner
Chorale (a 20-voice choir) along with a 10-piece brass section (conducted by
New York composer Peter Philips). This was the first of only three performances with the choir – they also featured at the Fillmore in San Francisco and
on the final night in Los Angeles.

During the band's performance at Pepperland on 17 October, Roger refers
to the first gig at the Fillmore being blighted by power failures. While edited,
the recording does not exhibit these power-outs, indicating that it is likely to
be from the second show.

*55.18, Astronomy Domine, 10.48, Green Is The Colour / Careful With That Axe,
Eugene, 14.01, Atom Heart Mother, 5.37, Fat Old Sun, 11.49, Set The Controls
For The Heart Of The Sun, 11.44*

Astronomy Domine

Thank you. >< Would all the characters that […] equipment at the side of the
stage please stop it 'cos it's getting boring. ><

Green Is The Colour / Careful With That Axe, Eugene

Thank you. ><

**Atom Heart Mother >< Fat Old Sun ><
Set The Controls For The Heart Of The Sun**

Thank you.

An advertisement for the show is to be found in *The Amazing Pudding*, no. 35.

TUESDAY 29

• **New York City Radio interviews the band.**

Full length version, 37.00

Common edited version, 30.45

The latter appeared as the second track on a *Limited Edition Interview Disc
& Fully Illustrated Book* in 1995. Perhaps its only recommendation is that the
'book' features a number of nice pictures! If this recording was in fact made
by New York City Radio, then it is likely that it was for research (non-
broadcast) purposes, since the quality is only that of a dictaphone.

OCTOBER

THURSDAY 1

- **Syd gets engaged to Gayla Pinion on her 20th birthday.**

  It only lasted a year.[213]

- **The Memorial Coliseum, Portland, Oregon, USA.**

FRIDAY 2 – SATURDAY 3

- **Moore Theater, Seattle, Washington, USA.**

SUNDAY 4

- **Gonzaga University, Spokane, Washington, USA.**

TUESDAY 6

- **Central Washington University, Ellensburg, Washington, USA.**

WEDNESDAY 7

- **Vancouver Gardens, Vancouver, British Columbia, Canada.**

  The band were interviewed by Mike Quigley for *Georgia Straight* and talked freely about the Roland Petit ballet, their sound system and free festivals.[214]

THURSDAY 8

- **Jubilee Auditorium, Calgary, Alberta, Canada.**

FRIDAY 9

- **Sales Pavilion Annex, Edmonton, Alberta, Canada.**

SATURDAY 10

- ***Atom Heart Mother* released in the UK and USA.**

  The band took out a full page display ad in *Melody Maker* featuring the 'Atom Heart Mother' herd in London's Pall Mall.
      Dave Croker, then head of Harvest records, having replaced Malcolm Jones, told Rick Sanders in his Futura book *Pink Floyd* that:

We'd seen some other group's advert in which they'd superimposed a flock of sheep onto a photo of the traffic in Oxford Street, so we decided to go one better. We arranged with the police to ban cars from the Mall at the crack of dawn one morning, and we brought in a herd of cows; the photos were brilliant.[215]

- *Pop 2*, **ORTF TV broadcast, France.**

Broadcast of the band's appearance at the St. Tropez Music Festival on 8 August.

- **Centennial Auditorium, Saskatoon, Saskatchewan, Canada.**

SUNDAY 11

- **Centre of The Arts, Regina, Saskatchewan, Canada.**

TUESDAY 13

- **Centennial Concert Hall, Winnipeg, Manitoba, Canada.**

WEDNESDAY 14

- **An interview with David Gilmour and Roger Waters appears in the** *Vancouver Free Press*, **published in Vancouver, Canada.**

THURSDAY 15

- **Terrace Ballroom, Salt Lake City, Utah, USA.**

FRIDAY 16

- **Pepperland Auditorium, San Rafael, California, USA.**

SATURDAY 17

- **Pepperland Auditorium, San Rafael, California, USA.**

This tape, which has been reproduced on a number of bootlegs, is easily distinguished by power cuts during 'Astronomy Domine' and 'A Saucerful Of Secrets'. Most recordings in circulation have been edited down, removing non-musical excess and an eleven-minute rendition of 'Set The Controls For The Heart Of The Sun', which should follow 'Careful With That Axe, Eugene'. We would recommend that the reader seeks out a version which resembles that which follows.

130.54, Astronomy Domine (with breaks for power losses), 22.04, Fat Old Sun, 11.51, Cymbaline, 10.29, Atom Heart Mother, 19.46, Embryo, 10.53, Green Is The Colour / Careful With That Axe, Eugene, 14.00, Set The Controls For The Heart Of The Sun, 11.20, A Saucerful Of Secrets, 19.54

Good evening, people, this is called 'Astronomy Domine'.

Astronomy Domine

[Power loss.] Thank you, for our next number! One. Hang on, we'll just find out what that was because the possibility exists that we may be able to split some power leads. [Person in the audience calls for 'Careful With That Axe, Eugene'.] Give us a chance John! I think we'll start that one again.

Astronomy Domine

[Power loss.] Third time lucky. Evidently that re-start was a little premature because they are splitting some leads – spreading some of the power out. So we'll start again in a minute. I hope so. There won't be enough left for us. This happened three times in our first set at Fillmore East a couple of weeks ago. Got quite boring after – oh you're a friendly little chap! ['Sorry!' from the audience.] You're forgiven. One.

Astronomy Domine

[Power loss.] Two, three, four …

Astronomy Domine

[Starts part way through.] K'you. This is a new song and it's on the album we've just released and it's called 'Fat Old Sun'.

Fat Old Sun

Thank you. >< This next song is something to do with a dream and it's called 'Cymbaline'.

Cymbaline

There's a very long cut out on our new album, called 'Atom Heart Mother', where we use some brass players and some choir. But before we put the brass players and the choir on, when we were recording it we used to play it live.

>< Atom Heart Mother ><

This is called 'The Embryo'. One. One, two, three, four.

The Embryo<

… do two things together now, the first of which is a song called 'Green Is The Colour' and the second is an instrumental off of our album *Ummagumma* and it's called 'Careful With That Axe, Eugene'.

Green Is The Colour / Careful With That Axe, Eugene

This is called 'Set The Controls For The Heart Of The Sun'.

Set The Controls For The Heart Of The Sun

Thank you. >< This is the last tune we're going to play and it's off one of our albums and it's called 'A Saucerful Of Secrets', and thanks very much [...].

A Saucerful Of Secrets [With seeming partial power loss after 18 minutes and another after 19 minutes.]

[MC: Pink Floyd!] Thank you, goodnight. [MC: ... '69 yellow Buic ...]

WEDNESDAY 21

• **Fillmore West, San Francisco, California, USA.**

The review in *Rolling Stone* magazine, published on the 26th lists: 'Astronomy Domine', 'Fat Old Sun', 'Careful with That Axe, Eugene', 'Green Is The Colour', 'Cymbaline', 'Atom Heart Mother', 'Set The Controls For The Heart Of The Sun' and 'A Saucerful Of Secrets' as being played at this show. The band performed 'Atom Heart Mother' with the Roger Wagner Chorale – the second time a choir and brass section were to play with the band on this tour. The Chorale performed 'Ave Maria' as an encore. The review, should you find a copy, is well worth seeking out.[216]

FRIDAY 23

• **Santa Monica Civic, Santa Monica, California, USA.**

136.08, Astronomy Domine, 8.39, Green Is The Colour / Careful With That Axe, Eugene, 15.48, Fat Old Sun, 12.30, Cymbaline, 12.24, A Saucerful Of Secrets, 22.39, Atom Heart Mother (with brass and choir), 22.40, Interstellar Overdrive, 13.46, Corrosion / Embryo, 21.23

Astronomy Domine

Thank you. First of the next two things we're gonna do is the song called 'Green Is The Colour', and second thing which we'll do immediately following that is an instrumental called 'Careful With That Axe, Eugene'.

Green Is The Colour / Careful With That Axe, Eugene

Thanks. Thank you. This next thing is a song of Dave's, it's extremely pastoral and it's called 'Fat Old Sun'.

Fat Old Sun

>< Thank you. >< [Footsteps.] >< This is a song called 'Cymbaline'.

Cymbaline

Thank you. ><

A Saucerful Of Secrets

Thank you. OK. We're ready now, I just … maybe we can welcome these other musicians to the stage. And this is Peter Kirks, who's our conductor this evening […] Right. We've got [unintelligible] eh, Pete? Er … this thing is called 'Atom Heart Mother' an' we … this song we already know about. Anyway, it's one side of an old Richardson's … sorry!

Atom Heart Mother

Thank you.

Interstellar Overdrive >< Corrosion / Embryo ><

This was the third and last show on the tour to feature a choir and brass section during 'Atom Heart Mother', and possibly the last time that 'Interstellar Overdrive' was performed.

'Corrosion' is our favoured title for the improvisation which the band performed as a prelude to 'The Embryo' during occasional gigs at this time. To our mind it is not simply a development of 'The Embryo', but an entirely unique piece, warranting some form of title to distinguish it from the highly extended versions of 'The Embryo' which were performed towards the end of 1971. Sadly, both suffer with cuts in the recording (similar problems proliferate elsewhere for our erstwhile recorder).

A 69-minute vinyl recording purporting to be from the concert suffers from a poor pressing, and would have improved upon the full-length tape, were this not the case.

SATURDAY 24

- *Pop 2*, ORTF TV rebroadcast of the St. Tropez Music Festival show, first aired on the 10th.

THURSDAY 29

- **Premiere of 'The Body', Piccadilly, London**

The soundtrack was radically remixed for the album, and took almost a year to see the light of day.[217]

NOVEMBER

- **Promotional interviews with Syd Barrett at the Brian Morrison Agency Office, Bruton Place, London.**

Syd was interviewed by Steve Turner for *Beat Instrumental* magazine and Michael Watts for *Melody Maker*.[218]

November 1970

Friday 6

- **Concertgebouw, Amsterdam, Holland.**

103.13, Astronomy Domine, 7.13, Fat Old Sun, 11.47, Cymbaline, 10.06, Atom Heart Mother, 15.50, Embryo, 9.13, Green Is The Colour / Careful With That Axe, Eugene, 12.37, Set The Controls For The Heart Of The Sun, 11.44, A Saucerful Of Secrets, 18.16

One, two. I'm sorry we're a […] we're a little late in starting […] half past ten, takes a long time to set up our equipment. This is called 'Astronomy Domine'. One two. Three four.

Astronomy Domine

[…] called 'Fat Old Sun' …' [Speaks extremely quietly.]

Fat Old Sun

OK. This song's called 'Cymbaline'.

Cymbaline

One … hello? One … [Whistles through echo delay, extended taped intro to 'Atom Heart Mother'.]

Atom Heart Mother

Thank you. ><

Embryo

>< [Inaudible introduction.]

Green Is The Colour / Careful With That Axe, Eugene >< Set The Controls For The Heart Of The Sun, A Saucerful Of Secrets<

Saturday 7

- **Grote Zaal, De Doelen, Rotterdam, Holland.**

135.42, Astronomy Domine, 8.45, Fat Old Sun, 12.36, Cymbaline, 10.47, Atom Heart Mother, 16.08, The Embryo, 11.12, Green Is The Colour / Careful With That Axe, Eugene, 13.06, Set The Controls For The Heart Of The Sun, 13.45, A Saucerful Of Secrets, 18.04, Blues 7.12

[DUTCH ANNOUNCER: … de Pink Floyd!]
Right, good evening. Could you people go and sit down, please. No? It would be nice if you could. Obviously […] Please sit down, or at least squat down. Right, this is called 'Astronomy Domine'.

Astronomy Domine

Thank you. This is quite a new song and it's one of Dave's songs that's called 'Fat Old Sun'.

Fat Old Sun

>< [Audience laugh, Dutch announcements, extended bass tuning >< bass and guitar tuning.]

Cymbaline

Thank you. [Roger seems to be having trouble tuning his bass.] ><

Atom Heart Mother

Thank you. We'll be back soon. >< [Roger runs some scales to the delight of the audience, Dave tunes up.]

The Embryo

Thank you. That was a song called 'The Embryo'. ><

Green Is The Colour / Careful With That Axe, Eugene

[Tuning.]

Set The Controls For The Heart Of The Sun

>< This is the last piece we're going to play tonight and it's called 'A Saucerful Of Secrets'. It's the last number so sit down.

A Saucerful Of Secrets

Thank you. Goodnight. [Extended audience outro.] We'll start again.

Blues

Thank you, goodnight. See you again I hope soon.

There are probably four versions of this concert generally available. The first, as listed above, is the most complete but is of fluctuating recording quality. The second, as listed below, is incomplete: it is missing 'Blues' but it does have some additional spoken comments that are not present on the 135-minute version. The reader should note the distinct differences in track timings as well:

119.17, Astronomy Domine, 8.59, Fat Old Sun, 13.20, Cymbaline, 11.37, Atom Heart Mother, 17.16, The Embryo, 11.23, Green Is The Colour / Careful With That Axe, Eugene, 12.29, Set The Controls For The Heart Of The Sun, 12.49, A Saucerful Of Secrets, 18.04

[DUTCH ANNOUNCER: ... de Pink Floyd!] ><

Astronomy Domine

Thank you. ><

Fat Old Sun

>< [Audience laugh, Dutch announcements, extended bass tuning >< bass and guitar tuning.]

Cymbaline

Thank you. [Roger seems to be having trouble tuning his bass.] There's a track on our current album which is […] takes up the whole of one side, and it's called 'Atom 'eart Mother', and before we decided to put brass and choir on it we used to do it in a slightly different form, without the brass and choir, and we're gonna do that now. When we've done that we're gonna take a short break and come back and do some more. ><

Atom Heart Mother

Thank you. We'll be back soon. >< [Roger runs some scales to the delight of the audience, Dave tunes up.]

The Embryo

Thank you. That was a song called 'The Embryo'. ><

Green Is The Colour / Careful With That Axe, Eugene< Set The Controls For The Heart Of The Sun >< A Saucerful Of Secrets [almost segued.]

Thank you. Goodnight. >< [Extended audience outro.]

The third is a 60-minute version of the set which features the complete encore, 'Blues', and the fourth is an 118-minute version, which is missing 'Blues', from a different source again – or at least we think it is: it could be an edited down version of the 135-minute version detailed above. Confused? We have been at times. Whichever your preference don't expect to find a recording of more than a very ordinary standard. Often the 60-minute version sounds best. The 135-minute version will suit the more patient listener as much of the additional material consists of Roger tuning his bass, etc.

WEDNESDAY 11

• **Konserthuset, Gothenburg, Sweden.**

THURSDAY 12

• **Falkoner Centret, Fredriksberg, Copenhagen, Denmark.**

Again, more than one tape exists. An 86-minute version is of superior quality but is incomplete. The full tape is 110 minutes and features complete recordings of 'A Saucerful Of Secrets' and 'The Embryo'.

110.30, Astronomy Domine, 8.29, Fat Old Sun, 11.54, Cymbaline, 10.58, Atom Heart Mother, 16.51, Green Is The Colour / Careful With That Axe, Eugene, 12.59, Set The Controls For The Heart Of The Sun, 11.40, A Saucerful Of Secrets, 16.17, The Embryo, 7.55

Good evening. [GIRL IN AUDIENCE: Good evening.]

Astronomy Domine

Thank you … this is a new song called 'Fat Old Sun'.

Fat Old Sun

[Someone whistles along to the first ten seconds, extended guitar tuning after.]
><

Cymbaline

>< We've got a new album out, one side of which is called 'Atom Heart Mother' and which has a choir on it and some brass people. Brass instruments. And er … and er, there's a version of it that we do without the brass and choir. We're gonna end first half of this concert with that.

Atom Heart Mother

[Rattling of mics during first few bars.] Thank you. We'll be right back after … […] ><

**Green Is The Colour / Careful With That Axe, Eugene ><
Set The Controls For The Heart Of The Sun**

>< [Tuning and a blast of feedback.] The powers that be tell me that our first set was too long, so we've got, this is going to have to be our last number, I'm afraid, and it's called 'A Saucerful Of Secrets'.

A Saucerful Of Secrets

Thank you. Very much. Good night [Rattling mics.] >< This is called 'The Embryo' and thanks again very much for coming, it's really nice.

The Embryo

Thank you.

FRIDAY 13

- **Vejlby Risskov Hallen, Åarhus, Denmark.**

The tape below represents two sources combined. The first source cuts after 'The Embryo'.

Combined source, 93.35, Cymbaline, 12.37, Atom Heart Mother, 17.43, The Embryo, 6.48, Green Is The Colour / Careful With That Axe, Eugene, 13.57, Set The Controls For The Heart Of The Sun, 12.43, A Saucerful Of Secrets, 18.36, Blues, 5.46

This is a song called 'Cymbaline'.

Cymbaline

Thank you. >< We've got a new album out, the moment. We'll just do a track off one side called 'Atom Heart Mother', and it's with a choir […] there is a version which we can do […] and we're going to do that now.

Atom Heart Mother

Thank you […] >< This is called 'The Embryo'.

The Embryo >Green Is The Colour / Careful With That Axe, Eugene >< Set The Controls For The Heart Of The Sun

Thank you. >< OK? […] it's called 'A Saucerful Of Secrets'. ><

A Saucerful Of Secrets >< >Blues<

[Much of the dialogue obscured by the hall's echo.]

'Blues' is cut on the above version, though it would appear that the person who taped the first half also recorded this song as well, since there is an uncut version available.

Second source, 7.38, Blues 6.41

There is also a second, poorly edited, sixty-minute version from the same source as above.

SATURDAY 14

• **An interview with Nick Mason appears in** *Disc & Music Echo* **newspaper, UK.**

• *Melody Maker* **magazine, UK, interviews David Gilmour in their 'Blind Date' record review feature.**

    Pink Floyd guitarist David Gilmour wasn't at all impressed with any of the singles played to him, and had most of them taken off before the end. He liked a couple of the album tracks, and asked if he could keep two of them.

• **Ernst-Merck Halle, Hamburg, West Germany.**

128.24, Astronomy Domine, 9.09, Fat Old Sun, 13.36, Cymbaline, 11.20, Corrosion / The Embryo, 26.56, Atom Heart Mother, 17.04, Green Is The Colour / Careful With That Axe, Eugene, 15.03, Set The Controls For The Heart Of The Sun, 12.02, A Saucerful Of Secrets, 18.22

'Corrosion' and 'The Embryo' are particularly interesting on this recording, which is available in extraordinarily high quality, should you wish to seek it out. Nick counts 'The Embryo' in, perhaps indicating the band's perception of these pieces as being autonomous, as we have suggested previously.

    This is called 'Astronomy Domine'.

Astronomy Domine

>< ... a new song and it's called 'Fat Old Sun'.

Fat Old Sun

>< This is a song called 'Cymbaline'.

Cymbaline

Thank you. ><

Corrosion

[Interpolates an extraordinary 'raving pict' act by Roger.]
NM: Two, three, four.

The Embryo

Thank you. ><

Atom Heart Mother

Thank you. We're going to take a break ... >< Right. OK. Burn it up, next ...
we're going to do two things now, cleverly run together, first of which is a
song ... [mutters under his breath] called 'Green Is The Colour', and the second one is an instrumental and it's called ... [mutters away, 'Pink Jungle' vocal
theatrics] and it goes like this.

Green Is The Colour / Careful With That Axe, Eugene

Thank you. >< My Lords, Ladies and Gentlemen. On my right, in the all red
kit, The Massed Gadgets Of Hercules. In the right corner in the all black kit,
The Knights Of The Teutonic Order!

Set The Controls For The Heart Of The Sun

>< OK. Hello. OK. Fine. One we go. Right. OK. On with the show. Good,
right, OK. Is everybody ready? No? OK. Fine ... it's OK. Good, great, that's
terrific. On with the show. [Chap shouts for 'Careful With That Axe, Eugene'.]
I beg your pardon, sir. [Audience shout for 'The Nile Song'.] I'll sing 'The Nile
Song'. OK. Right. Fine. Wonderful, good. Right, terrific, great, wonderful. 'The
Nile Song'. Yes. Erm ... never heard of it. Any other requests? Who's a no ...
fine, good, right. We've come to the end of the show now, and this is going to
be our last number, thanks very much for coming here tonight. And it's called
'A Saucerful Of Secrets', thank you very much. [Drowned out by audience.]

A Saucerful Of Secrets

Thank you! Thank you very much ...

FRIDAY 20

* ***Barrett* by Syd Barrett released.**

November 1970

- **Super Pop '70 VII, Altes Casino, Montreux, Switzerland.**

Pink Floyd were the first ever rock group to play at this 'serious music' festival. The orchestrated 'Atom Heart Mother' was performed with 'l'Orchestre Symphonique de la Suisse Romande'. They were to return to the Festival the following year.

It is rumoured that a recording of the show was pressed up on a limited acetate. *Through The Eyes Of ...* describes the acetate's track list as featuring, 'Just Another 12 Bar', 'Astronomy Domini' [*sic*], 'More Blues', 'The Embryo' and 'David Gilmour talks' (an interview, presumably).[219]

A source that has been in general circulation for some time doesn't feature the aforementioned, but does include additional tracks which reflect the tape set detailed below. Copies have been listed as Jazz Festival promotional acetate, though unfortunately, while the quality is extremely good, it would appear to be an audience recording (see note below regarding 'Interstellar Overdrive'). Copies of the acetate labels feature the misspelling 'Astronomy Domini', which further suggests that it is a well-conceived forgery.

Morning show, 144.17, Astronomy Domine, 10.23, Fat Old Sun, 14.15, Cymbaline, 12.05, Atom Heart Mother, 18.00, The Embryo, 13.50, Green Is The Colour / Careful With That Axe, Eugene, 14.59, Set The Controls For The Heart Of The Sun, 13.30, A Saucerful Of Secrets, 18.36, Interstellar Overdrive, 15.33

Astronomy Domine

Thank you. This is a new song, it's a song of Dave's and its called 'Fat Old Sun'.

Fat Old Sun

Thank you. This is a song we recorded for a film called *More* and the song is called 'Cymbaline'.

Cymbaline

Thank you. >< [...] What was all that about ...? [Tuning up.] Got a new album out at the moment and it's called *Atom Heart Mother*, and there's a track on it called 'Atom Heart Mother' which has got a ... brass instruments and a choir and we're gonna do that now, and then we're gonna take a break.

Atom Heart Mother

>< Are we ready? This is called 'The Embryo'.

The Embryo

Thank you. >< These next two thngs that we're gonna do we're gonna do together. First of which is another song from the film *More*, it's called 'Green Is The Colour', the second is an instrumental from *Ummagumma*, it's called 'Careful With that Axe, Eugene'.

Green Is The Colour / Careful With That Axe, Eugene

Thank you. [Tuning.]

Set The Controls For The Heart Of The Sun

Thank you. >< [Tuning.] ><

A Saucerful Of Secrets

>< ...called 'Interstellar Overdrive'.

Interstellar Overdrive< [Guy recording taps and blows into the mics during the first few bars of 'Interstellar'.]

A shorter version of the concert, which omits 'Interstellar Overdrive', is also in circulation. Of a distinctly lower quality than the fake acetate, it may easily be distinguished by its not being sourced from vinyl. The sound quality on this copy leaves a lot to be desired; in places, at its worst, the recorder's tape player seems unable to muster the energy to move forwards – at the top of its cycle the tape's happy and at its bottom it drops out. Very frustrating.

A far greater claim to the crown of having been sourced from the Jazz Festival promo has recently surfaced on CD. The sound quality is outstanding, soundboard, and unashamed stereo, bar a few minor blips. Roger is a lot more talkative than usual, suggesting maybe that it was the band's intention to make a recording.

The performances are all very competent, but make at the same time, oddly uninspiring listening. The tracks that are missing, judging by the fake acetate, would have been more enjoyable.

[AUDIENCE: Roger!] Good Morning. This is called 'Astronomy Domine'.

Astronomy Domine

Thank you >< ... song of Dave's and it's called 'Fat Old Sun'.

Fat Old Sun

Thank you. We've got a new album out at the moment and it's called *Atom Heart Mother* and there's a track on it called 'Atom Heart Mother', which has got some brass instruments and a choir on it, as well as us. But we do a version without the brass and choir and we're gonna do that now. Then we're gonna take a break.

Atom Heart Mother

... we recorded for a film called *More* and the song is called 'Cymbaline'.

Cymbaline

Thank you.

Just Another Twelve Bar

[COMPERE (?), partly inaudible – in German (?): Thank you – the Pink Floyd!]

Morning show; 59.50, Astronomy Domine, 9.56, Fat Old Sun, 13.33, Cymbaline, 11.07, Atom Heart Mother, 17.36, Just Another Twelve Bar / Blues, 5.09

SUNDAY 22

- **Super Pop '70 VII, Altes Casino, Montreux, Switzerland.**

We would acknowledge that the additional blues track at the end of the above CD is highly likely to not be from the 21st, as is 'The Embryo' part way through the recording.

Roger refers to its being too 'late' – presumably in the evening – to play anything other than the blues, a comment that goes against our explanation. The audience ambience that introduces 'The Embryo' suggests that the track is being played after a break.

Careful and repeated listening to the stereo separation, general dynamics, and recording levels of 'The Embryo' and 'More Blues' / 'Blues' has led us to believe that they have a lot in common with one another but not with the rest of the CD. The 22nd would seem to be the logical choice, if we are to accept the suggestion that the band were making recordings with a purpose.

Probable afternoon show, 22.17, The Embryo, 12.30, More Blues / Blues, 8.48

This song is called 'The Embryo'. [Clearly after a break because of unsettled audience.]

The Embryo

Thank you. >< OK it's a bit late for mind expanding so we're going to play some music to calm down to.

More Blues (?)

MONDAY 23

- **Grosser Konzerthaussaal, Wiener Konzerthaus, Vienna, Austria.**

WEDNESDAY 25

- **Friedrich Ebert Halle, Ebertpark, Ludwigshafen, West Germany.**

109.27, Astronomy Domine, 9.00, Fat Old Sun, 13.18, Cymbaline, 11.58, Atom Heart Mother (with orchestra), 16.04, The Embryo, 12.22, Green Is The Colour / Careful With That Axe, Eugene, 13.52, Set The Controls For The Heart Of The Sun, 11.36, A Saucerful Of Secrets, 16.04

Astronomy Domine

Thank you. Thank you. >< [...] a new song off our latest album. It's a song of Dave's, its called 'Fat Old Sun'.

Fat Old Sun

>< OK. This next thing is a ... song.

Cymbaline

Thank you. >< Eurgh ... I thank you one and all. >< [...] brass section or a choir. >< Ready, maestro?

Atom Heart Mother<

This song is called 'The Embryo'.

The Embryo

Thank you. >< [Echoed whistling and other curious vocal effects, segued into]

Green Is The Colour / Careful With That Axe, Eugene

K'you. ><

>Set The Controls For The Heart Of The Sun >< A Saucerful Of Secrets<

A tape of edited highlights, featuring no extra music or comments, is also in circulation, timing in at 75 min. 49 sec.

THURSDAY 26

- **'Pink Floyd – The Interstellar Band' published in *Rolling Stone* magazine, USA.**

  Writer Jack McDonough reviewed the band at Fillmore West, San Francisco on the 21st, and spoke to them about their live shows, *Ummagumma*, *Zabriskie Point* and Roland Petit. The article, reproduced in numerous other periodicals,[220] is well worth finding as an overview of this period in their career.

- **Killesberg Halle 14, Stuttgart, West Germany.**

  59.47, Fat Old Sun, 14.08, Green Is The Colour, 3.56, Cymbaline, 10.29, Atom Heart Mother, 17.48, The Embryo, 13.12

  Fat Old Sun

  Thank you.

  Green Is The Colour [Cut where segue to 'Careful With That Axe, Eugene' is expected.]<

Cymbaline

Thank you. ><

Atom Heart Mother< The Embryo

A fifteen-minute West German radio broadcast of 'Atom Heart Mother' is also in circulation.

SATURDAY 28

• *Melody Maker,* **UK announces 'four special concerts' under the front-page headline 'Pink Floyd Tour'.**

The article confirms that the band appeared with a ten-man brass band and an 18-voice choir at the following concerts: Birmingham Town Hall on 18 December, Colston Hall, Bristol, on the 20th, Manchester Free Trade Hall on the 21st, and at the City Hall in Sheffield on the 22nd. Promoter Peter Bowyer commented that 'it is costing the group about £6,000 to put on these shows because of the large number of people travelling with them'.

• **Saarlandhalle, Saarbrücken, West Germany.**

SUNDAY 29

• **Zirkus Krone, Munich, West Germany.**

109.36, Astronomy Domine, 8.03, Fat Old Sun, 12.56, Cymbaline, 10.40 Atom Heart Mother, 15.37, The Embryo, 12.15, Green Is The Colour / Careful With That Axe, Eugene, 14.25, Set The Controls For The Heart Of The Sun, 16.48, A Saucerful Of Secrets, 10.48

... called 'Astronomy Domine'.

Astronomy Domine

... this is a brand new song and it's called 'Fat Old Sun'.

Fat Old Sun

>< OK ... er ... this is a song we wrote some time ago for a ... for a film called *More* and this song is called 'Cymbaline'.

Cymbaline [Edited during footsteps.]

Thank you. >< Thank you very much. Erm ... what we do intend to do is a song off our most recent album. It's on ... it's an instrumental, it's called 'Atom Heart Mother' ... thank you. I propose to sing all the brass parts myself – you may not hear them, but I shall sing them quietly. When we finish that we're going to take a break, and then we're going to come back and do some more.

Atom Heart Mother

K'you. Thank you. We'll be back soon' ><

>The Embryo

K'you. Thank you. This is a song called 'Green Is The Colour', and following it very closely will be an instrumental called 'Careful With That Axe, Eugene'.

Green Is The Colour [Mic fumbles at start.]

Careful With That Axe, Eugene,
Set The Controls For The Heart Of The Sun [Edited in middle.]

Thank you. [Whistling, dog bark, echoed effects.] This is our last piece this evening. It's an instrumental and it's called 'A Saucerful Of Secrets'.

A Saucerful Of Secrets

[Fades out as mics fumbled.]

DECEMBER

- *Melody Maker* features a full page interview with Ron Geesin entitled 'Ron's Got It Taped'.

Roy Hollingsworth spoke to Ron about *Atom Heart Mother* and *The Body* album and film:

> I saw it as the propaganda of the misuse of the lower class body compared with the higher class body. I didn't know really what they wanted, neither did they …

- *The Body* LP by Roger Waters and Ron Geesin released in the UK.

It was never released in the US. The soundtrack LP to the movie is 44 minutes long, while the actual film runs a full 112 minutes. The film featured a scene narrated by Roger Waters. It had made its UK debut a month previously on 29 October. In the US it was first shown in New York City on 24 February 1971. The film is worth locating as the soundtrack is radically different to the album.

FRIDAY 4

- **Recording at ORTF TV Studios, Paris, France.**

241

December 1970

- **'Troubled Waters', an interview with Roger Waters, appears in *Melody Maker* newspaper, UK.**

Roger speaks further about the Roland Petit ballet project – 'I'm madly reading all Proust, because that's the basic idea, so they tell me.' The interview, by Michael Watts, sees Waters in introspective mood, somewhat disillusioned with the extra pressures which their increasing success was bringing.

> I want to stop going out and playing the numbers. I personally would like to stop doing that now today I would like to be creating tapes, songs material, writing, sketches of sets – whatever is necessary to put on a complete theatrical show in a theatre in London … sometime and see if the people dig it.

Also published in the same issue of *Melody Maker* was a full-page display advertisement announcing 'Atom Heart Mother Is Going On The Road'.

- **Recording at ORTF TV Studios, Paris, France.**

We have not been able to trace any details with regard to this supposed performance, and make note of it on the strength of a trustworthy source!

- **Big Apple, Regent Theatre Concert Hall, Brighton, Sussex, UK.**

The advertisement for the gig, originally featured in *Melody Maker*,
is reproduced in *Le Livre Du Pink Floyd*.[221]

* **Village Blues Club, Roundhouse, Dagenham, Essex, UK.**

VILLAGE, ROUNDHOUSE
LODGE AVENUE, DAGENHAM
SATURDAY, DEC. 12th

PINK FLOYD

Advance tickets 25/- ONLY
Available from: Dagenham Roundhouse on Saturdays, or Pomford King's
Head on Mondays, or by post (send s.a.e.) to: Asgard Enterprises, 645/7
High Road, Seven Kings, Ilford, Essex. Please send P.O.s (no cheques) cros-
sed and made payable to ASGARD ENTERPRISES.

Advertisement in *Melody Maker,* 28 November 1970

The details that follow have been attributed by some to 6 February 1971 – we know this to be impossible. Given the version of 'Embryo', and the peculiar introductions, a performance date of Germany, November 1970 is thought by many to be likely. Following our chronology this would be possible only if it were from their concert on the 28th.

Having listened to many concerts from the period we have come to have a feel for audiences, equipment, and ambience. Informed by the track listings proffered by Povey and Russell, our instinct, contrary to others', is that the recording is from either this date or 17 January, 1971.

78.38, Corrosion / The Embryo, 20.49, Fat Old Sun, 13.32, Atom Heart Mother, 14.19, Green Is The Colour, 3.26, A Saucerful Of Secrets, 17.44, Blues, 5.47

Your Majesty The Queen, my Lords, Ladies and Gentlemen. Mr Nicholas Mason.

Corrosion / The Embryo >< Fat Old Sun

>< Right then. This next thing ... answer, echoed, is driving me quite ... clearly over the edge ... ah ... when we've done what we're going to do now, we're going to take a break, and what we're gonna do now is, er, instrumental thing called, ah ... I am an echo! Called 'Atom Heart Mother' ... [Whistles and pants through echo unit, in similar fashion to November 1970.]

Atom Heart Mother [Runs fast.] ><

Green Is The Colour< [Fades out where segue to 'Careful With That Axe, Eugene' comes – further evidence that it is from around the end of 1970.]

This next piece, is our last piece, and it's instrumental again, some time ago, and it's called 'A Saucerful Of Secrets'. Thank you very much, all of you for ...
><

A Saucerful Of Secrets

>< This is something a bit less heated to end it, I thank you all very much once again for coming ...

Blues

>< [Audience to end.]

FRIDAY 18

- **Town Hall, Birmingham, West Midlands, UK.**

Dennis Detheridge of *Melody Maker* reviewed the concert, and declared the occasion 'an unqualified success ... unlike their Hyde park summer concert, when the music was lost to the birds and trees, they were able to fill the hall with glorious sounds. It was a moving and a truly brilliant exercise in combining the worlds of electronic, orchestral and choral music'.

His article makes reference to their having performed 'Atom Heart Mother', with choir and brass as well as 'Alan's Psychedelic Breakfast' (the opening number), 'Fat Old Sun' and 'A Saucerful Of Secrets'.[222]

New Musical Express, UK, also reviewed the performance in their 2 January 1971 issue.

SUNDAY 20

- **Colston Hall, Bristol, Avon, UK.**

MONDAY 21

- **Free Trade Hall, Manchester, Lancashire, UK.**

TUESDAY 22

- **Sheffield City Hall, Sheffield, Yorkshire, UK.**

133.08, Alan's Psychedelic Breakfast, 23.13, The Embryo, 12.01, Fat Old Sun, 14.30, Careful With That Axe, Eugene, 15.11, Set the Controls For The Heart Of The Sun, 11.00, A Saucerful Of Secrets (with power losses), 23.27, Atom Heart Mother (with orchestra), 30.56, Atom Heart Mother (reprise), 2.44

The above reflects the only live recording of 'Alan's Psychedelic Breakfast' in (general?) circulation. Nick Mason described the track in 1994 as not 'really working on record but [it] was great fun live'. The recording is available on two bootleg sources, both of which are of very good quality. The CD version, which is otherwise complete as far as the music is concerned, features 'Alan's Psychedelic Breakfast' minus Nick's dialogue following 'Rise And Shine', while the vinyl version, featuring only 'Alan's Psychedelic Breakfast' and 'Careful With That Axe, Eugene', features the track uncut.

It would appear that the band were able to sneak an overtly psychoactive reference past most Floyd fans with the song title 'Morning Glory' – a flower indigenous to the United Kingdom, the seeds of which, taken orally, create an effect far stronger than synthetic compounds such as LSD.

A copy of an advert for the above four gigs appears in *Le Livre Du Pink Floyd.*[223]

Alan's Psychedelic Breakfast
Rise And Shine

NM: A cup. That's it. Is that working? Where're the matches? What do you think he's going to do with the sugar? Is he going to pour it all into the cup? Or is he going to spoon it? He's going to spoon it all into the cup. No he's going to [...] Do you think it's going to work here, boys? Mmm ... eurgh! Oh. Oh, this is pretty disgusting isn't it?! Hardly music!

Sunny Side Up

NM: ... ah, that's it! Mmm hmm ... Ah ha, bloody! Yeuch ... [...] you go ... egg hmm hmm.

JIMMY YOUNG [BBC RADIO 2 PRESENTER, INFAMOUS FOR TALKING NONSENSE]:

Morning all, and [...] living in Yorkshire. Oh, they have, you live in Manchester [...] and then, um ... our, yes, Yorkshire I said didn't I. The lovely Greenwood. And that's, ah, Yorkshire, hence the expression get Knottingly. Ha ha. Anyway, as you've heard, hmm, I get worse from my husband unfortunately Uncle William was out of the room and he missed all that, any way oh dear oh dear, she says never mind all that stuff she says and I say congratu-latio-nes to you Dorothy, um [...] and I say here's a memory to take with you which will make you very glad you ever came ... anyway [...] well, I can if you write me a postcard, can't you, of course. But anyway, ah ha. The thing is I a, eh, ah. Nearly forgot to say didn't I. If you would like to, ah, phone you on the show, numero tele-phonio that's the thing. Ah, but as I say, if you'd like a message included, well, write one now, whack one, whack one off to me and we'll whack it in the show. You and I look forward [...] in the BBC (?) ... IA IAA [...] I see ... but this is Stephen's you see and, ah, I think it's Mr Cross, any-way, um ... the writing at the end's a bit rotten. And so, Mr Unreadable Cross, unreadable cross ... unreadable cross [...] this is for you. Get well messages to you, and Mrs Keatons and er, that's that actually, and they say Froggie says Monkeydo, and I say well I very much hope so, 'cos that's what I'm here for, so I hope I will help you both get better, out and about very soon. Meanwhile, on hand from Monkeydo to Stephen Crew. Er, actually it's rather nice, it's not only these commas that don't trust me you see, they've got, they've done it. Your funny phonetics again. Stephen TREW in brackets, pronounced CROOO Jim. [...]

Morning Glory

NM: One two. One … You together? You together – yet? Hang on a minute. You together? It's OK, Dave, I mean there's no hurry … an' it's only five past eight, I mean we only started at half past seven, I mean we have done one number! I mean you take as much time as you want, mate, I mean don't mind me standing here, you carry on, You jolly well know that […] the volume on this mic, eh. One two. One two. ONE TWO! A bit better. Are you together. […] OK, mate. OK. Great. It may take some time this evening 'cos everybody's in festive mood, but we will do it all in the end, and we'll start now, and this is er … this song is called 'Embryo' … four.

The Embryo

Thank you. ><

Fat Old Sun >< Careful With That Axe, Eugene >< Set The Controls For The Heart Of The Sun >< >A Saucerful Of Secrets [with power losses] **>Atom Heart Mother**

Thank you very much, goodnight. ><

Atom Heart Mother (reprise) ><

A fine way to end the year!

Rehearsals at Mike Leonard's house
on or about 20 January 1967

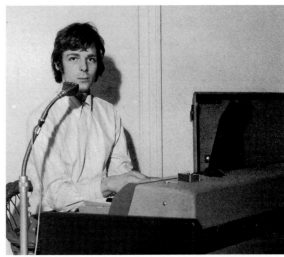

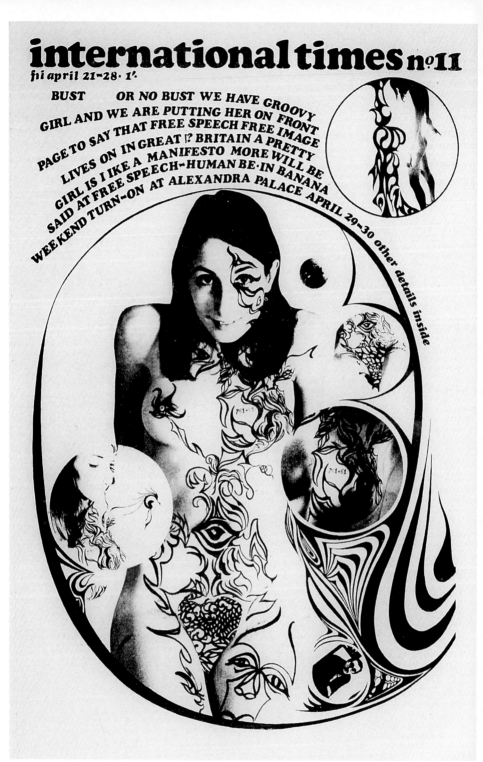

IT 11 promoting the '14 Hour Technicolour Dream'

Syd Barrett's Pink Floyd in flower-power garb for *Record Mirror* on 12 August 1967

Poster advertising the premiere of *The Committee* film at the Cameo Poly, Oxford Circus, London

Indecipherable and strange: the poster for 2–4 August 1968

San Diego Community Concourse, 17 October 1971

1971
The End Of The Beginning

- ***Crystal Voyager* movie soundtrack.**

  Crystal Voyager, 21.32, Echoes, 21.10, video

  It is often suggested that the take of 'Echoes' featured in the movie is different to that featured on *Meddle*. Having heard a low-generation copy, we are certain that it is the album version.

  In essence the film is a surfing documentary – the surfer being the 'Crystal Voyager' of the title – and features some great in-water photography. The band have used sections of the film in their own stage shows on numerous tours.

- **Weltweiter Superhit, West German TV.**

  Echoes, 16.43, video

  The show featured clips from the *Crystal Voyager* film.

- ***Barrett* album review appears in *Beat Instrumental* magazine, UK.**[224]

- **An article about the band appears in *Best* magazine, France.**

SATURDAY 2

- ***Soirée Roland Petit*, ORTF 2 TV, France.**

  Roland Petit and the band discussed plans for a ballet project. While footage of the band performing 'Set The Controls For The Heart Of The Sun' and 'Careful With That Axe, Eugene' exists, complete with ballet dancers, it is not in general circulation, and only about a minute of the show exists on tape.

  Beat Instrumental's Mason interview in April was to shed more light upon the project. Initially it was intended that the ballet be a presentation of Marcel Proust's *A La Recherche Du Temps* – an epic twelve-volume novel! This idea was abandoned, however, and the project was given the working title of 'A Thousand And One Nights'. Nick commented that:

  > Proust has been knocked on the head. Originally [Petit] was going to do a complete programme; a piece by Zinakist, a piece by us and a new production of *Carmen*. I think he has now decided to do just two pieces. Zinakist's and ours – which has meant doubling the length of the thing we are going to do.'[225]

The project would eventually see a public performance in January 1973, though the result was somewhat less ambitious!

MONDAY 4

*   **EMI, Studios 2+3, Abbey Road, London, UK.**

Work began on the *Meddle* LP. The musical parts of 'Nothing, parts 1–36', as 'Echoes' was originally known, were done early in the sessions. According to *Shine On*, these first sessions took place in Studio 2, and it is likely that they moved between the larger and smaller of the studios, depending upon which idea they were working on at the time. Nick Mason, in a contemporary interview, said that the band 'went in and played anytime that anyone had any sort of rough idea for something [and] we would put it down.' As evidenced by the live performances over the following year the lyrics were to be recorded far later in the sessions, as the band had tired of the romanticism of their earlier form and decided upon a re-write.

The sessions at EMI and AIR studios were engineered by Peter Bown and John Leckie. Leckie would go on to achieve a certain amount of fame as a producer of more 'alternative' bands in the 80s.

TUESDAY 5 – MONDAY 11

*   **EMI, Studios 2+3, Abbey Road, London, UK.**

It is likely that 'Seamus' was recorded fairly early on in the sessions. It is known that 'Echoes' was the product of musical experiments, and 'Seamus', which was recorded at Abbey Road, seems to fit this description. Seamus, it has been said, was Small Faces' Steve Marriott's dog – whom he'd trained to sing the blues ...226

SUNDAY 17

*   ***Implosion at the Roundhouse*, Roundhouse, Chalk Farm Road, London, UK.**

TUESDAY 19 – THURSDAY 21

*   **EMI, Studios 2+3, Abbey Road, London, UK.**

SATURDAY 23

*   **Leeds University, Leeds, Yorkshire, UK.**

- **EMI, Studios 2+3, Abbey Road, London, UK.**

David Gilmour interviewed in May 1971 and reproduced in *Sounds*,
17 August 1974:

> We spent about a month in the studio in January, playing around with various
> ideas and recording them all. Then we went away to think about them.

FEBRUARY

WEDNESDAY 3

- **Exeter University, Exeter, Devon, UK.**

SATURDAY 6

- **Royal Albert Hall, Kensington, London, UK.**

The Royal Albert Hall's archives confirm that Julie Felix performed on this
night. A concert recording miscredited by some collectors is noted earlier
under 12 December 1970.

THURSDAY 11

- **An interview with Roger Waters appears in *Disc & Music Echo*
  newspaper, UK.**

FRIDAY 12

- **Lecture Theatre Block 6 and 7, Essex University, Colchester, UK.**

Our tape, timing in at slightly over 90 minutes, is second generation, and
uncut. There is another version circulating which is cut onto a 90-minute
tape, which is incomplete. It should be noted that the first four songs and
commentary time in at almost 50 minutes, meaning that the recording will
not fit comfortably onto a ninety.

*90.46, Atom Heart Mother, 15.58, Embryo, 11.02, Careful With That Axe,
Eugene, 11.35, Astronomy Domine, 8.47, Cymbaline, 11.03, Set The Controls For
The Heart Of The Sun, 12.40, A Saucerful Of Secrets, 17.09*

From hereon 'The Embryo' is referred to as simply 'Embryo'. The band were
to revert back to the use of the title 'The Embryo' later in the year during
their American Tour.

OK. Here we go.

Atom Heart Mother

Thank you. This is a song called 'Embryo'.

Embryo

Thank you. >< ... do an instrumental called 'Careful With That Axe, Eugene'. [AUDIENCE: Oh great!]

Careful With That Axe, Eugene< Astronomy Domine

Thank you. ><

>Cymbaline

Thank you. ><

Set The Controls For The Heart Of The Sun

Thank you. ><

A Saucerful Of Secrets

Thank you. Very much. Goodnight.

<hr>

SATURDAY 13

* **Student Union Bar, Farnborough Technical College, Farnborough, Hampshire, UK.**

  86.17, Atom Heart Mother (with orchestra), 15.39, Embryo, 11.17, Careful With That Axe, Eugene, 11.48, Cymbaline, 8.02, Astronomy Domine, 7.25, Set The Controls For The Heart Of The Sun, 11.06, A Saucerful Of Secrets, 13.18

  ... 'Atom Heart Mother'.

  Atom Heart Mother

  Thank you. Here's a song called 'Embryo'.

  Embryo

  Thank you. Thank you. >< [Extended tuning.] Peter ... [...] One ... deux ... ONE ... and louder than that, Peter? This is a [...] it's called 'Careful With That Axe, Eugene'.

  Careful With That Axe, Eugene< >Cymbaline

  Thank you. ><

  Astronomy Domine >< Set The Controls For The Heart Of The Sun

  Thank you. >< OK, this is the last tune we're going to play [AUDIENCE: Ah ...]

'Ah ...' It's another oldie, and it's called 'A Saucerful Of Secrets'. Thank you all for coming.

A Saucerful Of Secrets<

TUESDAY 16

- **Syd Barrett session for *Bob Harris: Sounds Of The Seventies* at BBC Studio S1, Sub-basement, Broadcasting House, London, UK.**

The recording was broadcast on 1 March.

SATURDAY 20

- **Queen Mary College, Twickenham, London, UK.**

MONDAY 22

- **Théâtre du Huitième, Lyon, France (cancelled).**

WEDNESDAY 24

- **Halle Münsterland, Münster, West Germany.**

THURSDAY 25

- **Grosser Saal, Musikhalle, Hamburg, West Germany.**

93.04, Green Is The Colour / Careful With That Axe, Eugene, 13.54 Cymbaline, 10.26, Embryo, 10.09, Set The Controls For The Heart Of The Sun, 12.16, A Saucerful Of Secrets, 17.10, Atom Heart Mother (with choir and orchestra), 27.05

OK. We're gonna do a song now called 'Green Is The Colour' followed closely by an instrumental called 'Careful With That Axe, Eugene'.

Green Is The Colour / Careful With That Axe, Eugene >< >Cymbaline

Thank you. ><

>Embryo

Thank you. This is called 'Set The Controls For The Heart Of The Sun'.

Set The Controls For The Heart Of The Sun

Thank you. >< After we've done this next thing that we're going to do we're going to take a break 'cos we're going to do 'Atom Heart Mother' after the break and we need to change some things on the stage. And, but before we take a break we're going to do 'A Saucerful Of Secrets'.

A Saucerful Of Secrets [Note bird song at the very start.]

Thank you. >< OK. This is called 'Atom Heart Mother'.

Atom Heart Mother [Taped effect of someone unsuccessfully trying to start a car at the start – different to usual.]

There is also a 57-minute version and an excerpt of the concert features on the Italian 'Gong' EP. The EP was a freebie with a magazine, and was of course, unauthorised.

The Gong EP, 15.10, Introduction, 0.32, Green is The Colour, 3.15, Careful With That Axe, Eugene, 3.39, Embryo, 1.56, Set The Controls For The Heart Of The Sun, 5.26

Second source, 29.25, Atom Heart Mother (with choir and orchestra), 28.07

We'd like you to give a warm welcome to our brass section and choir, here, who're conducted by Jeffrey Mitchell. >< OK. This is called 'Atom Heart Mother'.

Atom Heart Mother

Right. Thank you very much, goodnight. OK. I'd like to say thank you to the choir who sang with us, and brass with us as well. Cheers.

FRIDAY 26

- **Stadthalle, Offenbach, West Germany.**

    109.16, Astronomy Domine, 8.40, Green Is The Colour / Careful With That Axe, Eugene, 14.51, Embryo, 11.25, Set The Controls For The Heart Of The Sun, 11.37, Cymbaline, 11.21, A Saucerful Of Secrets, 17.22, Atom Heart Mother (with orchestra), 21.02, Atom Heart Mother (reprise), 3.02, Blues, 6.10

    [What sounds like 'Atom Heart Mother' in the background.]

    Astronomy Domine

    Thank you. >< … two things together now, the first is a song called 'Green Is The Colour', and the second is an instrumental called 'Careful With That Axe, Eugene'.

    Green Is The Colour / Careful With That Axe, Eugene

    Thank y ><

    Embryo

    [AUDIENCE: Ow! Hee hee hee … ssh!]

    Set The Controls For The Heart Of The Sun >< >Cymbaline ><
    A Saucerful Of Secrets

Thank you.

>Atom Heart Mother >< Atom Heart Mother (reprise) >< Blues

SATURDAY 27

• **Recording for *Pop 2*, ORTF TV, France.**

The band performed a live take of 'Set The Controls For The Heart Of The Sun' which was broadcast on this date.

MARCH

MONDAY 1

• **Syd Barrett, *Bob Harris: Sounds Of The Seventies* broadcast, BBC Radio 1, London, UK.**

The show, which was recorded on 16 February 1971, was broadcast between 6.00 and 7.00 pm. Produced by John Muir and Pete Dauncey (for Transcription Services), engineered by John White. No additional personnel are listed on the session sheet suggesting this was a completely solo gig! This was not strictly a 'Peel Session' as it was recorded for Bob Harris' show.

7.00, Baby Lemonade, 2.24, Dominoes, 3.00, Love Song, 1.25

Syd also recorded one song listed as 'unknown' on the BBC session sheets. All copies of 'Terrapin' on tape have turned out to be from his first *Top Gear* session. It is worth mentioning that many tapes listed by collectors as the *Sounds Of The Seventies* broadcast, often substitute early off-radio recordings of the *Top Gear* session for certain of the songs, notably 'Baby Lemonade', so we advise careful listening to your copies to ensure they are the versions expected. As mentioned previously this second session was almost certainly solo and so features sparser versions of the songs, with little vocal double-tracking, and nothing more than a guitar as bass accompaniment.

SUNDAY 7

• **EMI, Studios 2+3, Abbey Road, London, UK.**

THURSDAY 11 – FRIDAY 12

• **EMI, Studios 2+3, Abbey Road, London, UK.**

March 1971

SUNDAY 14 – MONDAY 15

- EMI, Studios 2+3, Abbey Road, London, UK.

FRIDAY 19

- EMI, Studios 2+3, Abbey Road, London, UK.

SUNDAY 21

- EMI, Studios 2+3, Abbey Road, London, UK.

THURSDAY 25 – FRIDAY 26

- EMI, Studios 2+3, Abbey Road, London, UK.

SATURDAY 27

- An interview with Syd entitled 'The Madcap Laughs', appears in *Melody Maker* newspaper, UK.

  Michael Watts' article has been widely reproduced, most notably in Miles' *A Visual Documentary*.

SUNDAY 28

- EMI, Studios 2+3, Abbey Road, London, UK.

WEDNESDAY 31

- *Jackie* magazine reports that the Floyd are busy working on their ballet project, mentioned previously.

  The ballet, first reported in *Melody Maker* back in September 1970, would eventually see the light of day on 13 and 14 January 1973. *Jackie* reported that 'The plan is to stage it in Paris in the Grand Palais with an audience of 10,000 – no less – for a ten-day season. It would probably be seen on television all over Europe as well.'
  Dave was quoted as saying:

  > A leading French ballet producer approached us – saying he was looking for a fresh approach to ballet music. We were intrigued by the fact that we would have to write for a massive orchestra of 106 – and that we would be appearing with it.[227]

SPRING

- *The Asmoto Running Band* by Principle Edwards Magic Theatre released, produced by Nick Mason.

The album had been recorded in December 1970.

APRIL

- 'Until Recently We Were In Acute Danger Of Dying Of Boredom', an interview with Nick appears in *Beat Instrumental* magazine, UK.

Interestingly, the article reports that the Floyd are planning an idea to be staged in theatre form. Nick was to say that:

> Hopefully, it'll be something that settles in one place for one time. The idea being that we choose what we want to do – music, films, video, theatre, mime or dance – and then do it. We've been trying to do something like this for years, but we've only just achieved the financial independence necessary.[228]

SATURDAY 3

- **Sportpaleis Ahoy, Rotterdam, Holland.**

  144.02, Astronomy Domine, 10.11 Careful With That Axe, Eugene, 15.39, Fat Old Sun, 14.34, Set The Controls For The Heart Of The Sun, 14.42, Cymbaline, 12.22, Embryo, 12.16, A Saucerful Of Secrets, 24.04, Atom Heart Mother (with orchestra), 30.26

  One ... two. [Clicks tongue, whistles.] OK. Here we go.

  Astronomy Domine

  Thank you. [Extended tuning.] This is called 'Careful With That Axe, Eugene'.

  Careful With That Axe, Eugene

  >< This next thing's a song called 'Fat Old Sun'.

  Fat Old Sun

  >< One. This is called 'Set The Controls For The Heart Of The Sun'.

  Set The Controls For The Heart Of The Sun >< **Cymbaline**

  Thank you. ><

  Embryo

  [AUDIENCE: We want more!] >< OK. We're gonna do one more thing now, before we take a break. After the break we'll be doing 'Atom Heart Mother', but before the break we'll be doing 'A Saucerful Of Secrets'.

A Saucerful Of Secrets >< Atom Heart Mother

Thank you and goodnight. [...] Thank you.

There is also an edited version available on vinyl, notable since it features additional commentary, not available on the above tape.

87.27, Atom Heart Mother, 28.25, Embryo, 11.21, Set the Controls For The Heart Of The Sun, 14.21, Cymbaline, 11.15, A Saucerful Of Secrets, 16.59

OK. This is called 'Atom Heart Mother'.

Atom Heart Mother

>< [AUDIENCE: We want more.] OK. Now, this is called 'Embryo'.

Embryo

Thank you. Goodnight. ><

Set The Controls For The Heart Of The Sun >< Cymbaline

>< We're gonna do one more thing now, before we take a break. After the break we'll be doing 'Atom Heart Mother', but before the break we'll be doing 'A Saucerful Of Secrets'.

A Saucerful Of Secrets<

[Audience to fade.]

It is likely that the running order for this gig has been altered by whoever taped the show. Personal recollections of the show indicate that it ended with 'Atom Heart Mother', with 'Embryo' the encore. The concert began at 8.30 pm.

THURSDAY 8 – SATURDAY 10

• **EMI, Studios 2+3, Abbey Road, London, UK.**

SATURDAY 10

• **An interview with David Gilmour appears in** *Disc & Music Echo* **magazine, UK.**

TUESDAY 13 – WEDNESDAY 14

• **EMI, Studios 2+3, Abbey Road, London, UK.**

FRIDAY 16

- **Top Rank, Doncaster, Yorkshire, UK.**

A reader's recollection was published in *Brain Damage*, issue 36.

The concert opened with 'Atom Heart Mother (without orchestra), and directly after 'A Saucerful Of Secrets' 'Fat Old Sun' was interrupted by 'some jobsworth' who 'appeared on stage during "Fat Old Sun" and spoke into Dave's mic: "Would the owner of a grey Morris Minor registration number XXX please remove it from the front of the house" … Dave and Roger were gobsmacked but quickly returned to the song.' They also played (not necessarily in this order) 'Embryo', 'Careful With That Axe, Eugene', 'Set The Controls', and 'Green Is The Colour', and closed with 'Astronomy Domine', at the audience's request.

The band were supported by Quiver, Forevermore, and America.

MONDAY 19

- **Rehearsal at Cecil Sharp House, London, UK.**

WEDNESDAY 21

- **Rehearsal at Cecil Sharp House, London, UK.**

THURSDAY 22

- **University of East Anglia, Norwich, Norfolk, UK.**

Live debut (though not a public airing) of 'The Return Of The Son Of Nothing'. Obviously the band felt that the title 'Nothing, parts 1–36' wasn't enigmatic enough! The band recorded the performance, and used the tapes to help their continued work on the structure of the track, which was later to become 'Echoes'.

SATURDAY 24

- *Disc* magazine, UK, *Relics* preview and 15 May Crystal Palace concert announcement.

- *Melody Maker* newspaper, UK, publishes a two-page advertisement to promote 'An Afternoon At The Crystal Palace Bowl' on 15 May.

The same advert also appears the following week on 1 May.

April 1971

MONDAY 26

- EMI, Studios 2+3, Abbey Road, London, UK.

TUESDAY 27 – WEDNESDAY 28

- EMI, Studios 2+3, Abbey Road, London, UK.

MAY

SATURDAY 1

- 'Floyd's Search For Fresh Material', an interview with David Gilmour, published in *Sounds* newspaper, UK.

This article was the inauspicious first mention of the legendary 'Household Objects' project. Steve Peacock wrote that 'the Floyd have been experimenting for a piece of music made up from the sounds you can get from various household objects – glasses, a saw, and other odd things you might find lying about the house'. Dave was quoted as saying that:

> I don't think it will be for this album now. We got a lot of stuff down – enough for a whole side I think – but we've had some disagreement over it and I think the general opinion seems to be that it is not quite right for this LP. We got some jolly good sounds though, and it would be fun to show people what with a little thought they could get out of things they've got lying around the house.[229]

Nick Mason in *Mojo* magazine, 1994 on the subject of *Meddle*:

> We spent a long time starting the record. We'd worked through the Sounds of Household Objects project, which we never finished.

The band would still be working on the idea three years later.

- EMI, Studios 2+3, Abbey Road, London, UK.

SUNDAY 2

- EMI, Studios 2+3, Abbey Road, London, UK.

WEDNESDAY 5

- Technical rehearsal, Wandsworth Granada, London, UK.

The band hired the hall to evaluate a new PA system designed by Bill Kelsey, who had previously devised amplification systems for Emerson, Lake &

Palmer and King Crimson. Kelsey was to recall the session in a feature on the Floyd's live set-up for *Sound On Stage* magazine, published in March 1997.

> Peter Watts and Steve O'Rourke said they'd like to try a system so I went down with all the gear, and then found there was another PA company there and that it was to be an A/B test. Feeling a bit miffed that I hadn't been told, I set up the gear as did the other company, and they tried it out with the mixing console at the back of the hall.
>
> It seemed to be going alright, but Peter said, 'To be quite frank, I'm disappointed … it's rubbish.' And Steve cut in, 'You realise you've wasted my whole day, not to mention the cost of the hall.' Peter continued to push up one fader to produce this horrid, muffled sound, while the second fader produced a nice, clear sound. I just wanted the ground to open up. Suddenly they both burst into laughter and admitted they'd crossed the whole thing over.

Despite Watt's and O'Rourke's practical joke, Kelsey's system was later adopted for the 'Eclipse' Tour in early 1972.

It is often assumed that Wandsworth Granada was a facility owned by Granada Television. It was in fact a cinema, often used by bands as a rehearsal stage, and while it is no longer used for this purpose, it survives as a bingo hall (a case of the sublime to the ridiculous!)

THURSDAY 6

- **Morgan Sound Studio, London, UK.**

Mixing sessions by David Gilmour with Rob Black and Roger Quested engineering.

FRIDAY 7

- **Central Hall, University of Lancaster, Bailrigg, Lancashire, UK.**

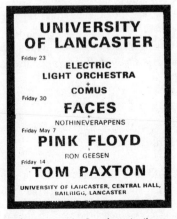

UNIVERSITY OF LANCASTER

Friday 23
ELECTRIC LIGHT ORCHESTRA
+
COMUS

Friday 30
FACES
+
NOTHINEVERAPPENS

Friday May 7
PINK FLOYD
RON GEESEN

Friday 14
TOM PAXTON

UNIVERSITY OF LANCASTER, CENTRAL HALL, BAILRIGG, LANCASTER

Advertisement in *Sounds*, 24 April 1971

May 1971

- **Melody Maker newspaper, UK, features a preview of the Garden Party concert on the 15th.**

The article announces that Floyd are to top the bill, and that they will play for two hours.

SUNDAY 9 – TUESDAY 11

- **EMI, Studios 2+3, Abbey Road, London, UK.**

FRIDAY 14

- ***Relics, A Bizarre Collection Of Antiques And Curios*** released in the UK.

It would perhaps seem sensible at this juncture to examine the differences between the versions of tracks on *Relics* and those which were released as original singles. We realise that this has been a matter of contention for some time, and the relatively recent release of the remastered CD further obfuscates the issue.

All the original single releases were in mono only, and are preserved in this condition on the *Shine On* box-set CD, *The Pink Floyd Early Singles* and the more recent *Pink Floyd / 1967 The First Singles* compilation.

The original *Relics* album featured 'fake stereo' mixes of 'Arnold Layne' and 'See Emily Play'. The fake stereo process adds nothing more than a hint of delay giving the impression of a fuller pseudo-stereo sound, as was common with a number of fifties and sixties re-releases at this time.

The remastered version of *Relics* has dropped these mixes in favour of the original mono versions, although in common with the original album the three other tracks released on 7-inch – 'Paintbox', 'Julia Dream' and 'Careful With That Axe, Eugene' are included as true stereo versions – unlike the actual single releases.

Please note that similar observations are made under our examination of the European-only *Best Of Pink Floyd* compilation, released in 1970.

SATURDAY 15

- **Melody Maker newspaper, UK, interviews Rick under the headline 'Another First For Pink Floyd'.**

The article adds detail to that published on the 8th amending the time the band are expected to play for at Crystal Palace to 2 hours.

'We are also planning a few other surprises during the act. We are getting quite a lot of money, so we are spending it on some extras to add to the act.'

Rick admitted that a certain amount of stagnation has set into the group as a result of their cutting down on live appearances – but hopes that the current activities will inject a new lease of life. 'We went through a stage of depression during the last few months, a sort of stagnation which occurs to everybody, but now we are going ahead again. It's very important for the band to keep together musically and not drift apart.'

- **An Afternoon At The Crystal Palace Bowl, Crystal Palace Bowl, London, UK.**

Sounds published a highly complimentary review entitled 'A Bowl Full Of Secrets At The Palace' on the 22nd:

As the magic of [the] first half hour began to fade, the Floyd's music took over as the dominant force, building moods of deep intensity, opening out wide, spacey areas, pushing out great waves of sound across the water to the back of the natural bowl arena and beyond.

Chris Charlesworth also wrote an interesting review – 'Rain Storms And Octopuses' – for *Melody Maker* on the same day.

… poor Floyd had to battle against the elements to keep the fans happy. It says much for them that thousands stayed to listen to one of their most spectacular sets ever.

Spectacular not only from a musical point of view but from the effects they brought with them. You can always rely on the Floyd to do something original, and Saturday was no exception. Not only did we have fireworks and coloured smoke rising from the lake opposite the stage, but a gigantic inflatable octopus – it must have been over 60 foot from end to end – rose out of the lake amidst clouds created by dry ice.

The creature, like something from a science fiction movie, needed a little prompting from a luckless roadie whose task it was to swim into the lake, extended to its full size as the group finished their act with the eerie 'Saucerful Of Secrets'. An encore was inevitable and the cheering crowds welcomed the Floyd favourite 'Astronomy Domine' despite the cold dampness of the afternoon.

It is clear from the above that the tape we have of the concert is incomplete. It seems that the band played for the originally intended two hours, and it is possible that while they planned on playing for longer, the performance was truncated due to the inclement weather.

81.51, Atom Heart Mother, 13.57, Careful With That Axe, Eugene, 10.00, Fat Old Sun, 12.00, The Return Of The Sun Of Nothing, 21.16, Set The Controls For The Heart Of The Sun, 10.10, Embryo, 8.46

Atom Heart Mother

[GUY IN AUDIENCE: 'Atom Heart Mother, Atom Heart Mother' ... I told you it was (ssh!) ha ha ha.] Thank you. [Unintelligible – distant recording with audience chatter very prominent. GUY COMPLAINS: Yeah, well don't keep talkin' – it's all going down on the tape.] This is [unintelligible!]. This is called 'Careful With That Axe, Eugene'. [Guy recording it debates going home or into a tent out of the rain.]

Careful With That Axe, Eugene [Edited in middle.]

Thank you. This is called 'Old Sun'. One two. One two.

Fat Old Sun >< The Return Of The Son Of Nothing

>< [Tuning.] >< ><

Set The Controls For The Heart Of The Sun

>< This is called 'Embryo'. One two. One. ><

Embryo

TUESDAY 18

- **Stirling University, Stirling, Stirlingshire, Scotland, UK.**

84.42, Atom Heart Mother, 14.01, Set The Controls For The Heart Of The Sun, 12.27, Fat Old Sun, 15.16, Careful With That Axe, Eugene, 9.53, The Return Of The Son Of Nothing, 20.42, A Saucerful Of Secrets, 11.35

Atom Heart Mother >< Set The Controls For The Heart Of The Sun ><
>Fat Old Sun >< Careful With That Axe, Eugene ><
The Return Of The Son Of Nothing >< A Saucerful Of Secrets<

The quality of this recording is nothing short of awful, although it has yet to be our pleasure to hear a copy which could be described as low generation with any certainty.

WEDNESDAY 19

- **Caledonian Cinema, Edinburgh, Lothian, Scotland, UK.**

THURSDAY 20

- **University Of Strathclyde, Glasgow, Scotland, UK.**

FRIDAY 21

- Trent Polytechnic, Nottingham, Nottinghamshire, UK.

MONDAY 24 – WEDNESDAY 26

- EMI, Studios 2+3, Abbey Road, London, UK.

FRIDAY 28

- EMI, Studios 2+3, Abbey Road, London, UK.

SATURDAY 29

- *Melody Maker* magazine, UK, publishes a half-page display advertisement for *Relics*.

The advertisement features a great line drawing which would appear to be drawn by Nick Mason. The design is different to that used on the European album cover, known to have been drawn by Mr Mason, and would in our opinion make a great poster – how's about it Hypnosis?!

JUNE

- An interview with Nick Mason appears in *Caio 2001*, an Italian publication.

WEDNESDAY 2

- EMI, Studios 2+3, Abbey Road, London, UK.

The band all but finished recording of the music for *Echoes* on this date.

FRIDAY 4

- Philips Verenstal Tungshalle, Düsseldorf, West Germany.

The first date on a European tour taking in Germany, Italy, France, Holland and Austria, ending on 1 July.

101.38, Atom Heart Mother, 15.12 Careful With That Axe, Eugene, 13.57, Fat Old Sun, 11.00, Embryo, 8.13, The Return Of The Sun Of Nothing, 22.06, Set The Controls For The Heart Of The Sun, 12.18, Cymbaline, 10.56, A Saucerful Of Secrets, 2.50

Atom Heart Mother

This is called 'Careful With That Axe, Eugene'.

Careful With That Axe, Eugene

K'you. ><

Fat Old Sun >< >Embryo<

Thank you, we're going to take a short break >< [tuning] >< OK. This, er, next piece is a new piece called 'The Return Of The Son Of Nothing'.

The Return Of The Son Of Nothing ><
Set The Controls For The Heart Of The Sun

>< 'Cymbaline.' [AUDIENCE: Cymbaline! Yeah! Yargh!]

Cymbaline

Thank you >< ... is our last tune for this evening it's er ... called 'A Saucerful Of Secrets'.

A Saucerful Of Secrets<

• **Berliner Sportpalast, West Berlin, West Germany.**

117.42, Careful With That Axe, Eugene, 10.14, Fat Old Sun. 13.48, Embryo, 9.49, The Return Of The Sun Of Nothing, 22.50, Set The Controls For The Heart Of The Sun, 13.46, Cymbaline, 11.16, A Saucerful Of Secrets, 18.29, Astronomy Domine, 7.05, Blues, 6.13

This's called 'With That Axe, Eugene'.

Careful With That Axe, Eugene

Thank you. >< [Guy yodels over the opening bars of 'Fat Old Sun'.]

Fat Old Sun

K'you. ><

Embryo

Thank you. We're going to take a short break. ><

The Return Of The Son Of Nothing ><
Set The Controls For The Heart Of The Sun >< **Cymbaline**

>< This is the last tune we're going to play and it's called 'A Saucerful Of Secrets'. Thank you all for coming. Thank you.

A Saucerful Of Secrets >< **Astronomy Domine**

>< This is hoping you'll calm down …

Blues

Thank you.

SATURDAY 12

• **Palais des Sports, Lyon, France.**

Broadcast on Europa 1 Radio, France, sometime in June 1971. 'Atom Heart Mother' was played with choir and orchestra. This show may have been the live debut of 'One Of These Days'.[230] Kevin Whitlock commented in an article in *Record Collector* no. 121 that 'Echoes' was played with the accompaniment of the choir!
   We have a first generation copy of the broadcast which is recorded on one channel only.

43.58, Introduction, 0.30, Set The Controls For The Heart Of The Sun, 15.04, Cymbaline, 9.49, Atom Heart Mother (with orchestra), 19.04

[French presenter's introduction.]

Set The Controls For The Heart Of The Sun

Thank you.

Cymbaline [The footsteps sequence is interrupted by the presenter.] ><

>**Atom Heart Mother**<

TUESDAY 15

• *Abbaye De Royaumont,* **Royaumont, France.**

ORTF filmed the show, and 'Cymbaline' was later broadcast.
   It would appear that most tapes in circulation are from the *Soirée Dim Dam Dom* show from 16 June 1969. These are sourced, in our experience, from the *Point Chaud* documentary broadcast, August 1974.

SATURDAY 19

• **Palazzo Delle Manifestazioni Artistiche, Brescia, Italy.**

124.28, Atom Heart Mother, 15.29, Careful With That Axe, Eugene, 13.44, Fat Old Sun, 14.37, Embryo, 11.16, The Return Of The Son Of Nothing, 22.33, Set The Controls For The Heart Of The Sun, 13.10, Cymbaline, 11.38, A Saucerful Of Secrets, 19.20

>Atom Heart Mother

Cheers. >< [Tuning.] ><

Careful With That Axe, Eugene

>< >< [Tuning.] ><

Fat Old Sun >< >Embryo >< The Return Of The Son Of Nothing ><
Set The Controls For The Heart Of The Sun

>< [Tuning.] >< 'Cymbaline' ><

Cymbaline

>< This last song's one we're gonna play an' it's called 'A Saucerful Of Secrets'.
Thank you for coming.

A Saucerful Of Secrets<

There is also a 108-minute version on vinyl, with the same content as above,
except 'The Return Of The Son Of Nothing' is cut.

SUNDAY 20

• **Palazzo Dello Sport E.U.R., Rome, Italy.**

*134.05, Atom Heart Mother, 17.57, Careful With That Axe, Eugene, 14.14, Fat
Old Sun, 14.15, Embryo, 11.15, The Return Of The Sun Of Nothing, 23.45, Set
The Controls For The Heart Of The Sun, 12.00, Cymbaline, 11.42, A Saucerful
Of Secrets, 18.22, Astronomy Domine, 7.44*

This concert could mark the last ever performance of 'Astronomy Domine'
(provided that is, you discount the 'version' performed on the 1994 tour).

OK. Here we go.

Atom Heart Mother

Thank you. Thank you. OK, this is called 'Careful With That Axe, Eugene'.

Careful With That Axe, Eugene

Thank you. This is a song of Dave's an' it's called 'Fat Old Sun'.

Fat Old Sun

Thank you. Thank you. ><

Embryo

Thank you. Thank you, we're taking a break for five minutes. [Italian
announcer explaining the same.] >< OK. This is a new piece an' it's called
'The Return Of The Son Of Nothing'.

The Return Of The Son Of Nothing ><

Set The Controls For The Heart Of The Sun

K'you. ><

Cymbaline

Thank you. Thank you. >< This is our last number, it's called 'A Saucerful Of Secrets'. Thank you all for coming.

A Saucerful Of Secrets

Thank you. Night. Thank you. [ITALIAN ANNOUNCER: The Pink Floyd! and else.]

Astronomy Domine

Thank you. Goodnight. [Italian announcements.]

SATURDAY 26

• **Amstel Free Concert, Amsterdamse Bos, Amsterdam, Holland.**

The band were supported by America and Pearls Before Swine.

First source, 60.26, Careful With That Axe, Eugene, 11.18, Cymbaline, 9.04, Set The Controls For The Heart Of The Sun, 11.29, A Saucerful Of Secrets, 18.21, Embryo, 8.46

[ANNOUNCER: … great joy we bring you The Pink Floyd.]

Careful With That Axe, Eugene >< Cymbaline

Thank you. ><

Set The Controls For The Heart Of The Sun

>< [AUDIENCE: We want more!] ><

A Saucerful Of Secrets

Thank you. Goodbye. ><

Embryo

Thank you.

There is a separate, short excerpt from a different source:

Second source, 13.46, Embryo, 8.36

ANNOUNCER: One two.
ROGER: One. One.
ANNOUNCER: My mic's just gone off.
ROGER: Gone off.

Embryo

[AUDIENCE: We want more!]

ANNOUNCER: Er ... we ... if, you'd like to help us, unfortunately the Floyd have to catch a plane, er ... they'd really like to go on all night. Ha ha. But, it would be really, really nice if you could just thank them one more time for getting through it, through such difficulties, 'cos it really was very very difficult. Er, and also, some people I'd like you to thank is their amazing road crew who've managed to keep all the wires intact throughout rainstorms throughout the whole day, that's the Floyd's road crew. Let's have a round of applause for them because they've been wonderful. That unfortunately winds it up. I'd like to thank the organisers and you especially, for sitting through all the rain.

The show, which took place at Het Amsterdamse Bos, a forest near Amsterdam, was blighted by rain, which caused all but the foreign bands' performances to be cancelled. Perhaps prophetically, the rain only stopped just as the Floyd took the stage.

JULY

THURSDAY 1

- **3 Internationales Musikforum Ossiachersee 1971, Stiftshof, Ossiach, Austria.**

A concert programme was produced for this week-long event, which reveals that the Floyd's appearance on stage was preceded by a performance of Mozart's KV 467 piano concerto by the famous Austrian pianist Friedrich Gulda.

88.45, The Return Of The Son Of Nothing, 22.16, Careful With That Axe, Eugene, 10.59, Set The Controls For The Heart Of The Sun, 12.19, Atom Heart Mother (with choir and orchestra), 27.26

One two. [Tuning.] One two. One two. >< [...] 'The Return Of The Son Of Nothing'.

The Return Of The Son Of Nothing

>< One. One two! This is called 'Careful With That Axe, Eugene'.'

Careful With That Axe, Eugene

Thank you. One two. This is called 'The Controls For The Heart Of The Sun'.'

Set The Controls For The Heart Of The Sun

Thank you, we're going to take a short break now. >< [Orchestra tunes up.] One. [...]

Atom Heart Mother

Thank you very much, goodnight. >< [Audience to end.]

MONDAY 19 – WEDNESDAY 21

- **Morgan Sound Studios, Kilburn, London, UK.**

16-track mixing sessions and overdubs for 'Echoes'. While the track had been completed back in early June at Abbey Road, the crow-like effects which link the two halves so effectively were finally added.

The various tapes which had comprised the opus 'The Return Of the Son of Nothing' were assembled both here, at Morgan Sound, and at AIR, which was also a fully equipped 16-track facility. AIR was owned by George Martin the ex-EMI staff producer, famous for his work with The Beatles. 'Echoes' itself was completed in July, and the rest of the album was recorded through the end of July and into August.

'One Of These Days' was also recorded and mixed at these sessions. Unusually for a Floyd studio recording, two versions of this track have found their way out of the archives, and make for interesting listening. As Cliff Jones notes in his somewhat disappointing book *Echoes: The Stories Behind Every Pink Floyd Song* [231] an experiment was made in which the voice of Radio 2 DJ Jimmy Young was 'cut up' into 'One Of These Days', and it is this which comprises these outtakes.

10.53, One Of These Days I, 4.32, One Of These Days II, 6.17

FRIDAY 23 – SUNDAY 25

- **Morgan Sound Studios, Kilburn, London, UK.**

TUESDAY 27

- **Morgan Sound Studios, Kilburn, London, UK.**

The day was spent recording the vocals for 'Echoes', along with a few guitar overdubs on the end section.

SATURDAY 31

- **Pink Floyd depart for Far East Tour of Asia and Australia.**

August 1971

AUGUST

SUNDAY 1

- **Arrive in Japan.**

FRIDAY 6

- **'71 Hakone Aphrodite, Seikei Gakuen Jofudai, Hakone, Kanagawa, Japan.**

According to the trivia test in the 1994 European Tour programme, the Floyd were supported by Buffy Saint Marie and The 1910 Fruit Gum Company.

The event took place in a forest, accessible only by a mountain railway as evidenced by the map that came with the programme / poster for the event. Particularly desirable items to collectors are the tickets for the concert, both of which are quite plain in design. The ticket for the 6th was green and for the 7th it was pink.

The band played late in the evening, and despite it being the height of summer it was a particularly cold night. Nevertheless the group kept their audience waiting for half an hour while they tuned up.

A 69-minute tape purporting to be from the concert is in circulation. Tracks from the recording suggest that the band played 'One Of These Days', 'Careful With That Axe, Eugene', 'The Return Of The Son Of Nothing' and 'Atom Heart Mother'. We however, have strong doubts as to whether the tape is truly from the 6th.

There is also a very good quality vinyl version that might either be from the 6th or 7th:

45.56, Green Is The Colour / Careful With That Axe, Eugene, 14.24, The Return Of The Son Of Nothing, 7.16, Atom Heart Mother, 15.43, Cymbaline, 7.13

[JAPANESE ANNOUNCER, GORO ITOI: Gentlemen, this is Pink Floyd.] ><

**Green Is The Colour / Careful With That Axe, Eugene ><
>The Return Of The Son Of Nothing** [Edited in middle.]

Thank you. ><

Atom Heart Mother

>< [ANNOUNCER: Pink Floyd!] >< [Firecrackers.]

Cymbaline [Edited.]

[Firecrackers.] Thank you. Thank you, goodnight.

SATURDAY 7

- **'71 Hakone Aphrodite, Seikei Gakuen Jofudai, Hakone, Kanagawa, Japan.**

A 45-minute recording in circulation featuring 'One Of These Days', 'Careful With That Axe, Eugene' and 'Atom Heart Mother' is most certainly bogus.

An excerpt from the concert on the 6th or 7th filmed by the local television station TV Kanagawa, was broadcast later on Japanese television and shows the band both arriving and leaving the airport, as well as performing on stage. The sound is badly dubbed and it may be that the footage was from one night and the sound taken from the other, or – equally possible – the sound is actually a particularly poor dub of the official release.

Atom Heart Mother, 16.06, video

MONDAY 9

- **Festival Hall, Osaka, Japan.**

122.50, Green Is The Colour / Careful With That Axe, Eugene, 15.24, Fat Old Sun, 14.32, Atom Heart Mother, 17.36, The Return Of The Son Of Nothing, 25.20, Set The Controls For The Heart Of The Sun, 14.13, Cymbaline, 11.34, A Saucerful Of Secrets, 21.33

> OK. This … first thing we're going to do is two […] together. The first is from the film *More* and is called 'Green Is The Colour' and the second is an instrumental called 'Careful With That Axe, Eugene'.

> **Green Is The Colour / Careful With That Axe, Eugene >< Fat Old Sun**

> >< [Taped sound effect of aeroplane taking off.] When we get this together it's gonna be a version of 'Atom Heart Mother' that we're now going to do.

> **Atom Heart Mother**

> Thank you. Thank you, we'll just take a short break. >< This is a new piece that we've been recording … […]

> **The Return Of The Son Of Nothing ><**
> **Set The Controls For The Heart Of The Sun ><**

> OK. This's … called 'Cymbaline'.

> **Cymbaline >< A Saucerful Of Secrets**

WEDNESDAY 11

- **Depart from Japan and arrive in Australia.**

FRIDAY 13

- **Festival Hall, Melbourne, Victoria, Australia.**

  79.20, Atom Heart Mother, 13.49, Green Is The Colour / Careful With That Axe, Eugene, 12.45, Set The Controls For The Heart Of The Sun, 10.46, The Return Of The Son Of Nothing, 18.37, Cymbaline, 9.56, A Saucerful Of Secrets, 5.00

  This was possibly the final performance of 'Green Is The Colour'. The band were supported by Lindsay Bourke and Pirana.

  > [Tuning.] >< Good evening. Right. This is called 'Atom 'eart Mother'.

  Atom Heart Mother

  > Thank you. This is gonna be two ... that we're gonna do two things together, first of which is our song off the soundtrack of the film *More*, which I think was banned over here, and it's called 'Green is The Colour', and the second is an instrumental called 'Careful With That Axe, Eugene'. ><

  Green Is The Colour / Careful With That Axe, Eugene

  > Thank you. ><

  Set The Controls For The Heart Of The Sun

  > Thank you ><

  The Return Of The Son Of Nothing

  > Thank you. >< This is called 'Cymbaline'.

  Cymbaline

  > Thank you. >< OK. this is it, our last tune, thank you all for coming. It's called 'A Saucerful Of Secrets'. Good to see you again some time.

  A Saucerful Of Secrets<

SUNDAY 15

- **Randwick Racecourse, Sydney, New South Wales, Australia.**

- ***Get To Know*, GTK TV, Australia.**

  Live footage of 'Careful With That Axe, Eugene' taken at the Randwick Racecourse was broadcast, although the music is taken from the *Ummagumma* album. The band were also interviewed for the show, but only the footage of 'Careful With That Axe, Eugene' is in circulation on video tape. The audio tape, which is available in surprising high quality, also features an extract of 'Set The Controls For The Heart Of The Sun', taken from the *Saucerful Of Secrets* LP.

Get To Know, Careful With That Axe, Eugene, 2.24, video

Get To Know, 8.41, interview and promos

TUESDAY 17 – THURSDAY 19

* **The band spent three days getting back to the UK.**

They left Australia on the 17th, and landed at Heathrow on the 19th, with a stop-over at Hong Kong on the 18th.

MONDAY 23 – WEDNESDAY 25

* **AIR Studios, Oxford Street, London, UK.**

'San Tropez' was recorded during these sessions; recorded in a very off-the-cuff fashion, it survives much as Waters' demo had described it.

FRIDAY 27

* **AIR Studios, Oxford Street, London, UK.**

The band completed the stereo mixes for the new album.

SEPTEMBER

SATURDAY 18

* **Festival de Musique Classique, Pavillon De Montreux, Montreux, Switzerland.**

The band played the evening show. L'Orchestre Symphonique De Vienne accompanied them on 'Atom Heart Mother'. Although the recording does not confirm this, *Shine On* records that 'The Return Of The Son Of Nothing' has been reworked and is now referred to as 'Echoes'.[232]

119.08, Echoes, 24.39, Careful With That Axe, Eugene, 12.14, Set The Controls For The Heart Of The Sun, 14.44, Cymbaline, 12.52, Atom Heart Mother (with orchestra), 30.04, A Saucerful Of Secrets, 20.51

Echoes

Thank you. [Unintelligible – obscured by crowds!] This is called 'Care ...' Dave, I mean Pete, can I have some top on this? One two, one two, one two, that's better. This is called 'Careful With That Axe, Eugene'. One two. Could I as well, Pete, please [inaudible – still concerned about the mic].

September 1971

Careful With That Axe, Eugene

OK.

Set The Controls For The Heart Of The Sun

Thank you. ><

Cymbaline

Thank you. Thank you, we're going to take a short break now. ><

Atom Heart Mother [And short trumpet solo in time with the audience's clapping.]

OK. This is called 'A Saucerful Of Secrets'.

A Saucerful Of Secrets

Thank you. Thank you. Thank you.

SUNDAY 19

- **Festival de Musique Classique, Pavillon De Montreux, Montreux, Switzerland.**

The band played the afternoon show.

TUESDAY 21

- **Command Studios, mixes for *Meddle*'s quadraphonic release.**

WEDNESDAY 22

- **Kungliga Tennishallen, Lindingövägen, Stockholm, Sweden.**

THURSDAY 23

- **KB Hallen, Frederiksberg, Copenhagen, Denmark.**

  III.44, Careful With That Axe, Eugene, 10.43, Fat Old Sun, 12.19, Set The Controls For The Heart Of The Sun, 8.49, Cymbaline, 11.24, Atom Heart Mother, 7.26, Echoes, 23.10, A Saucerful Of Secrets, 15.51, Blues, 6.13

  [Taped birdsong – same source to 'Cirrus Minor' et al >< birdsong continues; audience shout for 'Astronomy Domine' >< birdsong / tuning] 'One. One.'

  Careful With That Axe, Eugene [Roger 'shushes' the audience a few bars in.]

  Thank you. >< [Peculiar whistling effect.]

  Fat Old Sun >< Set The Controls For The Heart Of The Sun< Cymbaline

Thank you. ><

>Atom Heart Mother<

Thank you. Thank you. We're going to take a break. >< 'One two >< Terrific. OK. This is a new tune and it's called 'Echoes'.

Echoes >< >A Saucerful Of Secrets

Thank y >< you. >< OK. This is going to be very soft hopefully. ><

>Blues

There is also a 97-minute version available on CD, on which 'Atom Heart Mother' and 'Set The Controls For The Heart Of The Sun' are not present.

This is the first recording on which Roger can be heard using the title 'Echoes' as an introduction.

SUNDAY 26

• **Recording session at Command Studios, UK.**

WEDNESDAY 29

• **Setting up equipment at Wandsworth Granada, London, UK.**

THURSDAY 30

• **Rehearsals, Wandsworth Granada, London, UK.**

'One Of These Days' was rehearsed, amongst, presumably, other tracks which were to be played later that day. It has been preserved on tape.

6.05, One Of These Days

• ***In Concert* recorded at the BBC Paris Cinema, London, UK.**

The concert was broadcast on 12 October.

OCTOBER

• **'One Of These Days' / 'Fearless' promo-only single released in the US.**

The single featured different mixes to those available on the album.

SUNDAY 3

- **Napoli, Italy.**

MONDAY 4

- **An interview with Roger Waters appears in** *Melody Maker* **newspaper, UK.**

- **Roman Amphitheatre, Pompeii, Italy.**

Film recording for *Pink Floyd Live At Pompeii*. On its release the film was titled simply *Pink Floyd* and it would seem that the latter title was adopted for the video release. *Pompeii* was eventually released in the UK in late November 1972. A particularly fine set of US radio advertisements are available on a number of promotional singles (pressed up in 1974 to coincide with the delayed US release), and while these rarely come up in auction, they are available to collectors on tape

10.45, US radio advertisements for the Pink Floyd movie, twelve spots

1 'Pink Floyd, in concert, on the screen, the setting Pompeii ...', 0.55
2 'Pink Floyd ... music, electronics, space ...', 0.55
3 'Pink Floyd's music is a mixture of time and space ...', 1.02
4 'Pink Floyd in concert, on the screen. Pink Floyd sets up in an ancient amphitheatre near Pompeii to work their magic for the camera's eye ...', 0.55
5 'Pictures for your mind, the ruins of Pompeii ...', 0.27
6 'Pink Floyd. More than a movie, it's a cinemaconcert ...', 0.31
7 'Ah, I'm gettin' restless, you wanna go to a movie later ...?', 0.59
8 'I have in my hand raw electricity ...', 0.59
9 'Hello friends ...' (long version), 1.02
10 'When you see the Pink Floyd movie you just gotta marvel ...', 0.59
11 'The marriage of sound and cinema has continued for almost 50 years ...', 1.04
12 'Hello friends ...' (short version), 0.30

- **RTBF, Belgium, interview the band at Pompeii.**

TUESDAY 5 – THURSDAY 7

- **Roman Amphitheatre, Pompeii, Italy.**

Film recording for *Pink Floyd Live At Pompeii.*

SATURDAY 9

- **'Deep Waters' by Chris Welch, *Melody Maker* magazine, UK.**

He certainly is! Roger discusses recent morality drives such as the 'Festival Of Light', a censorship crusade led by Cliff Richard amongst others. He recalls visiting a live sex show in Denmark

> which was extraordinary. It went on too long, and certainly long before the end we were ready for hamburgers and chips. It was all very schoolboyish and patently obvious it was for people who didn't have the right schooldays.

Asked what his own plans were for a 'better, saner world' he muses that

> I'd like to help the revolution, when it comes. It would be nice if somebody could visualise the revolution, so we could have a slight idea of what to do. The trouble [with revolutionary theories] is, they all smell a bit. I'd sooner live here than in Russia and I'm not really into Soviet Marxism ...

SUNDAY 10

- **The Great Hall, Bradford University, Bradford, Yorkshire, UK.**

  117.12, Careful With That Axe, Eugene, 12.04, Fat Old Sun, 13.01, Set The Controls For The Heart Of The Sun, 13.59, Atom Heart Mother, 14.56, Echoes, 22.55, Cymbaline, 6.31, One Of These Days I'm Going To Cut You Into Little Pieces, 6.15, A Saucerful Of Secrets, 13.00, Blues, 4.15

  >**Careful With That Axe, Eugene**

  Thank you. >< [Roger clicks his tongue.] One two. One two. One two. Bit quiet isn't it? Don't worry about it. If it does get too qui … [cor, dear oh dear!] If it does get too quiet you will let us know, won't you?

  Fat Old Sun

  […] Thank you. One. [Almost total silence into]

  Set The Controls For The Heart Of The Sun [Edited about two minutes in.]

  Thank you. [Tuning.] Right, we're gonna do a … a version of 'Atom Heart Mother' now, obviously without the choir and brass … once we've finished that we're going to take a break, let you all have a drink.

  Atom Heart Mother<

  OK. This is a new piece, amazingly enough, and it's called 'Echoes'.

  Echoes >< >Cymbaline

  [Tuning.] >< This is another piece, and it's called 'One Of These Days I'm Going To Cut You Into Little Pieces'.

  One Of These Days I'm Going To Cut You Into Little Pieces [segued into] **A Saucerful Of Secrets<**

  […] psychedelics so we'll do something that isn't.

  Blues

MONDAY 11

- **Town Hall, Birmingham, West Midlands, UK.**

MONDAY, OCTOBER -11
at 7.30 p.m.
PETER BOWYER presents

PINK FLOYD

A N.E.M.S. presentation
All Advance Tickets Sold.
A few tickets available on night of
Concert only.

A review the following day in the *Birmingham Evening Mail* stated that:

Pink Floyd have one of the most imaginative sounds on the progressive scene. Their music starts like a storm; slowly, inexorably you are swept away … discovering quiet spots that lull before the compelling, moody, music takes hold once more. The silences before the applause proved the stunning effectiveness of this band.

There was a glimpse of their new album – 'Echoes', with its 'sonar' start, and 'One Of These Days'. Both show a movement towards wider experiments with electronic sound within the existing 'classical' development of themes that was so well exploited in *Ummagumma*, the album part recorded in Birmingham at Mothers.[233]

*   ***Sounds Of The 70s – In Concert* broadcast, presented by John Peel, BBC Radio 1, London, UK.**

The show, which had been recorded on 30 September, was broadcast at 10.00 pm on Radio One's medium wavelengths as well as Radio 2's FM frequencies – it was not until the late 1980s that Radio One got its own FM band. The producer was Jeff Griffin.

Pete Matthews wrote in his *Radio Times* column, 'This Week's Sounds' that:

> From their inception, The Pink Floyd have been a pleasantly confusing group. Classic Top 20 hits like 'See Emily Play' lured many an unsuspecting pop-picker into range of the harsh feedback of the early Floyd stage act; and the imposing version of their recent Ron Geesin-aided 'Atom Heart Mother' emphasised the relative feebleness of the songs on the other side of the album. Their fine sense of the dramatic lends itself to sound-pictures painted on a big canvas: hopefully a new work will be unveiled tonight.[234]

It should be noted that two mixes of the broadcast exist, the most notable differences being that one – for example, that available on the *Vintage Pink Floyd In Concert* transcription disc – features longer delay on the 'sonar' introduction to 'Echoes' than other recordings, which feature only subtle levels of reverb. Having spoken to a BBC engineer it would seem clear that Transcription Services often made their own mixes from the original multi-tracks, and that these would often differ from those broadcast at the time or held elsewhere. Please also note our comments regarding the previous Paris Cinema session broadcast on 19 July 1970.

In Concert, 60.00, Fat Old Sun, 13.48, One Of These Days I'm Going To Cut You Into Little Pieces, 6.35, Embryo, 10.02, Echoes, 26.05

> Radio 1. On Medium Wave ... And this is John Peel with another concert, and this one ... No! You blew it, you did it all wrong! Anyway, The Pink Floyd!

Fat Old Sun

> And er ... if you listened to this programme a year ago you'll have heard the Floyd do Dave Gilmour's 'Fat Old Sun' then, but it's, er, changed quite a bit

I think during the last twelve months. This next one is described by Roger Waters as a poignant appraisal of the contemporary social situation, er, you make what you will of that, erm ... during the course of it too, erm ... Nick Mason's vocal debut will come round, and, er, although you'll hear his voice, at no time, if you're here in the studio of course, at no time will you see his lips move, which is something of a technical tour de force, and it's called 'One Of These Days I'm Going To Cut You Into Little Pieces' or for the LP, 'One Of These Days'.

One Of These Days I'm Going To Cut You Into Little Pieces

Anyway, that's er, on the new LP and it's called 'One Of These Days I'm Going To Cut You Into Little Pieces' as you might have gathered. Erm, this next one has been released on a sampler LP by the Floyd's record company, and, er, they weren't too keen of the idea that it should be. In fact, they didn't know it was going to be until it was, er, because it was basically a demo recording that they'd done for their own edification and so it's radically different now as you'll hear, and its called 'Embryo'.

Embryo

Fine, fine music there from the Pink Floyd and that one's called 'Embryo', and er ... Programme's been produced by Jeff Griffin, sound balance by Wiper Lysett, leaping about by John Etchells. This last one takes up the whole of the second side of the *Meddle* LP, and the group's roadies, Pete and Scott say it's an extraordinarily good number and its called 'Echoes'.

Echoes

Of the above four tracks, only three appear to have been rebroadcast, and subsequently bootlegged. These are widely available and extremely high quality. 'Embryo' has been omitted from most, if not all repeat airings – most probably as a consequence of the band's never having given the track a full release (bar the US-only *Works* compilation).

In addition to the tracks listed above the band also performed an improvisation most commonly referred to as 'Blues', which has never been broadcast in the UK. It would appear to have only been transmitted once, along with 'Embryo', on New York City's WNEW-FM in the mid 1970s. *Record Collector* no. 115 comments, however, that a transcription disc of the show was pressed at the time.[235] If this is the case then it is most probably the rarest of any radio promos featuring the band. Interestingly, our research suggests that the BBC have retained 'Embryo', but no longer have the recording of 'Blues'.

WNEW-FM, 16.09, Blues, 5.06, Embryo, 10.38

WEDNESDAY 13

• **The band fly to the USA for their fifth American Tour.**

• **Winterland, San Francisco, California, USA.**

• *Cosmos*, **KPPC Pasadena, California, USA, radio interview.**

  36.42, interview with music

  A particularly groovy programme, which is well worth seeking out!

• **Santa Monica Civic, Santa Monica, Los Angeles, California, USA.**

  *150.03, Careful With That Axe, Eugene, 12.49, Fat Old Sun, 16.34,
  Set The Controls For The Heart Of The Sun, 12.58, Atom Heart Mother, 16.47,
  Embryo, 12.54, Cymbaline, 11.53, Echoes, 29.08, A Saucerful Of Secrets, 17.29,
  Blues, 5.50*

  [What sounds like an explosion into]

  Careful With That Axe, Eugene

  [Fumbling mics, church bells and birdsong into]

  Fat Old Sun >< >**Set The Controls For The Heart Of The Sun**

  >< [Tuning.] Peter, the stage one right speaker wasn't [...] very well, can you just check it out. Cheers. That's cool, that's [...] [Audience very vocal.] OK.

  Atom Heart Mother >< **Embryo**

  >< [Rick wigs out, tuning, mic fumbling.] >< ><

  >**Cymbaline** [Edited during footsteps.] ><

  Echoes >< **A Saucerful Of Secrets**

  Thank you, thank you all very much. [AUDIENCE: Here we go!] >< [Tuning, slow hand claps – GUY IN AUDIENCE: One, two three!] [Strange whistling effects, child crying.] 'This ... this time ... there ... er, y'know. I mean you'll have to feel for [...] so we're gonna do something else on *More*.

  Blues

• **Quadraphonic press presentation of *Meddle* at the Roundhouse, Chalk Farm, London, UK.**

  A presentation by EMI – the band was still on tour in the USA.

- **Convention Hall, Community Concourse, San Diego, California, USA.**

The poster for the gig features a collage of a flat-capped man in a field about to be attacked by alien craft. The view is seen through what seems to be a window that has wings. A notably high percentage of Floyd posters from 1971 and before feature images that suggest flying: the artists probably wanting to encompass the psychedelic experience. The band were lent support by Finnegan.

85.17, Careful With That Axe, Eugene, 13.08, Fat Old Sun, 15.21, Atom Heart Mother, 15.48, The Embryo, 11.24, Set The Controls For The Heart Of The Sun, 12.33, Cymbaline, 11.03, Blues, 4.50

[Wind and seabirds effects segued into]

**Careful With That Axe, Eugene >< Fat Old Sun ><
Atom Heart Mother >< >The Embryo ><
Set The Controls For The Heart Of The Sun ><**

... song called 'Cymbaline'. [Birdsong taped effect.]

Cymbaline

>< [Audience shout – someone requests 'Several Species Of Small Furry Animals'.]

Blues

Thank you again, it's really nice, we'll see you again, I hope.

TUESDAY 19

- **National Guard Armory, Eugene, Oregon, USA.**

One wonders how 'Careful ...' went down at this gig!

THURSDAY 21

- **Willamette University, Salem, Oregon, USA.**

FRIDAY 22

- **Paramount Theater, Seattle, Washington, USA.**

A reader's recollection of the show appeared in *Brain Damage* issue 35.
   The concert evidently started with the sound of footsteps circling the arena, after which the band came on and opened with 'Astronomy Domine'. They then played 'a somewhat abbreviated' 'Atom Heart Mother', along with 'Set The Controls' and 'A Saucerful Of Secrets'. 'Careful With That Axe, Eugene', 'Green Is The Colour' and 'Grantchester Meadows' were played

together. Electric again, the band performed 'Cymbaline' (with 'Roger performing lead vocal') as well as 'One Of These Days' and 'Echoes'.

SATURDAY 23

• **Vancouver Gardens, Vancouver, British Columbia, Canada.**

TUESDAY 26

• **Eastown Theater, Detroit, Michigan, USA.**

WEDNESDAY 27

• **Auditorium Theater, Chicago, Illinois, USA.**

139.32, The Embryo, 12.26, Fat Old Sun, 14.13, Set The Controls For The Heart Of The Sun, 13.04, Atom Heart Mother, 16.44, One Of These Days, 9.34, Careful With That Axe, Eugene, 10.36, Cymbaline, 11.25, Echoes, 23.15, A Saucerful Of Secrets, 14.40

The Embryo

Thank you. [Two guys in the audience discuss the merits of old versus 'new' Floyd while the band tune up in the background.] This is called 'Fat Old Sun'. [SAME TWO GUYS: What is it? 'Heart Of The Sun'? 'The Heart of The Sun'. 'Set The Controls For The Heart Of The Sun'?]

Fat Old Sun

>< [Mics rattle.] ><

Set The Controls For The Heart Of The Sun >< Atom Heart Mother

Thank you, we're going to take a break >< [Rattling mics.] >< [Tuning.] >< OK. This is a track off our new album and it's called 'One Of These Days'.

One Of These Days [Ends with the falling scream and bubbling effect familiar in earlier times as the intro to 'The Pink Jungle', over tuning, segued into]

Careful With That Axe, Eugene >< Cymbaline

[Rattling mics again.] >< OK. This is our last tune. Thank you very much for coming, this is called 'Echoes'.

Echoes >< [...] Astronomy Domine

[...] We're going to play 'A Saucerful Of Secrets' [...] [AUDIENCE: You hear what he said? Yeah. What'd he say? ... they don't play 'Saucerful Of Secrets' anymore because they've played it about 500,000 times. Oh.)

A Saucerful Of Secrets

Thank you. Thank you, goodnight. [...]

THURSDAY 28

- **Hill Auditorium, Ann Arbor, Michigan, USA.**

The group were supported by Guardian Angel. The gig was part of the 'Homecoming 1971'.

133.43, The Embryo, 12.43, Fat Old Sun, 15.09, Set The Controls For The Heart Of The Sun, 14.19, Atom Heart Mother, 16.43, One Of These Days, 9.26, Careful With That Axe, Eugene, 12.14, Cymbaline, 11.55, Echoes, 27.18, Blues, 5.34

[Audience] ><

>The Embryo

>< Thank you. That was a song called 'The Embryo'. This next thing is ... called 'Fat Old Sun'.

Fat Old Sun< **Set The Controls For The Heart Of The Sun**

Thank you. >< This next piece is called 'Atom Heart Mother' and when we've done this we're gonna take a break for quarter of an hour. ><

Atom Heart Mother

K'you. >< >< OK. This is called 'One Of These Days', it's off our next album.

One Of These Days

[Outro as previous night, tuning, segued into]

Careful With That Axe, Eugene [Edited moments after it starts.] >< >**Cymbaline**

K'you. >< [tuning] >< One >< This is erm, a cut from another, cut from our new album, *Meddle*, which doubtless you all […] one side and it's called 'Echoes' and I […] you all. ><

Echoes

Thank you and goodnight. >< […]

Blues

Thank you. goodnight. Goodnight.

SATURDAY 30

- *Meddle* **released in the USA.**

It was to be released in the UK on 13 November.

The April 1993 issue of *Q* magazine states with conviction that '"Dark Side Of The Moon" was originally the title of a song written by Roger

Waters during the recording of the *Meddle* album in 1971.' Some credence is given to the concept, if not the fact, under our Late December entry.

SUNDAY 31

• **Fieldhouse, University of Toledo, Toledo, Ohio, USA.**

81.44, Set The Controls For The Heart Of The Sun, 10.56, Atom Heart Mother, 15.17, One Of These Days, 8.15, Careful With That Axe, Eugene, 9.55, Cymbaline, 7.09, Echoes, 22.52, Blues, 4.53

Set The Controls For The Heart Of The Sun

OK. ><

Atom Heart Mother

Thank you. ><

One Of These Days >< >Cymbaline< >Careful With That Axe, Eugene

[AUDIENCE: Er ... OK!] ><

Echoes

Thank you. Goodnight. ><

Blues

[AUDIENCE: More! More! Woo!] Goodnight. [AUDIENCE: ... come right over.]

NOVEMBER

• **'One of These Days' / 'Fearless' single, USA.**

A general release for the promo released in October.

TUESDAY 2

• **Princeton University, Princeton, New Jersey, USA.**

WEDNESDAY 3

• **Central Theater, Passaic, New Jersey, USA.**

This show may have been replaced by Providence, Rhode Island.

November 1971

THURSDAY 4

- **Lowes Theater, Providence, Rhode Island, USA.**

FRIDAY 5

- **Assembly Hall, Hunter College, Columbia University of New York (CUNY), New York City, New York, USA.**

    149.22, Embryo, 17.29, Fat Old Sun, 14.10, Set The Controls For The Heart Of The Sun, 13.32, Atom Heart Mother, 17.23, One Of These Days, 10.45, Careful With That Axe, Eugene, 14.40, Cymbaline, 11.16 Echoes, 26.05, A Saucerful Of Secrets, 18.33

    This's called 'Embryo'.

    Embryo

    [Tuning.]

    Fat Old Sun

    Thank you. >< ><

    One Of These Days ['The Pink Jungle' gurgles, but no scream.]

    Careful With That Axe, Eugene

    Thank you. 'S called 'Cymbaline'.

    **Cymbaline >< >Atom Heart Mother ><
    Set The Controls For The Heart Of The Sun ><**

    >< ''Choes.'

    Echoes [Rubbing of mics during the opening minutes.]

    Thank you. >< ><

    A Saucerful Of Secrets

    Thank you, goodnight.

SATURDAY 6

- **Emerson Gym, Case Western Reserve University (CWRU), Cleveland, Ohio, USA.**

    An American contact of ours is quite sure that a tape of this gig exists. Copies in common circulation always (thus far) turn out to be mislabelled copies of the Taft Auditorium show on the 20th. Our friend says that the genuine copy is of inferior quality to that of the 20th and may be easily recognised by 'Embryo' not lasting the expected 27 minutes.

MONDAY 8

• **Peace Bridge Exhibition Center, Buffalo, New York, USA.**

TUESDAY 9

• **Centre Sportif, Université de Montréal, Montréal, Quebec, Canada.**

WEDNESDAY 10

• **Pavillon De La Jeunesse, Quebec, Canada.**

131.43, Embryo, 11.39, Fat Old Sun, 14.36, Set The Controls For The Heart Of The Sun, 12.03, One of These Days, 8.07 Atom Heart Mother, 14.07, Cymbaline, 11.58, Careful With That Axe, Eugene, 12.08, Echoes, 25.17, A Saucerful Of Secrets, 16.50

[ANNOUNCER: Bon soir, ha? Comment ça va?] >< Ah, ah, ee. Oh good, bon.

Embryo

Thank you. ><

Fat Old Sun

Thank you ... thank you. ><

Set The Controls For The Heart Of The Sun

Thank you. [Announces, in French] 'One Of These Days I'm Going To Cut You Into Little Pieces'. ><

One Of These Days

>< En va joue un morso qui s'appelle 'Atom Heart Mother' ... er ...[236] ><

Atom Heart Mother<

Soundtrack of the movie *More* and it's called 'Cymbaline'. ><

Cymbaline [Edited during footsteps.]

Thank you.

>Careful With That Axe, Eugene [Clips at start.]

Thank you. >< This is called 'Echoes'.

Echoes

Thank you goodnight. Thank you, bon soir. >< Thank you for coming. I hope we'll see you all soon, this is called 'A Saucerful Of Secrets'.

A Saucerful Of Secrets

Thank you, goodnight.

There is also an edited 65-minute version available on CD.

THURSDAY 11

- **Music Hall, Boston, Massachusetts, USA.**

FRIDAY 12

- **Irvine Auditorium, Pennsylvania State University, Philadelphia, Pennsylvania, USA.**

    First source, 71.47, The Embryo, 11.44, Fat Old Sun, 14.33, Set The Controls For The Heart Of The Sun, 13.50, Echoes, 26.10

    [Echoed bass thumps, tuning.] One, two. This is called 'The Embryo'.

    The Embryo

    Thank you. [Tuning, rustling mics.]

    Fat Old Sun

    Thank you. [Tuning.]

    Set The Controls For The Heart Of The Sun< >Echoes [clipped at the beginning, mics rustle during the sonar intro]

    [AUDIENCE: More ...]

    Second source, 47.47, Atom Heart Mother, 15.46, One Of These Days, 8.06, Careful With That Axe, Eugene, 12.32, Cymbaline, 10.54

    >Atom Heart Mother

    Thank you. ><

    One Of These Days >< >Careful With That Axe, Eugene >< >Cymbaline >< ><

SATURDAY 13

- *Meddle* **LP released in the UK.**

- **Capital Radio ads for *Relics* and *Meddle*.**

    While *Relics* and *Meddle* were of course released on different dates Capital Radio's advertisements are more often than not found together, so we have listed them as such.

    3.00, Relics I, 0.57, Relics II, 0.57, Meddle 0.55

- *Meddle* review, *Sounds* magazine, UK.

Steve Peacock's review was highly complimentary of the new disc, describing 'a side of surprises from the Floyd on this album, and on the other side a really effective and well executed piece of music called "Echoes".' The piece is accompanied by a picture of a rather confused Roger Waters – no doubt because they decided to caption it as 'Roger Walters'!

- *Meddle* review, *Record Mirror* magazine, UK.

Another reasonably interesting review appeared in *Melody Maker* around this time: 'Pink's Muddled Meddle'.[237]

- Convention Hall, Asbury Park, New Jersey, USA.

SUNDAY 14

- State University of New York (SUNY), Stony Brook, Long Island, New York, USA.

MONDAY 15

- Carnegie Hall, Manhattan, New York City, New York, USA.

39.54, One of These Days, 9.14, Atom Heart Mother, 5.37, Set The Controls For The Heart Of The Sun, 12.03, Fat Old Sun, 12.13

One Of These Days >< Atom Heart Mother [Fades in part way through.]
Set The Controls For The Heart Of The Sun

Thank you.

Fat Old Sun

The band were interviewed by *Disc* magazine, who also reviewed the gig:

The audience treated their Carnegie Hall concert this week as if it were almost a religious event. The incredibly loud, spacey music, accompanied by those great sound effects created an atmosphere that was really cosmic. Pink Floyd played for almost three hours, and despite some minor problems, they were a huge success with a totally sold-out crowd of 2,900 people.

Dave complained in the interview about having to play the same songs every night.

'In England it's different,' he said. 'We can do anything we like really. We've often gone on stage and done material that we've never done before and the audiences are used to us and they love it. But in the States, it's more or less like we have to play our "hits".'[238]

November 1971

TUESDAY 16

- **Lisner Auditorium, The George Washington University, Washington, District of Columbia, USA.**

  112.55, The Embryo, 11.32, Fat Old Sun, 13.49, Set the Controls For The Heart Of The Sun, 13.45, Atom Heart Mother, 15.24, One Of These Days, 8.38, Careful with That Axe, Eugene, 13.04, Cymbaline, 11.43, Echoes, 23.52

  [Audience] ><

  The Embryo >< Fat Old Sun

  Thank you. ><

  Set The Controls For The Heart Of The Sun

  Thank you. ><

  Atom Heart Mother [Mics hit during the intro.]

  Thank you. We're going to take a break now … ><

  One Of These Days [Edited seconds in.]

  >< Careful With That Axe, Eugene [Mics knocked during the final moments.]

  Thank you. ><

  >Cymbaline >< Echoes ><

  [AUDIENCE: More!]

FRIDAY 19

- **Syria Mosque Theater, Pittsburgh, Pennsylvania, USA.**

SATURDAY 20

- **Taft Auditorium, University of Cincinnati, Cincinnati, Ohio, USA.**

  129.10, The Embryo, 25.22, Set The Controls For The Heart Of The Sun, 14.02, Fat Old Sun, 12.08, Atom Heart Mother, 18.09 Careful With That Axe, Eugene, 11.50, Cymbaline, 11.08 Echoes, 25.34, Blues, 7.22

  This tape features the longest version of 'The Embryo' available. It has been suggested that the reason behind this was that the band were experiencing technical difficulties; whatever the cause, the result is sublime.

  One two. Good, and this is the first number an' it's called 'The Embryo'.

  The Embryo >< Set The Controls For The Heart Of The Sun

  [AUDIENCE: Yo!] ><

Fat Old Sun >< Atom Heart Mother >< ><
>Careful With That Axe, Eugene

[AUDIENCE: Yeah!] [Tuning >< more tuning.]
This next thing is a song from the soundtrack of a movie that you almost
certainly haven't seen called *More* an' it's called 'Cymbaline'.

Cymbaline

>< This is the last piece we're going to play an' it's called 'Echoes', and thank
you all very much for coming … tonight.

Echoes

>< >< …gig of our tour, we've been over here for five weeks, now I'm glad
we've finished here 'cos it's been good fun, tonight, really, so … this erm …
encore has really got nothing to do with us.

Blues

DECEMBER

• **Broadhurst Gardens, West Hampstead, London, UK.**

The band spent four days rehearsing and writing new material for what
would become *Eclipsed*.

MONDAY 13 – TUESDAY 21

• **Unknown TV Studios, Paris, France.**

Additional 'live' sequences were shot so as to tidy up the footage on *Live At
Pompeii*.

LATE

• **Bermondsey, London, UK.**

The group spent the rest of December writing and rehearsing *Eclipsed*. Roger
has gone on record as saying that they spent 5–6 weeks working on the
'Eclipsed' suite.
In *Vox Pop* Roger is quoted as saying:

Everything we got together we immediately put on the Revox. At the end of
four days we'd got half a dozen short pieces of music. It was exactly the same
technique we used when we put together *Meddle*. Just putting ideas down.
I had actually written a song previously when we were finishing the *Meddle*

album about the lunatic on the grass, and it had been running round my mind. We had Christmas off and then we reconvened on January 1st.[239]

THURSDAY 23

- **An interview with Syd Barrett – 'The Madcap Who Named Pink Floyd', appears in *Rolling Stone* magazine, USA.**

Syd, seemingly a broken man, commented, 'Everyone is supposed to have fun when they're young – I don't know why, but I never did.' Perhaps it is comforting to recall the more contented comments he made more than once in the happier days of 1967.

SATURDAY 25

- **'New Phase In The Busy Life Of The Floyd', part one of two interviews with Roger by Steve Peacock, appears in *Sounds* magazine, UK.**

The second part of the interview was published on 1 January 1972.

Intriguingly Peacock makes reference to talking to Waters about 'a film they're making', which is to appear in part two. Unfortunately no mention is made in the second part, though the film in question is most likely *La Vallée*. While it would be nice to end things on a high point, Roger's verdict at the time was that 'there's a feeling in the group that we've let things slide horribly.'

Part two of the interview is extremely interesting as an indication of the concerns which led to the creation of *Eclipsed*:

> We've got to step back from that whole career / money thing and make the right decisions, and take as little notice of all those pressures as possible. And I think that would cause us to make better music.

The irony would be that it is precisely these pressures which inspired the longest charting album ever ...

Notes

1 Glenn Povey and Ian Russell, *Pink Floyd: In The Flesh. The Complete Performance History* (London: Bloomsbury), 1997, pp. 8–19.

2 *Mojo*, UK, September 1996.

3 *Chapter 24*, no. 4.

4 See also 13 March 1967.

5 Michael Wale, *Vox Pop: Profiles Of The Pop Process* (London: Harrap), 1972, p. 135

6 *Mojo*, July 1995.

7 Nigel Fountain, *Underground: The London Alternative Press 1966–1974* (London: Comedia), 1988, p. 24.

8 Jonathan Green, *Days In The Life: Voices From The English Underground* (London: Heinemann), 1988, p. 54.

9 Miles, *Pink Floyd. A Visual Documentary* (London: Omnibus Press), 1980, unnumbered pages.

10 Pete Frame, 'The Year Of Love Including The Birth Of The Pink Floyd', *zigzag* 25 (undated).

11 *The Story Of Pop no. 26: A Trip On The London Underground*, BBC Radio 1, London, 12 July 1994.

12 *Joe Boyd: A World Of Music*, BBC Radio 2, London, 26 February 1997

13 See also 11–12th January, 1967.

14 *Underground*, p. 26.

15 Mike Watkinson and Pete Anderson, *Crazy Diamond: Syd Barrett And The Dawn Of Pink Floyd* (London: Omnibus Press), 1991, p. 42.

16 Mick Farren, *Watch Out Kids* (London: Open Gate Books), 1972, unnumbered pages. Roger Hutchinson reproduces the same in *High Sixties: The Summers Of Riot And Love* (Edinburgh: Mainstream Publishing), 1992, p. 91.

17 *New Society*, 27 October 1966, p. 637.

18 *Mojo*, May 1994.

19 See *Days In The Life*, p. 110.

20 Watkinson and Anderson, *Crazy Diamond*, p. 43.

21 *Omnibus: The Pink Floyd Story*, BBC TV 1, London, 15 November 1994.

22 *Melody Maker*, 14 January 1967.

23 *Kentish Gazette*, 18 November 1966.

24 Both articles have been helpfully reproduced in *Chapter 24*, no. 3.

25 *IT* 5, 12 December 1966.

26 Rick Sanders, *Pink Floyd* (London: Futura), 1976, p. 13.

27 See *Days In The Life*, pp. 132–140.

28 *Melody Maker*, 17 June 1967.

29 *Melody Maker*, 24 December 1966.

30 The *Daily Mail*, 2 January 1967.

31 Bruno MacDonald (ed), *Through The Eyes Of … The Band, Its Fans, Friends and Foes* (London: Sidgewick and Jackson), 1996, p. 194 and others. See also 17 April 1969.

32 *Days In The Life*, p. 112.

33 *The Pink Floyd Story Part 1: The Early Years*, Capital Radio, London, 17 December 1976.
34 Joe Boyd: *A World Of Music*.
35 See also 11 April 1967.
36 *Mojo*, July 1995.
37 *Days In The Life*, p. 108.
38 Watkinson and Anderson, *Crazy Diamond*, p. 51.
39 *Voxpop*, p. 135.
40 The *Kent Herald* reproduced in *Chapter 24*, no. 3.
41 The *Kentish Gazette*, 10 March 1967, reproduced in *Chapter 24*, no. 3.
42 *Mojo*, May 1994.
43 Michael English, *3D Eye*, p. 29.
44 Full details of the band's Beatles' connections can be found in *The Amazing Pudding*, no. 49.
45 *Mojo*, May 1994.
46 *Bristol Evening Post*, 28 March 1967, reproduced in *Chapter 24*, no. 2.
47 *Melody Maker*, 8 April 1967.
48 *Melody Maker*, 8 April 1967.
49 See also 26 February 1970.
50 *3D Eye*, p. 21.
51 Reproduced in *Chapter 24*, no. 4.
52 See also 8 April 1967.
53 Connor McNight, 'Notes Towards The Illumination Of The Floyd', *zigzag* 32 (undated).
54 Richard Neville, *Playpower* (London: Penguin), 1971, p. 26.
55 *zigzag* 25.
56 *Days In The Life*, p. 164.
57 *Melody Maker*, 6 May 1967.
58 *Days In The Life*, p. 163.
59 Authors' correspondence.
60 *Chapter 24*, no. 4.
61 *Q*, August 1987.
62 *IT* 13, 19 May – 2 June 1967.
63 *Mojo*, July 1995.
64 *zigzag* 25.
65 *Sounds Of The Sixties*, BBC 2 TV, London, 1993.
66 Malcolm Jones, *Syd Barrett: The Making Of The Madcap Laughs* (London: Orange Sunshine [Pill] Press). Malcolm Jones may also take a large degree of the credit for clarifying much of the detail with regards to the sessions through 1967 and 1968.
67 See also 20 March 1967.
68 *Melody Maker*, 20 May 1967.
69 *3D Eye*, p. 21.
70 Hopkins was to spend a year in prison on drug possession charges.
71 *IT* 15, 16 June 1967 (spelling is correct!).
72 *The Making Of The Madcap Laughs*, p. 27.
73 *Melody Maker*, 20 May 1967.

74 *Sounds*, 17 August 1974.

75 *The Making Of The Madcap Laughs*, p. 27.

76 *The Making Of The Madcap Laughs*, p. 27.

77 *Borge*, no. 17. Miles also mentions articles appeared in 1968. Perhaps it was as a result of Syd's departure that the band were forced to pull out.

78 *Mojo*, May 1994.

79 *Chapter 24*, no. 3.

80 *Melody Maker*, 27 March 1971.

81 *Record Collector*, no. 187.

82 Reproduced in *Chapter 24*, no. 1.

83 Reproduced in *Through The Eyes Of ...*, p. 48.

84 The track is also sometimes known as 'She Was A Millionaire'.

85 *Melody Maker*, 5 August 1967.

86 *Bouton Rouge: Ally Pally Stuffs*, ORTF TV, Paris, December 2 1967.

87 A reproduction of the poster appeared in *Brain Damage*, no. 24.

88 Reproduced in *Through The Eyes Of ...*, p. 21.

89 Both of which featured track-labelling errors; a trait that seems to be obligatory in the bootlegging world.

90 Quoted in *Chapter 24*, no. 4.

91 Karl Dallas, *Bricks In The Wall* (New York: Shapolsky) 1987, p. 49.

92 Display advertisement in *IT* 18.

93 *Melody Maker*, 9 September 1967.

94 *Borge* no.17, 17 August 1967.

95 *Borge* no. 23, 28 September 1967.

96 *Beat Club News*, Bremen, Germany, 26 April 1969.

97 *Melody Maker*, 9 September 1967.

98 This is tenuous. For further details see 5 November 1967.

99 *Chapter 24*, no. 4.

100 *zigzag* 32.

101 *Watch Out Kids*, unnumbered pages.

102 Richard Neville, *Playpower* (London: Penguin) 1970.

103 *Record Collector* no, 104.

104 *Mojo*, April 1997.

105 *Melody Maker*, 21 October 1967.

106 *Billboard*, 30 September 1967.

107 *Melody Maker*, 27 March 1971.

108 *The Art Of Rock*, p. 152.

109 Ken Garner, *In Session Tonight*, (London: BBC Books) 1996.

110 Storm Thorgerson, *Shine On* (London: Hipgnosis), p. 23.

111 Open City, 3–9 November 1967.

112 Nicholas Schaffner, *Saucerful Of Secrets: The Pink Floyd Odyssey* (London: Sidgwick and Jackson), 1991, p. 90.

113 After an unidentified press cutting in *Chapter 24*, no. 4.

114 *Mojo*, May 1994.

115 Date by implication, Watkinson and Anderson, *Crazy Diamond*, p. 74.

116 *Trouser Press*, February 1978.

Notes

117 *A Visual Documentary*, unnumbered pages.

118 *Dancing In The Street*, BBC 2 TV, London, 20 July 1996.

119 See 18 September 1967.

120 *A Saucerful Of Secrets*, p. 90.

121 *Melody Maker*, January 1970.

122 Reproduced in *Chapter 24*, no. 2.

123 *Saucerful Of Secrets*, p. 95.

124 Reproduced in *Chapter 24*, no. 3.

125 Reproduced in *Chapter 24*, no. 2.

126 Reproduced in *Chapter 24*, no. 3.

127 *Watch Out Kids*, unnumbered pages.

128 See also June 24 1969.

129 *Days In The Life*, pp. 164–169.

130 Joe Smith, *Off The Record: An Oral History Of Popular Music*, p. 359.

131 See for example, *Q*, August 1987.

132 *Omnibus: The Pink Floyd Story*, BBC.

133 *zigzag* 32.

134 Watkinson and Anderson, *Crazy Diamond*, p. 79.

135 *Melody Maker*, 27 January 1968.

136 *zigzag* 25.

137 *The Making Of The Madcap Laughs*, p. 29.

138 *Melody Maker*, 16 March 1968.

139 Watkinson and Anderson, *Crazy Diamond*, p. 83.

140 Display advertisement in *IT* 36.

141 *Through The Eyes Of...*, p. 200.

142 The same stills were used in an article about the film in *Brain Damage*, no. 39.

143 *Melody Maker*, 3 May 1968.

144 The concert poster is reproduced in *3D Eye*, p. 30.

145 Watkinson and Anderson, *Crazy Diamond*, p. 87.

146 Jeff Nuttall, *Bomb Culture* (London: MacGibbon and Kee), 1968, p. 239.

147 *Chapter 24*, no. 4.

148 *Melody Maker*, 17 May 1968.

149 *Chapter 24*, no. 4.

150 *Melody Maker*, 21 June 1968, *IT* 33.

151 *Shine On*, p.12.

152 *The Art Of Rock*, p. 278.

153 *Story Of Pop – part 26: A Trip On The London Underground*, BBC Radio 1, London, 12 July 1994.

154 *The Sixties At The Beeb: Radio 2 Arts Programme*, BBC Radio 2, London, 18 August 1996.

155 *The Art Of Rock*, p. 261.

156 *The Art Of Rock*, p. 283.

157 *Melody Maker*, 31 August 1968.

158 'Pinkos Return From United States', *Record Mirror*, 21 September 1968, reproduced in *Through The Eyes Of...*, p. 19.

159 *Record Collector* no. 187.

160 *Melody Maker*, 26 October 1968.

161 Reproduced in *The Amazing Pudding*, no. 18.

162 *The Making Of The Madcap Laughs*, p. 2.

163 *Sounds Of The Sixties*, BBC.

164 *All You Need Is Love: Rock Und Rausch*, German TV, 23 April 1993.

165 *Melody Maker*, 23 November 1968.

166 *Melody Maker*, 29 November 1968.

167 *In Session Tonight*.

168 *Omnibus*, BBC.

169 Advert in *Melody Maker*, 18 February 1969.

170 *Pi*, no. 271, 20 February 1969.

171 Advert in *Melody Maker*, 8 March 1969.

172 *The Making Of The Madcap Laughs*, p. 9. *In The Flesh*, p. 60.

173 See also comments under 1967.

174 *IT* 9, 27 March 1967.

175 See also 25 October 1969.

176 *Melody Maker*, 14 June 1969.

177 *Melody Maker*, 14 June 1969.

178 Watkinson and Anderson, *Crazy Diamond*, p. 90.

179 *Radio Times*, 17 July 1969.

180 *The Art Of Rock*, p. 312.

181 Alain Dister, Jacques Leblanc and Udo Woehrle, *Le Livre Du Pink Floyd* (Paris: Albin Michel), 1978, unnumbered pages.

182 *IT* 63, 21 August – 3 September 1969.

183 *Melody Maker*, 1 November 1969.

184 *Beat Instrumental*, January 1970.

185 See also 19 September 1969.

186 Reproduced in *Through The Eyes Of …*, p. 58.

187 See release date for details.

188 *Le Livre Du Pink Floyd*, unnumbered pages.

189 *Beat Instrumental*, January 1970.

190 Reproduced in *The Amazing Pudding*, no. 18.

191 *Chapter 24*, no. 4.

192 Watkinson and Anderson, *Crazy Diamond*, p. 158.

193 Reproduced in *The Amazing Pudding*, no. 34.

194 Translation of the original French in *The Amazing Pudding*.

195 *Le Livre Du Pink Floyd*, unnumbered pages.

196 *Chapter 24*, no. 4.

197 Interviewed in *The Amazing Pudding*, no. 56.

198 *Melody Maker*, 21 February 1970.

199 *Saucerful Of Secrets*, p. 144

200 Reproduced in *The Amazing Pudding*, no. 18.

201 *Shine On*, p. 37.

202 *The Art Of Rock*, p. 138.

203 Reproduced in *The Amazing Pudding*, no. 34.

204 See also 14 March 1970.

205 Reproduced in *Chapter 24*, no. 2.

206 *Le Livre Du Pink Floyd*, unnumbered pages.

207 Reproduced in *Through The Eyes Of ...*, p. 204.

208 The true title for the show is taken from *Radio Times*, 16 July 1970.

209 Once again, *Radio Times* is the source of the correct title for this, the rebroadcast.

210 Reproduced in the *Best Of The Amazing Pudding 6–9*.

211 Advertisement in *Melody Maker*, 15 August 1970.

212 *Melody Maker*, 14 November 1970.

213 Watkinson and Anderson, *Crazy Diamond*, p. 101.

214 Mike Quigley, *Georgia Straight*, October 14–21 1970.

215 Rick Sanders, *Pink Floyd*, p. 68.

216 If it makes it any easier it is reproduced in *The Amazing Pudding*, no. 8.

217 See also December 1970.

218 Watkinson and Anderson, *Crazy Diamond*, pp. 103–104.

219 *Through The Eyes Of ...*, p. 227.

220 Most notably the *Best Of The Amazing Pudding 6–9*.

221 *Le Livre Du Pink Floyd*, unnumbered pages.

222 *Melody Maker*, 26 December 1970.

223 *Le Livre Du Pink Floyd*, unnumbered pages.

224 Reproduced in *Through The Eyes Of ...*, p. 54.

225 *Beat Instrumental*, April 1970.

226 Cliff Jones, *Echoes: The Stories Behind Every Pink Floyd Song* (London: Omnibus Press), 1997, p. 83.

227 Reproduced in *The Best Of Brain Damage 1–7*.

228 Reproduced in *The Amazing Pudding*, no. 18.

229 Reproduced in *The Amazing Pudding*, no. 18.

230 *Shine On*, p. 33.

231 *Echoes*, p. 81.

232 *Shine On*, p. 33.

233 *Birmingham Evening Mail*, 12 October 1971.

234 *Radio Times*, 7 October 1971.

235 *Record Collector* no. 115.

236 Grave apologies to all French speaking readers; this is a vain stab at what Roger says, and it probably makes no sense whatsoever!

237 Reproduced in *Through The Eyes Of ...*, p. 56.

238 Reproduced in *Through The Eyes Of ...*, p. 43.

239 *Voxpop*, pp. 138–139.

Index

Index

Also available from

CHERRY RED BOOKS / THE RED OAK PRESS

Indie Hits 1980–1989
The Complete UK Independent Charts
(Singles & Albums)
Compiled by Barry Lazell

Indie Hits is the ultimate reference book for alternative music enthusiasts. Indie Hits is the first and only complete guide to the first decade of Britain's Independent records chart, and to the acts, the music and the labels which made up the Indie scene of the 1980s. The book is set out in a similar format to the *Guinness Hit Singles* and *Albums* books, with every artist, single and album to have shown in the indie charts over the 10-year period being detailed. The first Independent charts were published by the trade paper *Record Business* in January 1980, by which time they were well overdue. By that time, Mute Graduate, Factory, Crass, Safari and Rough Trade were just a few of the new breed of rapidly expanding labels already scoring hit records. They were producing acts like Depeche Mode, UB40, Toyah,

www.cherryred.co.uk

The Cult, Joy Division and Stiff Little Fingers, all to become major international sellers. Later years brought the likes of the Smiths, New Order, Erasure, The Stone Roses, James, The Fall and Happy Mondays (not to mention Kylie and Jason!) – all successful and influential independently distributed hitmakers. The A–Z section details every chartmaking 1980s indie act and all hit records in a detailed but easy-to-reference format. Also included are complete indexes of single and album titles, an authoritative history of the origin and development of the Indie charts during the 1980's, listings of all No 1 singles and albums with illustrations of rare original sleeves, print ads and other memorabilia of the period plus a fax 'n' trivia section including the artists and labels with the most chart records, the most No. 1s and the longest chart stays. If it was in the indie charts of the 1980s, it's in here!

Paper covers, 314 pages, £14.95 in UK

Also available from

CHERRY RED BOOKS / THE RED OAK PRESS

Cor Baby, That's Really Me!
(New Millennium Hardback Edition)
John Otway

Time was when John Otway looked forward to platinum albums, stadium gigs and a squad of bodyguards to see him safely aboard his private jet. Unfortunately it didn't happen that way. A series of dreadful career decisions, financial blunders and bad records left Otway down but not out. This is his true story in his own words. It is the story of a man who …

- has never repaid a record company advance in his life
- once put on a benefit concert for his record company after they had cancelled his contract
- signed himself to the mighty Warner Bros label simply by pressing his own records with the WB logo
- broke up with Paula Yates telling her it was the last chance she would get to go out with a rock star

This book is Otway's hilarious yet moving account of his insane assault on the music industry, a tale of blind ambition and rank incompetence, and a salutary lesson for aspiring musicians on how not to achieve greatness. But if the John Otway story is one of failure, it is failure on a grand scale. And it makes compulsive reading too!

Hardback, 192 pages and 16 pages of photographs: £11.99 in UK

Also available from

All the Young Dudes
Mott the Hoople and Ian Hunter
The Biography
Campbell Devine

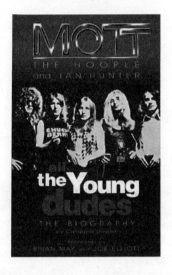

Published to coincide with the Sony 3-CD anthology of their music, *All the Young Dudes* traces Mott The Hoople's formation, their work with David Bowie, their rise to international stardom and beyond, including offshoots such as Mick Ralphs' Bad Company, Mott and British Lions, plus Hunter and Ronson's solo careers and collaborations with Van Morrison, Bob Dylan and Morrissey.

Devoid of borrowed information and re-cycled press clippings, this official biography contains new, sensational and humorous inside stories, controversial quotes and an array of private and previously unpublished views from the band, embellished with comprehensive appendices including discographies and session listings.

The author has collaborated with Ian Hunter and all of Mott's founder

members, Dale Griffin, Overend Watts, Verden Allen and Mick Ralphs –
who have provided their own anecdotes and photographs to illustrate and
enhance the project. There are further personal contributions from Luther
Grosvenor, Morgan Fisher, Stan Tippins, Diane Stevens, Muff Winwood,
Ray Major, John Fiddler, Blue Weaver and Miller Anderson.

This biography will be welcomed by both the committed and casual
rock reader, and by all Dudes, young and post-young!

Paper covers, 448 pages plus 16 pages of photographs, £14.99 in UK

'This book is by far the most comprehensive work on the subject, and
could well be the best book written about any band.'

– Adrian Perkins on his Mott web page

CHERRY RED BOOKS / THE RED OAK PRESS

We are always looking for any interesting book projects
to get involved in. If you have any good ideas, or indeed manuscripts,
for books that you feel deserve publication, then please
get in touch with us.

CHERRY RED BOOKS
a division of Cherry Red Records Ltd
Unit 17, Elysium Gate West,
126–8 New King's Road
London SW6 3JH

E-mail: iain@cred.demon.co.uk
Web: http://www.cherryred.co.uk

Available from

CHERRY RED RECORDS

A Saucerful of Pink
A Tribute to Pink Floyd

TRACK LISTING

PSYCHIC TV – Set Controls For The Heart Of The Sun

CONTROLLED BLEEDING – Another Brick In The Wall

SPAHN RANCH – One Of These Days

SKY CRIES MARY – Wots ... Uh The Deal

SPIRAL REALMS – Interstellar Overdrive

LEATHER STRIP – Learning To Fly

RON GEESIN – To Roger Waters Wherever You Are

EDEN – Jugband Blues

DIN – On The Run

continued overleaf

www.cherryred.co.uk

ALIEN SEX FIEND – Echoes

FURNACE – Hey You

NIK TURNER – Careful With That Axe Eugene

THE ELECTRIC HELLFIRE CLUB – Lucifer Sam

HELIOS CREED – Pigs On The Wing

PRESSUREHED – Let There Be More Light

PENAL COLONY – Young Lust

EXP – A Saucerful Of Secrets

MELTING EUPHORIA – Point Me At The Sky

FAR FLUNG – The Nile Song

Double CD – Over 2 hours of music

£11.95 in UK

Cat no CDBRED 120

Available in all good record stores.

Can also be ordered through Cherry Red mail order service on

0171 371 5844

Available in US on Cleopatra Records